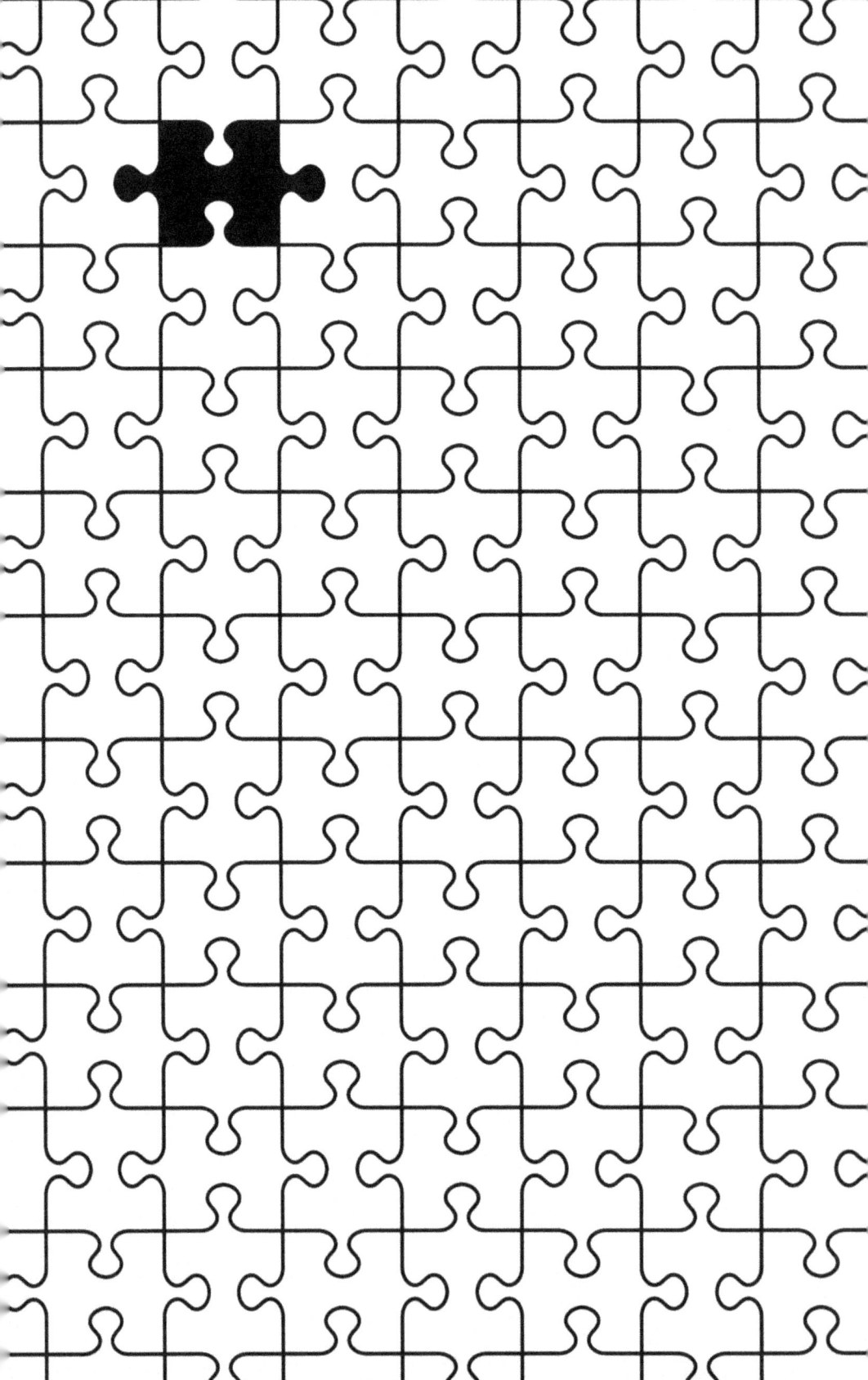

iHope

iHope

Life Hacks from the observations of a therapist's chair to help you cross the finishing line

Marcoco

iHope

Copyright © 2025 by Hopeful Scripts
Cover by Lynne Hollingsworth
Images by Lynne Hollingsworth

Hardback (Special Edition) ISBN: 978-10683890-4-7
Hardback ISBN: 978-10683890-9-2
Paperback ISBN: 978-10683890-0-9
eBook ISBN: 978-1-0683890-7-8

All rights reserved.
No part of this publication may be reproduced, stored, or transmitted in any form or by any means, electronic, mechanical, photocopying, recording, scanning, or otherwise, without written permission from the publisher. It is illegal to copy this book, post it to a website, or distribute it by any other means without permission, except for the use of brief quotations in a book review.

There is no authorisation to use this content to train Artificial Intelligence Software.

This book represents the bona-fide opinion of the author. Although it was written in good faith, the author or the publisher cannot take any penal or civil responsibilities for actions based on suggestions contained in this book.

Content

Preface 1

Introduction 5

Chapter 1: Subscribe to Change 10

Core elements are essential as we gear up for the race and set out on a journey of transformation.

Chapter 2: Formula 1 21

Provides key resources for iHope's race, using tyres as a strategy for better health, emotional awareness to enhance performance, and a flag system to guide our journey.

Chapter 3: All Clear! 42

Explores the opportunities for growth, self-development, womanhood, or stronger relationships that we often overlook.

Chapter 4: Move Over! 87

Experiences that compel us to see the bigger picture, helping us assess our choices with a wider perspective.

Chapter 5: Slippery Surface! 98

Adjusting to changing circumstances. Making decisions under pressure, navigating relationships and facing challenges hard on challenges head-on.

Chapter 6: Stop the Race! 116

We reach our limit, before we lose ourselves completely, it's crucial to hit the emergency brake and pause.

Chapter 7: Danger! 131

Difficulties in our lives that we find problematic, and have the potential to grow more complex, leading to additional complications.

Chapter 8: Unsportsmanlike Behaviour! 148

Times when emotional struggles ripple outward, driving us to act in ways that may harm ourselves and others.

Chapter 9: Mechanical Problem! 162

The intense challenges we face in our mental, physical, and emotional well-being.

Chapter 10: Immediately Return to the Pit! 178

Occasions when we feel overwhelmed, lose perspective, or even lose ourselves, prompting us to face the serious consequences of our choices.

Chapter 11: Victory - End of Racing! 188

This chapter provides solutions and life hacks to help us cross the finish line and achieve lasting transformation.

Chapter 12: Student 341

Looks into various aspects of studying and adopting a positive, healthy approach to stay focused and strive for better grades.

Chapter 13: Wheel Ups   356

Playlists - The positive impact of music on our well-being. Whether managing projects, strengthening relationships, or boosting motivation, discover how the right playlist fuels our drive and keeps us on track.

Chapter 14: Summary   376

Reflects on our journey, allowing us to assess the challenges we've overcome, and insight for the road ahead.

Attributions   381

Acknowledgements   384

Preface

People often ask me, ***"How do you do it?"***
I always answer, ***"Hope."***

It's the kind of hope that's bold, unapologetic and deeply personal, not just wishful thinking. It comes from deep within, shaped by a genuine longing for purpose and peace. That inner drive has helped me turn setbacks into lessons, pain into perspective, and a career into a calling.

That purpose is now this book.
That hope, I call *iHope*.

We live in a world that moves at breakneck speed, filled with responsibilities, pressures, and noise. In that rush, it's easy to lose direction or miss the signs telling us to slow down, reset, or shift course.

iHope was born to help you do just that.

It bridges emotion and ambition through a collection of brief, powerful reflections drawn from my work as a psychotherapist and my own life. These are not just stories or lessons, they're signposts. Moments of insight designed to guide, empower, and inspire you to move forward with clarity, purpose, and courage.

From my therapist's chair, I've witnessed thousands of life stories. While every person is different, many of the challenges are universal, feeling stuck, misunderstood, overwhelmed, or unsure of how to move forward. iHope is about feeling better, living with purpose, and achieving meaningful goals. Each chapter is linked to an F1 flag, offering a fresh start and a clear emotional structure, making the book both engaging and easy to follow.

Why Formula 1?

Because speed, strategy, and precision aren't just for the track, they're part of how we navigate life. If you're a motorsport fan, you'll recognise the references. If not, don't worry, the messages are universal. Whether it's a red flag urging you to stop and reassess, or a green flag encouraging you to go full throttle, these nine symbolic flags guide you to better understand when to pause, pivot, or accelerate. Real success is not about competing with others. It's about staying in your own lane, rising to what you're capable of, and becoming better than the person you were yesterday.

Your real race is not against anyone else. It's against your own procrastination, fear, self-doubt, and the comfort zone that holds you back. It's time to shift focus and run your own race, on your own track.

No journey is complete without music. Whether it's Chris Rea's *Driving Home for Christmas* or Tracy Chapman's *Fast Car*, music moves us in ways words can't. That's why *iHope* includes its own curated 101-song playlist, to accompany your moments of reflection, healing, and growth.

As a psychotherapist, I've heard it all!
We all wish for a world without judgement, the truth is, it's a survival instinct. That inner "no" is meant to protect, if left unchecked, it can also hold us back. Part of this journey is learning to judge wisely, choosing balance over fear. Whether it's reclaiming your voice, letting go of old wounds, or learning to care less about other people's opinions, this book is here to help you shine. To realign with who you are and what you're meant to do.

The idea for *iHope* came from something I saw again and again in my clients. People who were driven, talented, and full of potential, but emotionally out of sync. Their goals didn't match their inner world. They were chasing someone else's version of success. *iHope* bridges that gap. It helps you reconnect with what you feel, what you need, and who you are becoming. It's a framework for go-getters, people who are ready to lead their lives with intention, not just ambition.

Dr. Martin Luther King Jr. said,
"I have a dream..."
A dream born from hope, his unwavering belief in justice and equality.

Tina Turner once said,
"The future belongs to those who believe in the beauty of their own dreams."

Hope fuels vision. These timeless words remind us that without hope, dreams fade. Dr. King's hope inspired a movement. Tina Turner's hope turned pain into power. They both found their own unique version of iHope, and used it to leave a lasting legacy.

iHope is about helping you find your hope, your drive, your fire, your personal reason to keep going. This book is for the ones who still believe, the ones who rise again after falling. The ones who refuse to be defined by struggle, and instead choose courage, grit, and growth. The go-getters.

Stay the course. Your brave, beautiful, bold journey is just beginning.
Let's honour the hope that brought you here, and the future that's waiting for you.

Welcome to iHope.

Preface

Introduction

What do we do when hope has nowhere to go?

Somewhere in the back of our minds, we know that stress has steered us off track, and we've lost our way. It's a feeling many of us know when we're running on empty, overwhelmed by life, and out of touch with the values and dreams that once guided us. When uncertainty clouds our judgement, it can feel like there's no space for hope to land. We push through without a clear sense of direction, but let's be honest, *"wingin' it"*, just isn't cutting it anymore.

iHope recognises these struggles and offers a much-needed reset. A blend of life hacks and a clear roadmap to help navigate the chaos. When we feel burntout, and lost, it encourages us to shift gears, gain perspective, and make intentional choices. *iHope* rises above the noise to help us reconnect with what truly matters. We all have the capacity to face life's challenges with self-awareness and the right tools. *Life Hacks* doesn't skip the hard work of personal growth. It simply helps us avoid the detours that slow us down, guiding us more directly to what truly matters.

iHope

The title '*iHope*' encapsulates a powerful journey of self-reflection, growth, and empowerment. The 'I' represents the individual, a focus on our personal aspirations and the belief that we can create. meaningful change in our lives. It is not just about external circumstances; *iHope* is about tapping into our inner strength to reshape our lives. At its core, *iHope* is rooted in self-awareness and personal growth. As we become more in tune with our desires, strengths and limitations, we gain the clarity and confidence to navigate life's obstacles and make aligned with our goals. The foundation is autonomy, we can evolve into stronger versions of ourselves, owning our actions and directing our own path.

iHope offers a multi-dimensional approach to navigating life's complexities. Blending psychology, Formula 1 metaphors, and music, it delivers a holistic toolkit that supports mental clarity, emotional resilience, and motivation empowering lasting personal growth.

Components

The psychological component draws from my 25 years as a psychotherapist, offering deep insight into human behaviour, emotional regulation, and personal growth. Formula 1 metaphors add a dynamic, imaginative layer, reminding us that just like racing cars, we need strategy and awareness to avoid life's potholes, and collisions.
The use of flags act as warning signals, alerting us to potential risks and providing the insight needed to steer ourselves back on track.
Music adds energy, and motivation to the journey. A well-chosen playlist has the power to uplift us, focus us, and keep us going.

Together, these elements form the core of *iHope*. A guide to overcoming setbacks, making intentional choices, and crossing the finishing line with purpose and pride. Blending realism with fantasy, *iHope* uses racing metaphors to help us navigate life's challenges, manage emotions, and stay on course. From dashboard lights signalling our emotional states to tyre compounds representing different life phrases, each symbol offers a unique perspective on self-management and growth. Self-awareness is key. Like a skilled driver, knowing when to push, pause, or pit is essential to managing our emotional energy, focus, and momentum, and ultimately reaching our personal chequered flag.

The music chapter, titled 'Wheel Ups' introduces *iHope's* playlist. A carefully curated collection of tracks designed to uplift, motivate, and guide us through life's challenges. The diverse track list reflects different moods, experiences and themes from the book. Some songs reinforce key messages, while others are open to personal interpretation, allowing each listener to connect in their own way.

Ultimately the playlist acts as a soundtrack for growth, resilience, and reflection. Whether we embrace every track or skip a few. Its purpose is to enhance our journey and support us through life's highs and lows.

Students

The chapter focused on students is particularly relevant. Student life often comes with intense pressure, anxiety, and endless distractions. *iHope* offers a healthier approach to managing mental wellbeing, time, and focus. Serving as a practical guide for navigating both academic and personal challenges. My direct experience working with students ensures the advice is rooted in real-world understanding, making it relatable and easy to apply.

Blending candid life lessons with creative metaphors, *iHope* offers support to anyone who's ready to get back on track. Whether they are struggling with self-doubt, navigating educational pressures, or seeking a deeper understanding of themselves.

Real-life examples from my clinical practice add authenticity and depth, showing how these strategies have helped others overcome similar struggles. Whether it's managing stress, building confidence, or improving our mental health, these stories reinforce that change is possible, and offer a clear roadmap for lasting changes in our lives.

Couples

Couples seeking to strengthen their connection will find value in this book. While relationships rely on communication, expressing feelings or tackling difficult topics can often feel like driving through fog. *iHope* offers a structured yet creative way to spark meaningful conversations. Providing a fresh approach to connection and understanding.

Couples can engage with this book by selecting a track that resonates with their current situation or emotional state. After reading the corresponding section, they're invited to reflect or respond, either together or individually. This simple interaction acts as a gentle entry point for honest dialogue, helping to surface thoughts and feelings that might otherwise go unspoken. This approach creates a safe space for connection, empathy and growth.
In essence, *iHope* is about becoming the best version of ourselves by consciously choosing growth, embracing change and using hope as a catalyst to overcome and move towards personal goals.

It's natural to ask:
"I wonder why I am not progressing like my friends?"
"What's shaped me into who I am today, holding onto beliefs and perceptions that sometimes feel limiting?"

The self-critical beliefs that we carry can feel who we are, telling us we're,

Not good enough
Unlovable
Unworthy
Stupid

Yet these lies don't define us, and they don't have to hold us back.

Everything we experience leaves a mark on our spirit, especially during times of stress and uncertainty. These moments can shape how we see ourselves and the world, often amplifying limited beliefs, and silencing our self-worth. We can become our own biggest obstacle, building internal barriers that keep us from moving forward. Lasting change begins within, by understanding the beliefs that drive our actions.

iHope offers practical solutions for today's challenges. While the tools shared are general, they serve as a reminder that no one-size-fits all for everyone. Each journey is personal, and in a fast-paced world, staying grounded starts with reconnecting to ourselves.

This is the kind of book I once needed, something to lean on and guide me through life's twists and turns. With greater self-awareness, we can break free from self-sabotaging patterns, make choices that support our growth. and care less about the opinions of others. In doing so, we create space to live more authentically and thrive.

iHope

Chapter 1

Subscribe to Change

Subscribe to Change

This chapter touches on the key elements essential for engineering our iHope.
Building these foundations is vital before we embark on the race and commit to the journey of transformation. It emphasizes the importance of preparation as real change cannot take place without first laying the groundwork. Change requires us to confront what lies ahead, to challenge old patterns and mindsets that may have held us back.

This chapter invites us to recognize and embrace our unique qualities, and to understand that our individuality is a powerful asset in the process of transformation.

It is here, at the crossroads of self-awareness and commitment, that we make the decision to move forward. The journey requires us to take intentional steps toward positive changes; physically, mentally, emotionally and spiritually.

12 **Our Lives Are One Big Puzzle**
13 **Hope**
14 **A New Version**
16 **Difference**
17 **That's Life**
19 **Blue Sky Thinking**

"The first step to getting somewhere, is to decide you're not going to stay where you are." Steven Bartlett

Jend Backseat ♪

Our Lives Are One Big Puzzle

Our lives are one big puzzle,
We don't know how many pieces we've got.
There are people that fit in quite nicely
And people who try, but do not.

We're constantly adding more pieces,
All the memories of things we've been through.
We add laughter and tears and adventure,
And the lessons we've learnt to be true.

Everyone has their own puzzle,
There will be ones where we do not fit.
Don't you ever dare make your peace smaller,
Just so you can live there for a bit.

If you keep cutting off all your edges,
One day you won't recognise what you see
And you'll forget the person you once were,
Before the world told you who you should be.

Make the most of each piece in your puzzle,
It'll be a grand masterpiece when it's done,
So you won't have to look back when it's over,
And realise you've left out the sun.

Erin Hanson

I hope I can find an inner belief ...

Hope

An inner Belief that something Better lies Ahead

It's completely natural to question ourselves, doubt our choices, or feel as though we've lost hope. Yet hope rarely disappears, more often, it gets buried beneath layers of emotion: fear, anger, shame, sadness, the numbness of grief. At times, we may feel stuck, caught in cycles of overthinking, revisiting past mistakes, or unintentionally sabotaging our own progress and potential. Hope is the belief that the future can improve, even when the path is uncertain. It's about being open to realistic possibilities, starting with small, manageable steps. Hope isn't just a wish, it's an emotion, a mindset and a catalyst for action. It grows through constant micro actions and a sense of agency built over time.

The power of hope can transform us. It enhances our mental wellbeing, builds confidence, strengthens our relationships, and fuels a positive outlook. Hope can bring comfort and build strength, resilience, motivation, and inspiration. It offers a way to cope, helping us adapt to adversity and manage challenges that might seem insurmountable. It encourages persistence through setbacks, keeping us grounded and moving forward.

Hope has a profound impact on our health. It helps us to become more adaptable, less vulnerable to depression, and can reduce stress and anxiety. It provides a sense of optimism and the belief that things can, and will, get better. We have the power to shape our future and succeed in life.

When we've had enough, enough of feeling stuck; helpless, uneasy, or lacking self-esteem and confidence, we can still choose hope.

We can be **lost,** yet hopeful.
We can be **sad,** yet hopeful.
We can be **hurt,** yet hopeful.
We can be **angry,** yet hopeful.
We can be **afraid,** yet hopeful.

Hope is part of our own private world.
Our thoughts and feelings that empower us to believe in our ability to make things happen, no matter the obstacles.

Welcome to your iHope!

NF Hope ♪

I hope I can be a different me …

A New Version

The New version of Ourselves will Cost us our Old one!

We're heavily influenced by the world around us, almost hypnotized by external forces.

"This is what you're meant to do…"
"These are your expectations…"
"These are your labels to pick up…"

We're pushed to "mark this", to "do do do", and when we step away from it all, we find ourselves wondering.

1. Do we really need all of it?
2. Have we got enough stuff?
3. Do we need to buy into half the stuff that we think we need?

To validate our existence. We say "no".

In practice, Antonio, 27, underwent a transformation in his life…
"I stopped being influenced as much, and started questioning more, I became the lion that's awake, and not a sheep."

Becoming a new version of ourselves through self-development or therapy requires growth and change. Transformation means letting go of old patterns or beliefs to make space for something new, often in unexpected ways. The old version demands focus and comes at a cost: releasing what no longer serves us so we can. evolve, grow, and move forward. If we've been stuck in a bubble for a while, our social circle can shrink, leaving us out of touch with how our others think or behave. Before starting our self-development journey, we may have compared ourselves to others and felt we were falling short; perhaps that's what's led us to seek help.

The first stage of personal growth is awareness: becoming aware of our actions, behaviours, our decisions, how we perceive ourselves and others. With this awareness self-development becomes a tool to upgrade both ourselves and our quality of life. Over time, self-development gives us focus on ourselves as individuals, from our needs to our comfort zone, eventually we gain a new sense of direction. The upshot is, we will grow as a result of investing in ourselves, we will gain a more responsible approach to our needs and naturally outgrow and surpass our peers. We find that their attitudes towards the opposite sex, relationships, dating, sex, and their expectations of life are outdated and different from ours. We have our own thoughts and opinions from making autonomous decisions. This breeds confidence, and we find that we're different from our tribe, we have grown, evolved and left our tribe behind after breaking free, we can clearly see the limitations of the tribe's comfort zone. Their comfort zone maintains their culture, beliefs, values or parental expectations, we find we're in a league of our own, we have redefined ourselves.

We're no longer in a tight restricted bubble of life. Imagine the bubble as being like a sock made up of culture, indoctrination, religion, or traditions that restricts our thoughts and behaviours. Over time, self-development will take the sock off and peel back the layers to understand who we are and how we tick. We begin to see the world through different lenses and view things differently, to question more, become curious, take risks, and challenge ourselves; thus, we become our own shape, we're dancing to our own tune, to the beat of our own drum.

On reflection, we will find our tribes, opinions and behaviours are outdated, they don't align with ours, our tribe no longer shares the same values, or has different expectations of how to live life. This can feel like a lonely place because our world has expanded, bigger than the sock that they are in. We've outgrown them, we're out of our comfort zone, there is less in common. They may seem boring simply because they represent the 'old and familiar'. What interests us now is 'the new', to be excited about the 'new' us and our future, the new challenges that are coming and inevitably a new tribe will emerge. This is the time to say "yes" to meeting new people, to invite them into our life, and to build a new tribe that's to our level, our frequency, speaking the same language, energy and curiosities. This helps us to feel seen and heard, alongside a comfort zone centred around positive things that supports us in moving forward. Being with like-minded people will encourage change, a different version will emerge, we're entitled to grow, losing what supported the outdated version of us that no longer serves us is healthy.

Outdated versions of ourselves that overstay their welcome stunt our growth. By staying loyal to one version. We do ourselves a disservice and limit our potential.

There are many versions waiting for us!

Fasten our seatbelts, time to update the satnav.

Basia A New Day for You ♪

I hope I can be myself ...

Difference

Distinction, Variety and Contrast of Humanity

"If you are always trying to be normal, you will never know how amazing you can be." Maya Angelou

Different is not right or wrong. This book is for everyone, it celebrates being individual whatever our social-class, background, colour, race, religion, gender, (LGBTQIA+) sexuality, financial status, qualifications, size or age, we are all welcome on this journey.

Please keep in mind that the behaviours described in this book are generalisations. A man may display some of the behaviours thought of as a-typical, and the same goes for a woman and vice versa. Everyone is different none of us are easily bundled into just one or two types, or groups of people.

Our identity makes us unique from one another, the more we focus on our individuality, who we are, the more powerful we can become. We can be happier, not dancing to other people's tunes, not bending to the point of breaking, or losing ourselves in trying to meet others' expectations.

We have the right to be ourselves, and with our unique life experiences, talents and gifts that make us 'brilliantly bonkers', we all have something valuable to offer to the table of life. If we aren't hurting others, it is our right to live our lives differently even if others may not understand simply because we are different. We were not born to fit in, we were born to stand out, to shine, our job is to learn how to manage and handle our light.
We all have our own unique puzzle to figure out, our identity, who we are, our own personal aspirations, desires, dreams and our iHope.

Every one of us can excel at something because our DNA is completely distinct from anyone else. Enjoy finding that spark to light our fire on this journey, to steer us in the right direction towards achieving our iHope.
Be proud of who we are, own it and celebrate our differences!

We all share the same sky yet see different shades of colour. None of us sit high enough to look down on anyone, we all have a place in the world so dare to be different.
No one is exactly like us, that is our power!

Subscribe to Change

You are an original.
Be you! 🪶

Cultural Warriors & Errol Dunkley A Little Way Different ♫

I hope life is like the fairytale ...

That's Life

A Privilege!

"Life teaches us how to live, if you live long enough'."
Tony Bennett

Life is a serious business!
We may all want to live a life that we consider blessed, be under no illusion, life is not easy. Life is tough, life is hard, life is a journey, it's not as simple as black and white, the magic is in the numerous different shades of grey for us to learn. There's no fairytale and no rehearsal so make the most of it. Some say life is about a bunch of problem-solving, we make mistakes, fail and we get over them, but what if we're not strong enough to solve them, we've not become bulletproof to life's knocks?

Life is abundant with cliches, we become bored of our childhood and rush to grow up, and then wish we were children again. Or, we lose our health through working too hard making money, to then spend our money trying to regain our health. Or we become so anxious about the future that we neglect being present to then spend time in our past trying to work out why we were anxious. See, naturally as human beings we take life's gifts for granted. We change as human beings, life can take its toll, with the ups and downs that come along that sometimes we have to allow ourselves to enjoy life again.

So, let's look at the alternatives, a different path that gives us opportunities and guidance to meet our needs and find joy, contentment and hope again in life in a different way. There will be good days and bad days, and we must be grateful for them all.

Life isn't supposed to be easy.

Let's stay with change. From iHope's perspective, life moves in cycles, repeating, shifting, stopping and restarting, endings and beginnings. New relationships start, others end. We begin a new job, or lose one. The death of a grandparent, a friend, a parent. The birth of son, or daughter. Over again and again. Round and round we go. We must learn to ride the waves of life, and with each cycle, we gain more experience and resilience. Life is a game of continual adjustments; nothing stays the same forever. Time softens the sharp edges of our memories, gently blurring certain pains. Life is made up of experiences that teach us who we are and what we're made of, whether through failure or success. Failure is the secret ingredient, it's nothing to fear. Try to understand life on life's terms and not take it too seriously. Falling is a part of the process; getting back up is where the living begins.

Life is a grand adventure, amazing; incredible, wonderful, breathtaking, magnificent, sublime and supreme, yet it can also be cruel and bittersweet. There is darkness in the world that can unravel us, glance at it, but don't stare. Live with no regrets. Embrace the adventure, take risks, otherwise we risk nothing at all. Some people settle for the ordinary sprinkled with the occasional extraordinary moment, and that's okay too. When it comes to others in our life, the key is to peace is simple, lower our expectations, or better yet, have no expectations, we'll enjoy life a whole lot more.
Life is for living!

When we find life is coming at us fast, pick ourselves up, dust ourselves down and get back in the race of life.
That's life!

Frank Sinatra That's Life ♪
The Verve Bitter Sweet Symphony ♪

Subscribe to Change

I hope I can embrace, limitless possibilities without constraints...

Blue Sky Thinking

Unrestricted thinking without Limitations

We all have the power to change and reach our potential by being content with who we are!

Blue Sky Thinking refers to a creative and unrestricted way of thinking, where there are no limits or constraints. It encourages exploring new possibilities, brainstorming without judgement, and thinking outside the box to generate innovative ideas or solutions. This type of thinking is open, imaginative, and often leads to breakthroughs by removing traditional boundaries or preconceived notions.

Let us imagine we're in our driver's seat, hands on the wheel, steering our vision, guiding our journey with focus and purpose. As we cruise along, enjoying the rhythm of life's playlist, we stay present, with our eyes on the horizon and the best views ahead.
Every now and then, we glance into the rear-view mirror of life, reflecting on the past to help us understand where we've been, while keeping our eyes on the blue skies of the future towards growth and fulfilment, confident that we're on the right track.

What vehicle will we choose to drive our best life forward?
What dreams do we want to achieve in 12 months?
What are the objectives to our dreams?
What's our reason to succeed?
What tools do we need?

Let's steer our vision toward iHope!

Justin Timberlake Let's Take a Ride ♫

Subscribe to Change

Chapter 2

Formula 1

Formula 1

Welcome to the 75th year of Formula 1.
The home of British motorsport. The fastest sport on earth.

This chapter provides the resources and requirements for iHope's race.

23 **Vehicles**
24 **Circuit**
25 **Horsepower**
26 **Tyres**
28 **Soft Tyre**
29 **Medium Tyre**
30 **Hard Tyre**
31 **Intermediate Tyre**
32 **Wet Tyre**
33 **Dashboard**
36 **Flags**
39 **Formation Lap**

Vehicles

Choose our wheels, hatchback, saloon, coupe, 4x4, or SUV whatever we're cruising in.

They offer endless choice, from the colour to the brand, the shape of the engine, every detail matters. the battery, headlights, grill, tyres, rims, and hubs all play their part. Each modification brings us closer to our ideal ride.

Imagine the journey we would like to experience?

We know what to expect on the familiar route, feeling worn down from the tough, bumpy roads we've travelled, marked with deep potholes and loose debris, leaving us with undeniable wear and tear.

Now that we've chosen our vehicle it's time to embrace a fresh approach and head in a new direction. A more scenic route, filled with fresh ideas, strategies, tips and hacks for a less travelled road, where the views are clearer and the 'blue skies' of life await.

The headlights are on full beam, it's time to hit the straights!

Steppenwolf Born to Be Wild ♪

Circuit

Currently there are 24 races. The distance of each circuit is around 305 Kilometres, the laps vary on each circuit depending on the length of the lap. There is a street, road, or permanent facility for a race. Legendary tracks like Spa and Silverstone, or Monaco's tight street circuit, not to mention the smallest, fastest, hottest, and oldest venues. Choose from the famed 'Cathedral of Speed' to the 'Wall of Champions.' We each might choose our own 'home race.'

Each circuit has its own corners with cambers at the kerb or the crown. Infamous corners to slam on the anchors or pick up some slipstream on the straights. With ground breaking apexes to gain good traction on the exit, or a notoriously tight and twisty street circuit. Each lap of a track is split into three sectors using a colour to symbolise each sector to the driver.

There are three different colours to mark our performance. Our engineer will inform us of the data to tell us If we are above or below our potential. The different performances are represented in green, yellow and purple. The green light tells us we've set our personal best. Yellow means we fell short of our best, and we are slower than our personal best. Purple means setting the fastest time out of any of the drivers, and if we light all three sectors, we've set the fastest lap.

With each track we must devise our strategy accordingly. The strategists and the engineers work behind the scenes to devise the masterplan. What isn't part of the masterplan is to get bumped out of Q3 or do a full French kiss, and the car's been totalled, this is why they work ahead of several races to build analysis and data for each upcoming race.

Strategy involves which tyres to start the race to gain or keep pole position, that are used in qualifying. This depends on how technical the track is and the track temperature. When to use DRS (Drag Reduction System) or KERS (Kinetic Energy Recovery System) on track, when to pit, how many pit stops to make or how to overtake another opponent and there's more, helps to know how to take advantage of a collision, when the safety car is on track to using the correct tyres according to the changeable weather.
We might have to abort the lap especially if our car starts to aquaplane. If there is heavy rain the DRS system is not used, at best we can pick up a slip stream to gain speed in these conditions. DRS is enabled when the track is

safe, so be sure not to cook our tyres if we stay on the 'wets' for too long. Whatever tyre we are on, keep to a strategy.

Are we going to start aggressive, and then pit early to make position, or the opposite and go long to bring ourselves into play later?

Choose the circuit.

Horsepower

Formula 1 cars change with the seasons. Currently, they are pushing 1.6-litre, four-stroke, turbo charged 90-degree V6 double- overhead camshaft (DOHC) reciprocating engines. F1 Cars have been known to drive 3-litre engines on V10 layout, reaching speeds of up to 375km/h/233mph.

The official top speed stands at 246.908mph and to give extra push with KERS and the DRS that reduces the drag. This helps the drivers catch up and make a move to gain an extra dose of straight-line speed, adds an extra 10 - 12 km/h or 6.2 - 7.5mph by the end of the activation zone. There are three changes of engine per season, plus upgrades are allowed, costing around $16 million for the engine alone. Insane!

Choose what power we are pushing.

Tyres

Without a good set of wheels, we can't drive anywhere. These are the basic staples that are necessary to maintain and build a healthy life. There are different sets of tyres to represent various times in our lives to support our different journeys.

We need to go through quals. Qualifying gives us the opportunity to have the best Grand Prix starting grid position. There are three sessions of qualifying: Q1, Q2, and Q3. These sessions determine which tyres we choose to give us the best opportunity to be on pole position on the grid.

There are five different elements that will serve us well if we keep them consistent. Some tracks will use the rear tyres more and the front tyres less, we need to get our 18-inch tyres in the window for the best performance by making the right decisions and choices in our lives.

The profile of the tyres is optimised for our durability and stress control, The lifespan of tyres, depends on the compound can last between 50 to 330 miles. The best way to maintain our overall health is daily, once our tyres are worn, our handling deteriorates and the danger of a blowout increases, or worse causes a collision, or crash, or it's time to be towed back to the pit, either way we DNF (Did Not Finish) and the race is over.
The journey's over, we're unable to reach our goal.

Our tyres are essential to our racing, they are the only contact that touches our track. The degradation of the surface can be an issue, causing blistering, graining, flat spotting, or a steady loss of tyre performance, called degradation that can lead to blowouts. It is imperative that we take care of the tyres, without tyres the race is over. There are soft, medium, hard, intermediate, and wet tyres, they all have different tyre compounds to suit different tracks. These five different compounds will represent different times in our lives to get different trade-off's. The five different compounds are marked in different colours.

It is important that we keep loading our tyres to generate as much temperature as possible to obtain the best performance. We all start our race with slicks, (soft tyres), they are predominantly used for qualifying. In a

Formula 1 race we are required to only use two of the dry compounds during the race unless wet weather plays a part on the track.

iHope provides a range of different tyres, to change as many times as required for challenging situations to help us to the chequered flag.

Different Tyres

- **Soft** - more grip/speed - short journeys.
- **Medium** - less grip, good start off - medium journey.
- **Hard** - long haul more durable.
- **Intermediate** - grooves to give more traction for partially wet conditions.
- **Wet** - deeper tread that gives maximum contact for dramatic weather conditions.

Choose a set of fresh tyres to support whatever phase, episode, season, or year of our life we are presented with. Additionally, there are different ages in our lives that will naturally dictate different tyre compounds. There are different compounds we can use depending on the challenges in our lives that may require a different speed, or attention to meet all weather conditions.

Each compound indicates a situation when we are seeking versatility or durability to withstand certain conditions we find ourselves in. Strategy is an important part of Formula 1 racing, knowing which tyre to change to can be crucial to our race. Making autonomous decisions at the right time can support us in steering clear of or prevent a circumstance from accelerating or becoming out of our control. It is key to make the right call at the right time in our lives to take care of our mental, physical, and emotional health to ensure we can stay in the race. We might have times when we need to be somewhat of a 'tyre whisperer' to get those tyres to go a little further.

Tyres generally determine who wins the race, or who doesn't, depending on the compounds we choose. The rubber on the track helps to assist us on our journeys to cross the finishing line and achieve iHope.

Look after our tyres and our tyres will look after us!

We're ready to hit the ground running!

Limp Biztic Rollin' ♪

 Soft Tyre

Accountability and Focus

We require slicks (soft tyres) for training and our attention for speed. They represent the fastest rubber with the most grip to give more downforce. These compounds are entirely smooth, with no grooves designed for rapid momentum for a short space of time. The soft tyre helps us to optimise our mood to the max. These tyres are ideal when we are up against a deadline, a life-changing deadline, when nothing else matters, and at the top of our priority list to succeed.

These times command accountability, our full attention, focus, dedication and commitment to ourselves to start cleanly off the line, ensuring no lockups, and maintain a smooth first sector of the lap, allowing us to break away and stay at the front of the field. We accelerate and launch ourselves full throttle to gain some time on the track for intense, short and brief episodes in our lives.

⚙ This compound requires. Cold Shower. High Protein Breakfast. Morning Walk. Meditation.

- **Cold Shower** Acceleration. Foot on the throttle and away we go. Gives us a head start. Kick-starts our day and floods our body with endorphins, serotonin and dopamine and oxytocin.
- **High protein Breakfast** Quick acceleration - quickest way to help to build and repair tissue, gives us the right energy boost and gets our metabolism motoring and sustaining pace for the day.
- **Daylight** Outdoor exercise - jogging- important for High intensity exercise like Running in the morning. Gets the heart/engine pumping, clears out the cobwebs, keeps our minds sharp and gets rid of any negative emotions that prevent us from stealing our day. Having a moment to self-reflect and process emotions, helps to boost our productivity for the day.
- **Meditation** Anytime, to start, or end our day, whatever we need to stay focused or supports us in staying calm and grounded for the day.
- **Exercise** 'The Fifteen'. Fifteen minutes sprinting on a treadmill. pauses are necessary, for 30 second intervals only. Try to beat our longest time sprinting within the entire 15 minutes.

Medium Tyre

Regulating Alertness and Sleepiness

We require a medium tyre for versatility. The medium tyre strikes a balance, combining and compromising between the soft and hard compounds. It isn't as quick off the mark as the soft tyre, nor as tough and long-lasting as the hard one, but it offers a versatile middle ground. Whether the track is wet or dry, the medium tyre adapts well to changing conditions, making it the go-to choice when flexibility and steadiness are key. Much like this tyre, in life we encounter new and unexpected tracks. These are moments when we must rely on our bodies and minds for consistent performance. The medium tyre reminds us of the importance of resilience and adaptability, offering just the right blend of responsiveness and durability to help us navigate through uncertain times with confidence. It is a reliable partner in our journey, supporting us when we need to stay steady and strong amidst life's twists and turns.

Our circadian rhythms regulate our alertness and sleepiness by responding to light. Our bodies have a master clock that controls and coordinates all the biological clocks in our body, including our circadian clock.

Our circadian rhythm regulates our biological functions, including our sleep, eating, digestion and our moods, which impacts our physical, mental, and behavioural changes and our hormonal activity. This requires consistency and the ability to hold firm boundaries, especially regarding time.

- This compound requires, Food. Daylight. Exercise. Sleep.

    - **Food** Eating schedule - regular smaller meals. No skipping meals, especially breakfast or eating late at night.
    - **Daylight** Enhances natural light exposure, gets us outdoors and walk for 20-40 minutes helps to set the clock and gives us our daily vitamin D.
    - **Exercise** Regular Physical activity that's calm helps to manage stress, and stretches the body's limbs - Yoga, Pilates or Tai Chi. Qi Gong and many more.
    - **Sleep** Practice good sleep hygiene. A regular sleep-wake schedule, and a regular bedtime routine, our brains love routine, they also need to rest and repair.

 Hard Tyre

Balance and Maintenance

We require a hard tyre to go the full distance. The hard compound is the most durable tyre, doesn't suffer too much graining, and they provide the least grip yet remains in working order the longest.

This classification allows us to travel the longest distance on the same tyre. This compound can cope with most conditions in a race. If we're at a time in our lives in a situation, feeling under pressure, this compound is for maintenance and balance, to focus on the fundamentals of our engine, our nutrition, and to maintain our social network, exercise and sleep. To go the distance given any situation requires maintaining our health and fitness. Steady energy for a prolonged period to see things to completion, such as going through a divorce, or starting a new business.

⚙ This compound requires; Me-Time. Social Network. Exercise. Sleep. High Wellbeing. Spiritual Hygiene.

- **Me-Time** Taking time-out for ourselves to re-group, for self-reflection and introspection helps us to process emotions, improve our mental health and increase our productivity. Zen. Nature Walking. Me-Dates
- **Social Network** Spending time with close family and friends, to unwind, switch off from the daily grinds of life, enhances our psychological wellbeing, boosts our spirits to keep us lifted and reduces our stress.
- **Exercise** Keeps us fit, maintains strength and health and bone density, mobility and flexibility in our bodies. Soothes stress, - running, swimming, yoga or resistance training.
- **Sleep** Helps keep our heart and immune system strong, supports maintaining weight and improves concentration. Additionally, to rest, cool the engine down from our day, a regular 6-8hrs. Washes our brain.
- **High Wellbeing** Practicing good health, self-discipline, independence and having a varied lifestyle.
- **Spiritual Hygiene** Cleansing our energetic and spiritual bodies, clears negativity, aligns our energy and creates space for new opportunities.

Intermediate Tyre

Support

These tyres are best suited for racing when there is light rain. The compounds provide better grip and good resistance, they are required for saving energy by improving fuel economy in light standing water conditions. Intermediates are a versatile compound that can manage a wide range of conditions. They can be used on a dry or wet track, when the road is slightly slick, if we're not aquaplaning, and we can get through the puddles and find grip, there is no need for wets.

These compounds are required when we need extra support. When we are undergoing unwelcome small, yet significant challenges that have the potential of becoming permanently life changing if there is no action taken to move forward. For example, if we've failed an exam/ course, or a redundancy imminent, a separation.

This compound requires; Friends/Family. Socialising. Exercise. Therapy. Spiritual Hygiene

- **Family** Our tribe is our main support network. Talk. Share and keep them in the know.
- **Socialising** Life still goes on. To keep ourselves ticking over, it is essential to interact, and have fun to lift our spirits, meet new people and mix 'n' mingle.
- **Exercise** 1hr. regular physical activity. High cardiovascular exercise or aerobic activity we enjoy, getting our hearts pumping and our bodies releasing endorphins to make us feel good. Cardiovascular exercise promotes a good night's sleep and deters sleepless nights. Four times a week - Running, spinning, or trampolining.
- **Therapy** Additional support is always an option. Find a therapist for us to disclose any other information that we prefer to keep to ourselves. Brief therapy is available to help with sticky moments.
- **Spiritual Hygiene** Cleansing our energetic and spiritual bodies, clears negativity, aligns our energy and creates space for new opportunities.

 Wet Tyre

Calm and Relaxation

Wets are specifically required for wet weather conditions. They heat up quicker in these conditions than any other tyre, designed with a deeper tread to disperse standing water, causing more friction to give maximum contact with the ground.

Sometimes life challenges us to slow down, be kinder to our bodies, or to heal ourselves, physically, spiritually and mentally. In adversity, we require heavy resistance to weather the storms in life, and find our own pace.

If we are feeling burned out, sleep deprived, stressed, incapacitated or in need of rebalancing our hormones. This is a time in our lives when we need to drop the pace and slow down, relax, re-energise, and renew our souls. Here are a few suggestions.

◉ This compound requires Breath Work. Meditation. Relaxation. Journaling/Manifesting or Mindfulness. High Wellbeing. Spiritual Hygiene.

- **Breath Work** Release stubborn feelings that have no vision or sound or words.
- **Meditation** in the morning or at night or 10 minutes to break up our day.
- **Relaxation** Allow our vibration to rise -zen, sound baths, gongs, or massage for stillness.
- **Journal/ Manifesting** Connect with our internal world. Stay focused and maintain a clear mind.
- **Spiritual Hygiene** Cleansing our energetic and spiritual bodies, clears negativity, aligns our energy and creates space for new opportunities.
- **High Wellbeing** Practicing good health, self-discipline, independence and having a varied lifestyle.

See if we can stay in clean air to manage our tyres!

Dashboard

Emotional Awareness to Optimize our Performance!

When driving the car, we need to have constant access to useful information.
The dashboard is a control panel set within the cockpit that alerts us to how the car operating. Our dashboard consists of a speedometer, temperature and battery indicators, and a fuel gauge to display the amount of fuel in that tank.

The DRS (Drag reduction system) button and the car warning lights and symbols, also relates to internal components, and our emotions which extend to the steering wheel.

The internal components are represented by a set of different coloured lights signalling to the driver.

The colours are red, purple, blue, green, yellow, and orange. They signal to the driver to stop, slow down, be cautious, or keep going. These colours represent different emotions, they are illustrated in the 'Feelings Wheel' diagram formulated by Dr. Gloria Wilcox.

Our gears are displayed on two paddles either side, one for down shifting and the other for upshifting. They consist of eight forward gears, evenly divided and one reverse gear. The gears are either manual or semi-automatic.

The engine warning light is the most important warning light of all the indicators. If we feel like the car is on a knife edge and the engine light is flashing, there is a mechanical issue, something has failed in the engine or transmission, and we need to act immediately.

If the engine light stays on, we need to turn off the ignition, it's a DNF (Did Not Finish) the race. This signal represents a rapid deterioration of our mental health or physical health that would prevent us from continuing the race.
If we become high-risk, we need to seek professional help and obtain immediate assistance.

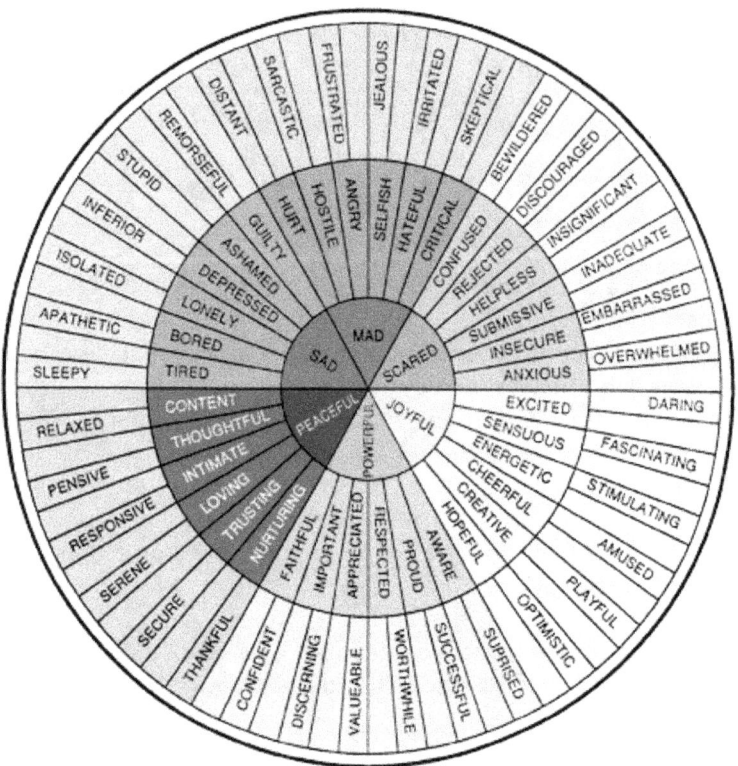

Figure 1. **Feelings Wheel**, *Dr. Gloria Wilcox.*

- **The Red light indicates: Stop!**
  - **Mad:** Angry. Hurt. Hostile. Selfish. Hateful. Critical. Sceptical. Irritated. Jealous. Frustrated. Sarcastic. Distant. Trauma. Burnout. Stress., Dirrty Thoughts.

These emotions are associated with **angry (mad).**

- **The Orange light indicates: Caution!**
  - **Scared:** Confused. Rejected. Helpless. Submissive. Insecure. Anxious. Overwhelmed. Embarrassed. Inadequate. Insignificant. Discourage. Bewildered. Procrastination. Ego. Not Good Enough

These emotions are associated with **fear.**

● **The Purple light indicates: Action Required: Check Rear View Mirror!**

- **Sad:** Tired. Bored. Lonely. Depressed. Ashamed. Guilty. Remorseful. Stupid. Inferior. Isolated. Apathetic. Sleepy. Rock Bottom

These emotions are associated with **sadness.**

● **The Yellow light indicates: Pick Up Pace!**

- **Joyful:** Excited. Sensuous. Energetic. Cheerful. Creative. Hopeful. Optimistic. Playful. Amused Stimulating. Fascinating. Daring. Playful Story Wheel.

These emotions are associated with **joy.**

● **The Green light indicates: All Clear!**

- **Powerful:** Aware. Proud. Respected. Appreciated. Important. Faithful. Confident. Discerning. Valuable. Worthwhile. Successful. Surprised.

These emotions are associated with **power.**

● **The Blue light indicates: Leisurely slow the pace down!**

- **Peaceful:** Content. Thoughtful. Intimate. Loving. Trusting. Nurturing. Thankful. Secure. Serene. Responsive. Pensive. Relaxed. Meditation. Gongs

These emotions are associated with **peace.**

When the red; orange, yellow, green, blue or purple lights flash on our control panel, we must respond accordingly. The aim is for us to dial into our own race, so we can become more in tune with ourselves. Just as drivers adjust their cars to find that sweet spot, we must tend to our emotions to prevent the different coloured lights on our internal dashboard from flashing the unhealthy warnings.

Time to enjoy showcasing our skills on track and bringing our car home.

Flags

When the Flag drops!

A beginner's guide to the Formula 1 flags.
Each Marshall post around the track is equipped with a full set of flags, and each colour has its own specific and unambiguous meaning. Getting to know them will enhance our understanding of a race in progress.

The flags are deployed by the marshals to communicate certain messages to the driver. The coloured flags have different meanings and are used to share messages about different changes that occur on track for a Grand Prix race, including speed, weather, traffic ahead, and car and driver conditions.

We are juggling acceleration, braking, steering, the wheel, switches, and Information radio messages, whilst travelling at lightning speeds. We will also need to pay attention to the flags that will navigate us through the track of our lives. They will give assistance to help us to recognise obstructions that lie ahead, depending on the issue and circumstances we find ourselves in, and the decisions we make to ensure we cross the finishing line of our iHope.

We are governed by 9 different flags for each track: yellow, red, black, blue, green, black and white, orange and black, red and yellow striped and the chequered flag.
Each flag will navigate us around the track.

Yellow Flag

Indicates danger.
There is a hazard on the track.
Overtaking is prohibited.
Approach with caution.
Drive within our limits; we cannot overtake and must be prepared to change direction. It must be evident that a driver has reduced their speed during the relevant sectors.
Slow down considerably. It is often used when Marshalls are on track.
Be prepared to stop!

Red and Yellow Striped Flag

Slippery surface up ahead on track due to oil, water or another substance, causing a lowering and deterioration of grip levels.
Rain has rendered the service hazardous. We need to slow down and be careful through this section

Green Flag

All clear. End of danger zone.

Blue Flag

A faster car is going to overtake. Move over. We are about to be lapped.
At all times, it is shown to inform a driver, leaving the pits, that traffic is approaching.

Red Flag

The race has now stopped in the interest of safety.
Stop the race due to a serious accident or extreme weather.
Reduce our speed and proceed back to the pit lane.
Line up at the exit and await instructions.

Black Flag

Warning! Immediately return to the pit.
We are in trouble, make sure we recognise the situation.
To disqualify a driver, return to the pit immediately.
This flag is only waived based on the decision of the stewards.

Black and White Diagonal Flag

Warning. Unsportsmanlike behaviour.

Black and Orange Flag

The car has a mechanical problem.
Mechanical problems detected we are a danger to ourselves.
We must stop at our own pit on the next lap.
Our back-up crew at the pit wall are notified.
The car has damage or a mechanical issue, which could be dangerous, we must return to the pits as soon as possible!
The car may return to the track if the chief scrutineer is satisfied that the issues have been resolved.
Penalties for infringing the warning flags, or for speeding in and out of the pit lane can be costly in championship points, and positions in the race.

Chequered Flag

End of racing.
Signals the finish of the race.
The race has officially ended.

Sash Adelante ♫

I hope I can see I'm progressing ...

Formation Lap

Sow the Seed and see it Grow!

A Formation Lap is the lap before the race begins.

The driver will drive around the track at a slow speed of 50 mph, each driver will keep to their grid position, no overtaking is allowed. This gives the driver the opportunity to familiarise themselves with the track conditions and check the performance of the car. It also allows them to warm up the tyres and the brakes ready for the race. Once the formation lap is complete, the cars will form into position on the grid to start the race.

Nature can lie alongside us.

Even in the most hostile environments, we may come across a weed in the small cracks of a concrete slab or a brick wall, somehow nature finds a way. If not a person or a pet, choose a plant to love unconditionally on this journey. Plants thrive on the same sources as us, food, water, oxygen and light, they grow towards the light. Whilst starting any journey of self-development, a plant can keep us company along the way, it's visual, we can witness the growth, new roots, shoots, and leaves. We will need to tend to our plant each day, so why not give our plant a name?

The formation lap is a chance to prepare our plant, robust, with high tolerance to the climate and conditions in our home. Our plant can be a wonderful teacher, so choose our seedling wisely. if it's the first time for us, try not to be too overly ambitious in finding a plant that's unforgiving. A very young plant, indoor or outdoor, every plant requires nurturing; feeding, watering, and general maintenance, we can practice taking care of and learn how to nurture it.

A plant is a great metaphor for growth, mirroring our own development as we both start the journey together. A plant is visual and can be used symbolically in line with our own personal growth. Witnessing seeing the first green shoots, the growth of our plant can lift our spirits and encourage us to stay on track with our own self development. We're not alone on this journey.

Take regular photos to track our plant's growth, while watering our soul with good thoughts, open-mindedness, patience, compassion, kind words, self-belief, love, and hope.

What we focus on, grows.

Imagine we're in the last race of the season with it all to play for. We've sealed the deal for qualifying on track, we start from pole position. It's time to start the formation lap to leave the grid for the Grand Prix.

All focus on the five lights of the gantry to start the countdown to the race.

LIGHTS OUT

Ed Sheeran Drive 🎵

iHope

Chapter 3

All Clear!

The chapter of the Green Flag is announcing ...

Green Flag

Track is all clear.
End of danger zone

Sometimes life signals us to go forward, and we hesitate and fail to notice the opportunity.
This chapter discusses the "green flag' moments in our lives.
The green flag represents a moment of opportunity, a time when the path ahead is clear and it's safe to accelerate and move forward. We sometimes overlook these moments, whether they are opportunities for personal growth, career development or improved relationships. These moments can often be disguised as quiet opportunities or subtle changes in our lives. This is a time to recognise these moments of potential and embrace them with confidence. They require us to be present, aware, and ready to act!

The track's clear, it's time to accelerate, don't leave any margin, our engines will be singing away in 8th gear.
Hit the limit!

DRS Enabled!

44	**My Culture**	66	**His Reign**
46	**ManTalk**	67	**Birthday Vs. Work**
48	**Opinions**	68	**Parenthood**
49	**Quitting**	70	**Sorry**
51	**Firsts**	71	**Dear Girlfriends**
52	**Kindred Spirits**	72	**Skullful of Brilliance**
53	**Kindness**	74	**Equal Exits**
55	**Eavesdropping**	75	**Healing**
56	**Vibes**	78	**Friendship Reshuffle**
58	**Compassion**	80	**Meantimers**
59	**Swearing**	81	**Power of Feminine Energy**
60	**A Friend in Need**	82	**Trust Thy Self**
61	**Forgiveness**	83	**Change Becomes Habits, Habits Becomes Change**
63	**Boredom**		
65	**Self-Enquiry**		

I hope I can make a change my way of life ...

My Culture

Who do You think You Are?

Dashboard The Green Light indicates: All Clear!

I am a woman of colour, in my fifties, shaped by a lifetime of curiosity, passion, loyalty, honesty, creativity, kindness, and ambition. Raised in a working-to middle-class family in the UK, and growing up in a predominantly white society, my experiences have profoundly shaped the person I am today. These qualities, rooted in my culture and upbringing are woven throughout the fabric of this book.

> Culture is a defining force, that shapes
> who we are and sets us apart.

Just like a dish, we all start with the same base, but the seasoning we add creates a flavour that makes us different. Our culture is deeply personal and rooted in our DNA, ancestry, and the tribe we belong to. It influences our values, morals, relationships, language, emotions, beliefs, and traditions. It shapes how we perceive the world, our customs, social behaviours and experiences.

Culture is not just a part of us; it's the very way we live and breathe.
It's a way of life!

What is our culture?

By asking ourselves key questions, we can begin to shape a life and culture that truly reflects who we want to be, not just who we were conditioned to be.

The Key Questions

- What elements of our culture no longer serve us anymore?
- What is our culture depriving us of?
- What elements of our culture are we proud to maintain?
- What new experiences can we seek to broaden our perspective?
- What fears and insecurities are holding us back?
- How can we create space in our life for self-love?

If we don't like the life we lead, we can always shift our own culture and step out of our comfort zone to embrace new possibilities. Being brave can be a lonely place. However, having the courage to create and live the culture we desire begins with exploring new practices.

The Key Practices

- Enhancing our wellbeing.
- Say "Yes" to self-development.
- Unlearn old behaviours to change our belief system.
- Set boundaries by saying 'No' to what isn't serving us anymore.
- Make a decision.
- Account for our emotions.
- Become mentally and physically fit.
- Becoming debt-free.

We are entitled to set our own culture!

⚙ Consider changing to a different compound. Soft Tyre.

Pulp Common People ♪

I hope I can make connections ...

ManTalk

The Language of Men

Dashboard The Green Light indicates: All Clear!
For women to understand men better, we must recognise that males and females think differently and communicate differently from one another, dependent on their communication needs.
One way is not better than the other, they are simply different. In general, men are less likely than women to express their emotions openly or show vulnerability through crying.

In practice, Lewis, 32, explains,
*"There is a process we must go through before we get to the **emotion** (204). We don't go straight to the emotion, we need to understand what the problem is first, and that can take time. We struggle to express something that we don't fully understand yet, and if we haven't figured out the issue, women add to the issue because of their impatience, they want us to communicate like they do."*

Men and women are wired differently. For example, if both are given the task of getting to the other side of a forest, most women are likely to walk and talk their way through the forest to figure out how to get to the other side. Men would prefer to stay where they are, prepare themselves, get a map, a torch, and check if they need a machete or a tractor. Once they have gathered all the information and sorted out the route of how to get through the forest, only then are they ready to move. Much like communication, once they have figured out what's happening in their head and their heart, then they might be ready to talk.

Many men from diverse cultures often hold themselves to rigid restraints, creating barriers that prevent them from expressing their feelings openly. This pattern is rooted in societal expectations that equate vulnerability with weakness. Yet, the truth is quite the opposite: vulnerability is a superpower. It allows us to confront and feel our emotions, which in turn builds strength, courage and resilience. To embrace vulnerability is to be brave enough to acknowledge and own our feelings, rather than suppressing or dismissing them.

Male interaction, in general, often follows certain patterns. It tends to be either task-orientated, focusing on practical objectives and problem-solving, or involves banter, where the casual exchange of teasing or mocking becomes a form of bonding. This type of camaraderie, though seemingly playful, can range from light-hearted to antagonizing, serving as a means of testing each other's wit and ability to think on their feet. It's a way to establish mutual respect, gauge emotional **boundaries** (215), and build trust within their group dynamics. However, while this style of interaction fosters connection in some ways, it can also limit the depth of emotional expression. The cultural norms around masculinity often discourage open discussions about vulnerability, personal struggles, and emotional pain. Yet, it is in these honest, and raw conversations when barriers are lowered, that true bravery and strength emerge. Men tend to keep their thoughts to themselves often feeling they aren't worthy of attention. They seldom discuss their problems and sometimes they assert dominance to downplay others.

Their primary focus seems to be on gaining respect, rather than seeking to be liked. When it comes to intimate stuff the bigger things aren't discussed, which means close bonds aren't formed, leaving them nowhere to go. The demands of rigid masculinity create barriers to fully expressing their emotions and needs.

Men tend to focus on fact-based, or unemotional conversations, they are not receptive to the deeper story unless they are active: exercising, doing chores, watching sport, playing cards, driving, or attending external events. This approach is the opposite from women who prefer full attention, face to face, eye contact to talk about emotional disclosure, like a therapy room.

The closest to a **therapy** (284) room for some men could be going to the barbers. The barbers are a place for community, that's the time to rebuild friendships, where bonding, sharing stories may occur. This resource sometimes can disappear, due to financial difficulties, or fatherhood gets in the way, we may have less time to rebuild friendships.

Where do we forge new friendships?

As we grow older, many of us find it harder to make new friends. Often, men build connections through shared environments, e.g. school, work, hobbies, or sports. Personal matters are more likely to be shared with a partner than with friends. Strengthening friendships takes intention, and it's never too late to start. Just keep talking!

- Consider changing to a different compound. Intermediate Tyre.

Mr Probz Waves (Robin Schulz remix radio edit) ♫

I hope making informed judgements matters ...

Opinions

Stand for Something, rather than Nothing!

Dashboard The Green Light indicates: All Clear!

Opinions don't appear overnight; they're formed through experience. We gain perspective that can't be taught, only lived. Each challenge, success, or setback, teaches us something new, shaping our value and principles over time. These lessons become markers of maturity, strengthening our backbone and helping us define who we are. As we align ourselves with certain beliefs or values, we begin to form a clearer sense of identity. From that, our opinions take shape, not just as quick reactions, as reflections of deeper understanding. In turn, those opinions help build and express our character.

Opinions are the spice of life!

To form a meaningful opinion, we need interest, information, knowledge, and personal experience about the subject to support our ability to assess, evaluate, and offer a perspective that is truly own.

Opinions are valuable, they take our own experiences, emotions, and beliefs into account to form an opinion; they matter. When we share our opinions, it shows that we are willing to engage in meaningful conversation. If someone agrees with our views, we have a sense of inclusion or validation. As a collective, we can make a difference, they can bring new ideas to the table and inspire change. Without a voting system there wouldn't be change. To vote is to create change, to change laws, and to vote, we are expected to have an opinion. Expressing our opinion can build stronger relationships, opinions can bond and unite people or create an alliance about a subject we feel passionately about that aligns with our values, thoughts and feelings.

It's okay to have some strong unshakeable opinions.

To have an opinion, however 'unshakable' the opinion might be, does not mean we have to force our opinions on others, or validate other opinions for our own means. We can respect other opinions, regardless of whether we agree, there are more than one right answer.

Stand up and be counted, make a difference and stand for something, rather than nothing, or we are likely to be floating wherever the wind takes us. Form an opinion for a richer conversation and a richer life.

I'm of the opinion that our opinions count!

I hope I recognize the right time to let go ...

Quitting

Ending is as fundamental as Starting!

Dashboard The Green Light indicates: All Clear!
"Quitting is a skill. Knowing when to quit, change direction, leave a toxic situation, demand more from life, give up on something that wasn't working and move on, is a very important skill that people who win at life all seem to have." Steven Bartlett

Knowing when to cut ties, whether out of loyalty, fear or habit, is one of the hardest and most necessary parts of growth.
Holding onto what no longer serves us can keep us stuck. To move forward, we must make room by releasing the outdated, the draining, and the unhelpful, opening space for new opportunities, growth, and meaningful experiences.

This process isn't easy, several challenges can hinder our progress, such as avoiding the confrontation of core values:

- Being loyal, or pleasing people, feeling obliged to stay.
- We're a 'finisher' in life.
- An over-achiever.
- Heavily invested in the old and too afraid to jump.
- Think we're a loser and we've failed.

Choosing our battles is as important as knowing when to quit. Staying until the bitter end to prove a point, or overstaying our welcome never serves anyone, its time wasted, and our confidence is bruised. The job that's trading our health for cash, it's time to quit. The job that is degrading and dragging us down, it's time to quit. Or the job that is 'taking us for a steal,' taking our fresh, innovative, genius ideas that we can use to set up our own business that means, it is time to quit. There is no point in settling for a job when we know we are better than the job. To upgrade ourselves, it is time to quit while we are ahead, not when we are spent. A relationship that has passed its expiry date, long stale and unfulfilling, often keeps us stuck. We have clung to a deadbeat partner, holding on to the illusions of a "couple" status, at the expense of our friendships.

Those friends who offered honest advice, eventually grew tired of telling us,

"You've changed."
"They're not right for you."

As they watched us lose ourselves in a relationship that no longer served us.

In prioritizing the façade of a partnership, we sacrificed meaningful connections with those who truly cared for us. We stayed hoping they'd one day appreciate us, treat us better, pay back the money they owe, or stop with the jealous accusations and hurtful put-downs. We clung to the belief that they might transform into the potential we once saw, only to realise later, they had no intention of changing.

In hindsight, if we had quit the relationship sooner, we might have preserved precious memories with friends, avoided missing opportunities to meet a suitable partner, and protected our time, self-respect, **self-esteem** (144), and self-worth. Overstaying our welcome past its expiry date comes at a high cost. It's more expensive than walking away sooner.

Quitting is just as fundamental as starting.

We need closure to move forward and embrace new beginnings. To be a winner, we must know when to take the risk, let go, and quit to pursue the next opportunity. Without taking risks, life becomes stagnant, offering diminishing returns from doing the same things and pressing the same old buttons. Quitting is not for losers. It is for the shrewd, those who recognize that sometimes letting go opens the door to greater possibilities.

In the process of upgrading ourselves we need to know when it's ripe to quit. It is a part of progression and moving on!

Pick up the slipstream to gain speed and overtake.

Primal Scream Movin' on Up ♫

I hope trying something new is worth it ...

Firsts

Sometimes, we can all find ourselves 'winging it!'

Dashboard The Green Light indicates: All Clear!

Most of us get to a place in our lives where we don't want to try anything that we're not any good at doing, because we don't want to fail or feel vulnerable. No one wants to fail!
So, we avoid trying new ways of doing things, like saying,

"I'll take that new class!"

At times life presents situations in which we need to step out of our **comfort zones** (118) and step into 'first times'. This can make us feel incredibly vulnerable. That 'muscle' that we use when we do 'first times' can be the 'secret sauce' to life, in gaining confidence, when we flex our 'independent' muscle and meet new people or start a new hobby. We learn something new about ourselves, this wouldn't happen in our comfort zones.

In practice, Amelia was going through a separation, living alone and working remotely. She became lonely, her social circle had halved after separating from her partner. Amelia enjoyed running, so rather than running alone, I encouraged her to join a running club to meet people with similar interests. Over time, her social circle expanded, where she met her future wife. Her life changed significantly, simply doing something new for the first time.

The Outcome

'First times' are like pressing the 'restart' button on our devices, they clear away the old stuff to update our souls. They can refresh, reset, and re-energise our spirit to new empowering levels. Take that step to discover what makes the 'new version of ourselves' tick.

🟢 Consider changing to a different compound. Soft Tyre.

We've gone purple and set the fastest lap

Annie Lennox Little Bird 🎵

I hope I can be open to connect deeply with a friend…

Kindred Spirits

Good friends are better than Pocket Money!

Dashboard The Green Light indicates: All Clear!
One of the most powerful and meaningful connections we can experience is the bond we share with our friends. These relationships hold a unique place in our hearts. Our friends are the family we choose, our confidants, our kindred spirits. Rich, supportive friendships are essential to our wellbeing, offering love, laughter, and loyalty through every season of life.

Clients often ask me, with a mix of curiosity and reflection, how they can truly recognise a best friend is someone who genuinely stands the test of time, trust, and connection.
Every friendship is unique. Soulmates are special, they're the truly good, wholesome friends in our lives I call kindred spirits. Kindred spirits are like-minded souls who share similar beliefs, common interests, and sense of humour. They mirror us, creating instant positive and **emotional connections** (302) and it feels like we've known them for a lifetime.

The qualities of good, healthy friendships begin with honesty, trustworthiness, openness to different perspectives, emotional sharing, and a willingness to invest time in the connection. If we make a mistake, it's not permanent, they are open to repairing ruptures by apologizing, it strengthens the bond. These attributes alone can sustain a positive lifelong relationship.

Kindred spirits are emotionally supportive, understanding and respectful, and they genuinely care about our well-being. They are loyal, there in the good times and the bad. They accept us for who we are, and are willing to share, help and expect nothing in return. Real friendship is built on care and intention, where our happiness truly matters to someone. These friends lovingly encourage us to grow, holding space for our flaws with love and understanding. Together, we share moments that become treasured memories. With healthy **boundaries** (215), these bonds deepen, becoming lifelong connections filled with warmth, wisdom, and light.

Kindred spirits are defined by how they make us feel. We recognise it when we're in their company. They offer a safe space that allows us to show up as

ourselves. When we part ways, we leave feeling better, seen heard, and lighter. Super good friends have a lasting, positive impact in our lives.
We never know who we might bump into in life. If we haven't yet experienced a kindred spirit, we must remain open to meeting new souls and embracing fresh energy as we journey through life's seasons. There's a whole world of souls out there who are meant to cross our path.

If we're lucky enough to share our lives with a kindred spirit, celebrate the premier of all friendships!

International friendship day 30th of July.

I hope I know how to be kind to myself ...

Kindness

The Best Version of ourselves, requires Kindness!

Dashboard The Green Light indicates: All Clear!
We often hear the phrase,
"Be kind to yourself!"

In my practice, I've met many thoughtful souls who quietly ask,
"What does it really mean to be kind to ourselves?"

It's a powerful question, one that invites us to pause and reflect. Let's begin with the very foundation of who we are: the body we live in, the temple we inhabit each day.

How often do we give ourselves good news or gentle words?

The truth is, we never stop listening to ourselves. Yet, much of our inner dialogue is far from kind. Negativity often takes up residence in our heads, lingering for far too long. That internal committee of critics is usually stuck on repeat.

When we hear the phrase, *"Be kind to yourself"* many believe it means an abundance of treats and spoiling ourselves into existence. Sometimes we need to be cruel to be kind.

Being kind to ourselves means we treat ourselves how we would treat our own best friend to convey love. Kindness looks like care, respect, compassion, understanding, encouragement, reassurance, acceptance, loyalty, patience, ease, support, emotion, attentiveness, gentleness, and mindfulness. Being kind means keeping ourselves out of harm's way, to 'feel safe', meaning feeling safe in our environment, externally as well as internally. This includes feeling complete emotional comfort.

Resting is an act of kindness to ourselves, giving permission to step back from the grind of life every now and again. We all feel guilty for having some time off. It's okay to do nothing, have a duvet day. Treat ourselves to a day of snuggling under the duvet for regular snoozes, or with a book or a boxset; it is a time to chill, catch breath, restore ourselves and tuck up!

Kindness will rarely lead us in the wrong direction, particularly when we are guided with love and awareness. When we'd prefer to change a behaviour that is not working for us, speak kindly to ourselves, gently and supportively. This is more likely to elicit positive change by validating and understanding rather than beating ourselves up.

Treat ourselves the way we would look after our new car, new kitchen, or new sofa. We might take pride in maintaining its newness. This suggests **emotional maintenance** (229), little and often, to nurture and care for ourselves.

Remember, we're always listening, be kind!

⚫ Consider changing to a different compound. Medium Tyre.
Pick up the slipstream to gain speed and overtake.

HNNY Kindness 🎵

I hope I can pay attention to hear myself think ...

Eavesdropping

Mind our Language

Dashboard The Green Light indicates: All Clear!

Do we really hear the words we say to ourselves?
Notice the tone of our inner voice?
We often assume we're always listening to ourselves. After all, there's a constant stream of chatter in our minds, keeping us company, especially when we're alone, in quiet moments.

Are we really paying attention?

It's one thing to have thoughts; it's another to consciously listen to the language and the content we use within. It is not unusual for us to lose our way and follow a path that's not ours. We often run on autopilot. Thoughts flit through our heads non-stop, some helpful, others toxic and shaped by the beliefs we hold. Our beliefs are incredibly powerful: they guide every thought we have. What we think influences how we feel; how we feel dictates our behaviour; and our behaviour looks for evidence to validate those beliefs. Without realising it, our beliefs can steer us down narrow, unhelpful paths, this is known as "tunnel vision". Tunnel vision keeps us locked into our own mental loop, preventing us from seeing the full picture. That's why it's important to 'eavesdrop' on our thoughts to catch the ones circling in the background and pull ourselves back into a wider, healthier perspective. It helps to pause and reflect: When we feel stuck, pause and take a moment to re-evaluate. Tune into our inner voice, and ask ourselves,
"Is there any truth in this belief?"
Beliefs are learned and can be unlearned.

Incorporating this into our daily routine makes it easier to check in regularly, helping to sustain the habit. Make inquiries to ask some key questions:

The Key Questions

- How am I doing today?
- How am I feeling?
- Have I been holding my breath, or breathing shallow or deep?
- Any aches or pains, does my heart feel heavy or light?

- Notice repeating thoughts, and how we've been self- talking?
- Am I being kind or critical - what words am I using about myself?

Our personal check-ins are a moment of calm and orderly thinking in a noisy world of chaos to give us a chance to keep up with ourselves. Checking in can boost our emotional intelligence as we reveal our deepest thoughts and feelings, from our innermost fears to our deepest desires. We become aware of our unconscious thoughts, which improves our mental health and in turn creates calm and orderly thinking amid the demands of a disordered world. Checking in with ourselves makes a difference in how we feel about ourselves and helps us to understand our world, highlighting the aspects that require attention to help us change and feel genuine improvements.

Listening is plenty of doing!!

I hope my presence can be felt by others …

Vibes

This is me, my energy, my essence!

Dashboard The Green Light indicates: All Clear!

Everything is energy.
We are all a ball of vibrating energy. We are all giving off a vibe, even the thoughts we think give off a vibration, we are attracted to things by energy.

Emotion is the experience of feeling energy moving through our body and we give that emotion a name, joy, sadness, excitement, nervousness, or anger. Others can experience our emotions from a frequency of vibration. We all vibrate at a certain frequency; these energies can impact other souls. Energy becomes contagious to those that share a similar frequency or are particularly sensitive to energy that may feel familiar.

Ever felt drained for no reason after being around someone?

We all have an energy centre that runs through our body, made up of eight chakras that are in our astral body starting from the base of our spine to the crown of our head. These chakras are mapped to different emotional and psychological issues that can be used to help identify imbalance in the body.

On the other side, there are other emotions such as feelings, enthusiastic, positive, upbeat, lively, contagious, vivacious, bubbly, vibrant, or high-spirited. We all have a vibration, vibrations occur from energy, the higher the vibration the more positive the energy, when our energies are synchronized, we feel good vibes.

We attract what we radiate.

The people around us reflect the energy we carry, often mirroring what feels familiar and attractive to us.

We are all energy fields and our quest in life is to keep our energy vibrations high. It's helpful to incorporate different practices to maintain or strengthen our vibrations, being active: exercise, having fun, eating healthily, **meditation** (293), or prayer to support our frequencies.

Keeping ourselves internally connected and balanced is key. We all would like to feel good vibrations to free our soul and spirit to thrive.

Our auric field is an extension of us, an energy field that surrounds and extends beyond our physical bodies. We can start by clearing our auric field, which is like clearing out our dustbins, getting rid of old, dead energy that's been hanging around and weighing us down.
Once we've cleared our energy, we can nurture it through dance, stillness, music, movement, rest, and meditation. These practices help us stay grounded and vibrant—because positive energy grows where positive vibes flow!

Positive vibes breed positive energy!

Our energy creates ripples like a stone dropped in water.

Children of Zeus Vibrations ♪

I hope to embrace empathy, and acceptance in myself and others...

Compassion

We are All deeply Connected!

Dashboard The Green Light indicates: All Clear!

Compassion is essential to our well-being to ensure permanence.
It's the opportunity to consciously stretch ourselves to deepen the emotional connections that define who we are.
Compassion is often mistaken as simply, being 'nice', yet it's vital for our well-being. True compassion connects us with our inner selves, helping us face difficult emotions like fear and sadness, and strengthening our overall existence. This process takes courage to look inward honestly, connect with another's pain and respond with genuine empathy and respect.

Compassion is a universal language that begins from within!

Self-compassion deepens our presence, allowing our emotions to move through us with greater ease and acceptance. As we begin to understand and honour our true selves, including our flaws, gifts, and everything in between, we start to see reflections of ourselves in others. We realise we're not alone in our struggles or joys. We are all part of something bigger, deeply woven together in our humanity. When we align with our inner wisdom, we connect with the essence of who we are. And in that space, we become more open, more empathetic, and more capable of truly seeing, feeling, and connecting with those around us.

"Unfinished Sympathy," captures the essence of compassion by exploring the human experience of heartbreak, the hope in possibility, and the strength found in emotional vulnerability and understanding. It invites us, as listeners, to reflect on our own lives and relationships, encouraging a deeper sense of empathy, both for others and ourselves.

Compassion is a daily practice of holding space for ourselves and others.

We've gone purple and set the fastest lap.
- Consider switching to a different compound. Wet Tyre.

Massive Attack Unfinished Sympathy ♪

I hope I can express exactly how I feel …

Swearing

Beeeeeeeeep!...Beeeeeeeeeep!!!!!!!!

Dashboard The Green Light indicates: All Clear!

Every language, culture, or religion has its taboo words. Words that are forbidden or seen as distasteful or disrespectful and swearing may be one of those taboos. However, in the expression of passion, swearing has its uses.
I don't advocate swearing to be the only words in our vocabulary, having full use of our rich and colourful language is there to be used appropriately, nevertheless, swearing has a place.

It's healthy to swear, to fully express ourselves appropriately can feel liberating. Pain is physical and physiological. It is scientifically proven swearing helps to release or numb the pain.

Swearing helps especially if we find ourselves in a situation feeling **angry** (224), frustrated, or frightened, and we don't have any other outlet to release the feeling. Swearing helps us to process those emotions by externalising them. Letting go and releasing frustration through verbal expression allows adrenalin levels to simmer down, which helps us to feel better.

It is necessary to let off some steam; sometimes swearing can relieve, reduce and save us from many confrontational situations or physical fights. Cursing and cussing has its place.

Sometimes a beep, beeep, beeeeeeeeeep!!!!!!... is necessary!

Serial Killlaz Traffic Blocking ♫

I hope I can show my support ...

A Friend in Need

Be there!

Dashboard The Green Light indicates: All Clear!

When we find our tribe, the friends that we can laugh, connect and embrace with, they become our people, the ones who lift us up and remind us that life is worth living.

Friends are special souls we cherish. When they start to withdraw, distance themselves, become unusually quiet, or simply seem not quite themselves, it's important that we notice and reach out with care and compassion. Let's start by asking:

"How are you doing?"

We often speak in riddles when it comes to expressing how we feel:
"I'm doing alright, I suppose I've been better..."
"I'm not doing great as I should be at the moment."
"Yeah, I'm so so.."

Ask them again,

"How are you doing?"

Ask them until they have answered the question, and we understand clearly, allowing us to step in and offer help and support. This may also involve contacting their family or professional services.

There are other practical things we can do to make a difference to their daily lives that might ease the pressure.

What can we do?

Offering our best help may look different each time.

The Key Practices

- Cooking a meal for them.
- Picking the children up from school.
- Listening and providing advice.
- Taking them out to be social.
- Babysitting the children to give them space.
- Being a shoulder to cry on.
- Speaking to friends or relatives on their behalf.
- Regularly checking in on them, letting them know they're loved.

There are many other ways to support and **help** (283) friends in need, we know them well.

All we must do is be there. Show up for them. Physically be there, be beside them, no need to say or fix anything. Let them know we are on their side, simply by being beside them...that's enough!

Just be there!

Kate Bush and Peter Gabriel Don't Give Up ♫
Snow Patrol Chasing Cars ♫

I hope I can move on ...

Forgiveness

Turn our painful past to Dust!

Dashboard The Green Light indicates: All Clear! 🟢
Pride can quietly take root in our hearts, often becoming the silent force behind our disagreements, quarrels, and everyday bickering. It keeps score alike a seasoned referee, stockpiling memories that justify our feelings and replaying them like comforting reruns.
Whether we're right or wrong, holding onto conflict can be exhausting. It takes real energy to keep the battle and defend our position.

What about us?

The crusade has cost us our peace of mind, gambling with our time and relationships. Whether we're right or wrong, it is toxic and onerous, and has a negative impact on our life, and our health.
Trying to validate ourselves in conflict comes at a huge cost to our soul, the stereotype of both parties keeping a stiff upper lip, pursed lips and being uptight keeps us on guard. While holding onto toxic energy, negative thoughts, and pain, we ignore the damage it may cause to our body and soul.

What's left of us?

Firstly, put the weapons and the shields down, take the gloves off and look in the mirror. The most important person to forgive is ourselves. Forgive ourselves first, for all that we've put our body and soul through at the cost of our time, relationships and energy, that's distracted us from focusing on what really matters, just to prove a point. Forgetting is not part of forgiveness; we will remember it. Neither is forgiveness excusing the harm done to us. By offering ourselves compassion and respect to free ourselves from the burdens of past grievances, we can allow the wound to **heal** (75).
Secondly, we can allow them to learn the lesson.

How are things going to change?
If a person has made a mistake, let them learn the lesson, there is a difference between someone who makes a mistake and somebody that refuses to learn and continues to replay a pattern. Mistakes can be forgiven, patterns must be broken, for the sake of themselves and others in the firing line.

Give them the space to come back, to apologise, to say,
"I could've done things differently, and I've learned something..."

Choosing not to forgive and holding onto resentment keeps pain alive for both parties, allowing toxic emotions to take root. This can manifest as dis-ease in the body and harm our health.

Is it worth it?
Aren't we worth more? Let go!

Forgive ourselves!

Forgiveness releases us from toxic, negative energy. Embracing acceptance encourages peace and contentment, setting us free to grow and thrive.

Step out of the past. It is time to move forward, full throttle ahead!
Pick up the slipstream to gain speed and overtake.

Alanis Morissette Thank U ♫

I hope I'm not twiddling my thumbs ...

Boredom

When boredom strikes, Creativity Awakens!

Dashboard The Green Light indicates: All Clear!

There is so much to one person.
We can spend our whole lifetime getting to know ourselves as we evolve with time. Time doesn't stand still and neither do we.

There are all the different spheres that make us who we are, our personality, our experiences, our memories, our likes and dislikes, curiosities, or peccadilloes. There's so much information out there to learn about: books, podcasts.
How can we be bored?

Boredom is usually the time when we scroll through our phones to distract ourselves with the latest, news, podcast, Instagram, Tinder, or Tik Tok posts, when instead, this time could be channelled into getting to know more about who we are.

The remedy to boredom doesn't come from external means; to unravel our boredom we need to look within ourselves, as boredom is connected to the emotion of sadness.

There's so much more for us to get to know, by tuning into ourselves to go deeper, we can discover more of who we are and give ourselves the attention we deserve. Through general self-enquiry, we may have some unanswered questions about ourselves, such as.

What's missing in our lives?

Do we have any unfinished business in our life, any old hurts?

We miss ourselves if we're not tuning in or responding to the attention our spirit requires from us.

When our children are bored, allow them to be bored, boredom will not hurt them in any way. This is how they learn to roll up their sleeves and get stuck into entertaining themselves. Typically, creating their own entertainment is something 'only children' or those who have much older siblings, often with,

6-7-year age gap, they can't relate to. With no peers at home to play with, they often learn early on how to entertain themselves. Most become very creative, thinking creatively by getting in touch with their imaginations, or creative writing through storytelling, poetry or expressing themselves through drawing, building, inventing, crafts and so on.

It is never easy being a parent, however this area doesn't have to be our responsibility, it's important to let go of the obligation to entertain our children. Children need to learn to be bored, it allows them to develop their own interests creatively, being resourceful with themselves it makes life much easier for teachers to teach in the classrooms.

This is where entrepreneurs and inventors are born. It's a lot cheaper than sending them on a course ten years down the road.

We have all the answers for ourselves, kindly listen.

I hope I can understand what I do to cope with my feelings ...

Self-Enquiry

Coping with our Emotions?

Dashboard The Green Light indicates: All Clear!

Spend some time alone.
Pay attention to what we are feeling. Investigate our thoughts and assess our activities. Self-enquiry helps us understand where we are emotionally.
We all develop coping mechanisms to manage our **emotions** (204).

How do we manage our emotions?

The Key Questions

- Dance it away?
- Sex it away?
- Run it away?
- Write it away?
- Cuss it away?
- Game it away?
- Bash cushions?
- Box it away?
- Scream it away?
- Snort it away?
- Game it away?
- Pierce it away?
- Shop it away?
- Eat it away?
- Drink it away?
- Gamble it away?
- Porn it away?
- Breathe it away?
- Deny it away?
- Doomscrolling it away?
- Smoke it away?
- Tattoo it away?

....many more.

- Consider switching to a different compound. Wet Tyre.

Solange Cranes in the Sky ♬

I hope I can get this off my chest …

His Reign

Rise up, Reach Out

Dashboard The Green Light indicates: All Clear!
Whether we are struggling with fatherhood, brotherhood, manhood, relationships, family, work, career change, loss, failure, low self-esteem, or other ongoing struggles, talking helps!

It's a struggle from a young age. We are told we must behave differently when it comes to our emotions – *"Stop crying"* (235), as this demonstrates weakness.

As life goes on, we grow into men believing certain stereotypes of being 'a man' refers to being brave, tough, the one with big shoulders, in control and emotionless, put simply, we're taught that masculinity means:

> **tough and silent type.**
> **man up.**
> **take it like a man.**

Over time, we internalise the idea that being 'a man' means we sort out problems on our own, without talking about them or involving outsiders.

I have encountered many who act out to suppress or mask feelings of insecurity, they often bypass emotions of denial, anger and frustration, and turn to pornography, alcohol, smoking or gambling as a distraction to keep depressive feelings away. However, these choices won't bury the problem. Instead, they get in the way of the problem. It is worth talking through our pressures with someone who's neutral in the situation to be supported to gain a deeper understanding and a different perspective of what's going on, allowing us to sort the problem out.

It is not easy being vulnerable in society, especially when we feel the social pressure to be tough. It's time we let go of outdated stereotypes, get them off our chest, so we can release the pressure, the isolation, shame and frustration.

There's not a problem that can't be solved with a little **help** (283).
No need to suffer in silence.
It takes strength to admit we need help!

🟢 Consider changing to a different compound. Intermediate Tyre. We've gone purple and set the fastest lap

Donae'o | 🎵

I hope I can make the most of my birthday ...

Birthday Vs. Work

Happy birthday Dear Soul

Dashboard The Green Light indicates: All Clear!
Being born is the most traumatic journey our little souls experience, coming down the birth canal to take our first breath of life as we enter the world. Sadly, some don't make it, and some souls don't make the age we have become today.

Whether we choose to have a gathering, involve friends, family, or not, we can still forget everyone else. Our birthday is a day for us as individuals to acknowledge and celebrate ourselves living another year.

A birthday is an anniversary, to mark the occasion and acknowledge a year has passed in our lives. We made another year; we're still here. Hopefully healthy and well, whether it's a 'cheap and cheerful' to toast and cheer, a party, a rave, a dinner or a dance, it's an occasion allowing us to indulge in ourselves and be celebrated. Whatever our vibe, it's an affirming occasion and a chance for others to express what we mean to them.

Our one-day of the year to celebrate, why go to work on our day?

We spend most of the day away from loved ones. Work does not give us the freedom to do what we want, turn the alarm off, rest and relax, or play, have fun, pleasure, and entertainment, participate in interests that we like. A day to do something different that's all about us, just 24hrs a year we can call 'ours'. Why choose to be confined at work on our birthday, to have a person in charge of us, managing our day, instructing us, a person we're answerable to?
"Is it okay to take a break now?"
Running our day. Choosing to disregard our day tells us a lot about who we are, and how we value ourselves.

The day we were born is an important day, after all our biological mothers went through a lot for us to be here, it is still a momentous day. We are worthy of being celebrated simply because we were born. Celebrate life, revel in our own self-importance if only for one day, do as we please. Embrace the freedom to do whatever we like, whenever we like, with whomever we choose. For 24 hours, indulge, spoil, treat or pamper ourselves, we deserve to spend at least one day dedicated solely to us. We matter.

Celebrate the year gone by, our experiences, achievements, triumphs and good time. Even just getting by, just making it, or simply being alive. **Celebrate** (326).

Life can have its ups and downs.
We don't always feel like we want to celebrate. However, when life is going well, take it and run with it, dance, sing, and laugh with it, have fun. When the chips are down, the cards are stacked, and life's dishing out lemons, we must do what we have to do and make lemonade.

Take the opportunity to enjoy our day and celebrate.
Margarita please!

I hope I'm setting a good example …

PaRenting

Children are borrowed, give them wings and let them Fly!

Dashboard The Green Light indicates: All Clear!
The best gift we can give our children is our wellbeing. To be a healthy parent, we need to bring our whole self into raising our children because they are going to teach us stuff about ourselves that we may have left behind, or never realised was there. Our journey of being a parent will naturally bring up certain areas of our childhoods that we will be challenged to address. How we were raised, our relationship with our parents, others, our beliefs, and values will be tested, all of which may need updating to accommodate raising our child for tomorrow.

When we take on life's biggest responsibility, a child, and life gets in the way, naturally, things can get missed. There's no such thing as 'perfect parenting' we'll never get parenting one hundred percent right, or at least not all the time, and that's okay. Sometimes, children who need the most love can ask for it in the most unloving ways. Simply the nature of the parent-child relationship is up and down. Try not to lie, we know, the big whoppers, such as, "I'm not your dad".

It's not worth it in the end.

Whether it's social media influences, google, reading books, or theories, try not to complicate, trust and follow what we feel, it's honest and our child will respect us because it's us. Our children naturally want to love and respect us, so let's show them affection, physical closeness, warmth, hug and cuddle them, show them we love them, unconditionally.

This helps them to learn about intimacy and closeness in romantic relationships. If we smother our children or try to keep them on a tight leash for fear of them making the wrong decisions in life, overtime they will deceive and do the deed without our knowledge and consent, or resent us and withdraw, they have their own journey and life to lead.

This is a natural process that happens in all families. It is nature's way for our children to detach from us, if we have loved them well, we have done our job, they will pass on the love that we have taught them to nurture in their own family. As much as we love our children, it's not their duty to give it back.

Children are a gift.
They're not ours to keep!

Madonna Notting Really Matters ♫

I hope I can be a responsible parent...

Sorry

An apology to our Minor Demonstrates we are Major

Dashboard The Green Light indicates: All Clear!

The word 'sorry' is a sacred and powerful word.
For some, we may say the word flippantly without meaning or without hesitation because we're embarrassed. Some people can overuse "sorry", diminishing its significance and the true power of an apology. For others, however, "sorry" feels like the hardest word to say, making it a rare yet meaningful confession.

When things cut deep, not apologising allows things to remain unresolved with room for the issues to fester. The word 'Sorry' can make a difference in people's lives and relationships. An apology takes acknowledgement and accountability; 'sorry' means we are regretful of our actions. There will not be a repeat; it will not happen again. It's important to say "sorry" when we hurt a loved one's feelings, make a big mistake, or, upon reflection, wish we had done things differently, Even little people need to hear 'I'm sorry' too. It helps our children feel valued and learn humility. Without the word 'sorry' in our vocabulary, relationships can lack depth, trust or struggle to move forward. We must admit to ourselves that we're not perfect for us to keep improving and developing the role of being a parent.

I've seen many people hurting and needing an apology to help them to **forgive** (61) and move on. Refusing to apologise creates division and resentment in relationships, which is likely to manifest into further friction down the road. Withholding an apology demonstrates a lack of trust and a disrespect of their feelings. This sends a message to our children that they are not important, their hurt is unseen, and their feelings don't count, in turn, we have set the bar, a standard of how they expect to be treated in the world. Admitting we are sorry can elevate the relationship, rather than demote the connection, especially with our children. Sorry carries clout, whether it comes ten years later, an apology can make all the difference.
After all, we are only human.

"I'm sorry"

expresses regret, a recognition of the issue, and an intention to remedy the situation.
Prioritise our relationships over our ego!

Pick up the slipstream to gain speed and overtake.

I hope you understand, I'm still your friend ...

Dear Girlfriends

Low Maintenance Friends

Dashboard The Green Light indicates: All Clear!

Dear Sisters,
Women communicate differently from men. We tend to be natural communicators, often multitasking with ease, which sets us apart. In friendships, there are often 'unspoken' expectations about how and when we should communicate, which can sometimes feel overwhelming. Generally, women tend to value regular contact with their girlfriends and often feel more pressure than men to maintain daily or weekly communication. However, when we have demanding careers, family obligations, or simply a time and energy-consuming lifestyle, maintaining those communication expectations can become challenging to stay consistent.

For the record, it's nothing personal. There are no issues. We haven't turned our backs on you. Life's a hustle. We simply may not have the capacity to meet the expectations of constant communication. Our needs might differ, but we're still here. When it counts, we're there!
We care, love and will support you.

So, girlfriends ease up on us. We miss you; we do want you in our lives, and we're doing our best.
Much love,
Your 'low maintenance' friend.

Let's all support each other's crowns.

Little Simz Woman (feat. Cleo Sol) ♪

I hope I don't take advantage of my mental health ...

Skullfull of Brilliance

The CEO of our Being

Dashboard The Green Light indicates: All Clear!

We all want to take care of our bodies, but do we take care of our brain?

Our amazing brain is the most complex structure we humans have.
The brain controls our thoughts, emotions, memory, breathing, motor skills, vision, touch, hunger, temperature, and all that regulates our body. Our brilliant brains are the CEO of our beings and take leadership over our mental and physical health.

It is the only organ that can rewire itself, called neuroplasticity. Our brains never stop operating for us. Even when we're sleeping, our brains are still functioning, repairing and re-organising their connections based on what we have learned from the previous day, as well as washing our brains ready for the next day.

We are only human, and at times we have all taken our brains for granted. Whether it's being high on alcohol, drugs or whatever other substance, we expect our brains to carry on giving one hundred percent to us whilst we abuse ourselves. When we choose to burn the candle at both ends, we expect our brains not to falter, but to keep providing for us moment by moment.

Our brilliant brain controls the nervous system. The nervous system uses neurons to transmit messages from our brains, through our spinal cord, to the rest of the nerves throughout our body. This allows us to think, remember, dream, move, hear, talk, sleep and feel. Our mind controls our thoughts and our experiences and changes with the experiences we encounter. The modern-day world we live in is full of health hazards that cause inflammation, oxidative stress and a loss of neuroplasticity.

Here are just a few:
- Chronic **stress** (164).
- Sedentary lifestyles.
- Poor **sleep** (212).
- Constant screen time.

- High sugar and processed foods.
- Anything that lowers blood flow to the brain.

To improve brain function:

- Anything that increases blood flow to the brain.
- Omega 3 fatty acids.
- Gingko
- Exercise

Everything starts with a thought.

Our brains are designed to carry out the tasks they're given by doing what they're told. We can change how we experience the world by teaching our brain to change our perspective. Becoming intentional about the reality that we are creating is essential to how we experience life. Let's say, if the story in our minds is,

"I'm a loser"

our brain will cherry pick everything in our lives to reinforce that notion. Instead, consider asking our brains to show us positive, fruitful things,

"Show me life will get better!"

As a result, our brains will then seek evidence and cherry pick examples which support this notion instead, for it to be true, to become our reality. Our brains will seek proof of reality that we, ourselves, have created in our lives. See, we can take the lead and help our brains to help us if we take the time to be conscious and work with our brains.

Our brains can heal given the right conditions, if we feed them with the proper nutrition and plenty of water, rest, mental stimulation, and movement. Don't take our brain for granted; without our brains fully functioning, we're unable to achieve our ambitions, the brain understands routine, so let's give our brains a helping hand to help us.

There is always the opportunity to change our brain to whatever we're experiencing. We have the power to change the narrative, our perspective, and our ways of thinking.

Help our brain to help us!

- Consider changing to a different compound. Medium Tyre.

I hope I can make the best of life …

Equal Exits

No one leaves this world Unscathed

Whether it's the beginnings in childhood, mid-way through our lives, or in our autumn years that we face adversity, these are our biggest challenges in life. We all level out in the end.

Everyone has their own battles; we don't know when they will come. Take our noses out of other people's lives; envy will keep us off track. Stay focused in our own lane. Life has a funny way of bringing us down a peg or two or knocking us off the top of the ladder when we least expect it. We all get our fair dose of lemons that life throws at us. Life can deliver pain that brings us to our knees, PTSD, breaks hearts, the deepest sorrow, crippling fear, quivering shame, trembling hopelessness or devastating loss at some point in our lives for us all to bear.

In the end, we're all equal.

If we count our blessings and focus on the rise and not the fall of our lives, opportunities won't pass us by, the harder we work the luckier we become. Wherever we are on life's journey, whatever cards we've been dealt, the power of changing our mindsets is key.
Are we a glass half empty or a glass half full?

- Discomfort equals growth, or growth equals discomfort.
- Problems equal challenges or challenges equal problems.
- Pain equals power, or power equals pain.
- Failure equals lessons or lessons equal failure.
- Rejection equals redirection, or redirection equals rejection.

How we approach life makes a difference, our fears can become our reality, and our habits can position our future.

We all have to put in the effort, if we want to get the most out of life.

Life will humble us all!

John Lennon and Yoko Instant Karma (We all Shine On) ♫

I hope I can repair, recover and restore ...

Healing

We cannot Heal without Awareness!

Dashboard The Green Light indicates: All Clear!
When life is coming at us at breakneck speed, sometimes we approach our issues and our hurts by putting plasters on our wounds as a temporary fix to get by or to get through a period in our lives; however, the wound remains.

The good old remedies that never fail when it comes to quick, effective ways to feel better is an abundance of **good nutrition** (254), plentiful deep **sleep** (212), and regular **exercise** (238). These timeless pillars work in harmony to nourish the mind and body. If returning to basics isn't enough, we may need to consider more for a deeper level of healing. We may need to take the plaster off to address our hurts, so our wounds have a better chance of completely healing and fully recovering. Sometimes that takes time. Our struggles can improve our lives. Pain can be an integral part of the healing process. Healing is not suppressing, numbing or avoiding pain. It is about embracing it. Pain can serve as a guide, an indicator in life, showing us where attention is needed. It can be a powerful teacher and motivator for growth, highlighting what we need to change, heal, or let go of. In this process, pain helps us to build compassion, resilience and a deeper understanding of ourselves.

Healing begins with awareness, being well-informed and mindful of:
What? Who? Why? How?

Behind our wounds. It allows us to understand, reconnect with our bodies, and avoid repeating the same patterns. Self-awareness supports our self-development, allowing us to consciously explore ourselves which leads to emotional awareness so we can meet our needs to heal. On reflection, sometimes we may have negative thought patterns and behaviours that have kept us hooked into our suffering, or old stories that we lug around without us realising that they hold us back in certain areas of life. This usually requires alternative therapies, such as talking **therapy** (284), to reinvest and pour into ourselves.

Life is full of flaws and contradictions. Through observing a variety of souls, I've recognized that we can learn and understand the principles of the healing process from our parents. Their imperfections, or dysfunctions, are the most valuable gift we can receive. If we have reconciled, we have learned the essence of life's lessons. By learning to be aware, understand, accept, have **compassion** (58), learn **forgiveness** (61), and heal from it. These are the teachings of life's lessons that they have given us, the journey of how to heal.

Once we understand the fundamentals of healing, other alternative therapies are available to enhance and complement our journey.

- **Sound bath** – Resets energy and turns off the sympathetic nervous system.
- **Breathwork** – Moves energy and emotions through the body.
- **Homeopathy** – Stimulates the body's own healing response to disease.
- **Massage** – Speeds up healing by encouraging blood flow.
- **Reiki** – Helps to return the body to a state of relaxation.
- **Acupuncture** – Stimulates the central nervous system – releases pain-relieving endorphins.
- **Aromatherapy** – Essential oils to improve mood and relaxation.
- **Hypnotherapy** – Reframes negative thought patterns.
- **Reflexology** – Stimulates the nervous system to reduce stress and pain.
- **Cupping** – Encourages blood flow and increases circulation to reduce pain.
- **Visualization** – Creates positive images to change emotion.
- **Yoga** – Improves breathing, reduces levels of stress, and lowers blood pressure.
- **Mindfulness** – Practices being present. Enhances awareness. Reduces stress.
- **Meditation** – Induces deep relaxation to reduce stress and improve sleep.

Therapy can reveal options and new choices, allowing us to commit to our healing process. Once we feel a sense of safety in the therapeutic relationship, trust will emerge as a cornerstone, creating space for vulnerability to transpire.

Naturally, this foundation encourages transparency, which allows truth to be revealed. That is when the true healing begins, and transformation starts to take root.

Our spirits may need varying levels of discipline. We may need to relearn how to love ourselves, as our old patterns no longer serve us. This requires discipline, **kindness** (53), respect, patience, accountability, and the courage to step out of denial, along with acceptance and forgiveness to aid in our healing journey.

Integrate new thought patterns and behaviours into daily life to spark real change and discover a renewed sense of self.
Healing is an invitation to rediscover love for ourselves and for life.

- Consider switching to a different compound. Wet Tyre.

Ram Dass (feat Krishna Das) I Am Loving Awareness ♫

I hope I'm in good company …

Friendship Reshuffle

Pick our Friends like we pick our Fruit

Dashboard The Green Light indicates: All Clear!

"Before you diagnose yourself with depression or low self-esteem, first make sure you are not, in fact, surrounded by assholes" Sigmund Freud

Souls can come into our lives for a reason, a season, or a lifetime.
Friendships are more than just companionship, they are the family we choose, the trusted few who show up, stand by us, and earn their place through loyalty and love. various stages of our lives, we may need different friends at different times to support, challenge, and grow with us.

Friends can either be an asset or a liability. It's okay to reconsider our social circle if they no longer serve us, weigh us down, or hold us back. If they've become toxic or leave us feeling negative or uncertain. There are many types of friends, from those we share secrets with, to fun-night out companions, to lifelong treasures we can call at 4 a.m. Each friend serves a different purpose in our lives, whether for support, fun, or even friends we just love to bits, and then there are our kindergarten friends. After twenty years, what still connects us?

What company do we keep?

The people we choose shape our lives, influencing our thoughts, beliefs and perspectives, reflecting different parts of who we are. Do we enjoy being surrounded by, e.g., the talented, shiny-happy people, wounded warriors, caring or angry, critical people?

Look around. What value do they add to our lives?

Here's a list of different types of people and what they might represent to us.

Are they unwell people; self-absorbed people, loving people, oppressed people, abusive people, helpful people, narcissists, avoidants, manipulative people, passive people, workaholics, angry people, funny people, caring people, considerate people, supportive people, nurturing people, selfish

people, people pleasers, show-offs, complainers, calm relaxed people, silly light-hearted people, motivating people, adventurous people, practical people, the listeners, scary people, confident people.
Each of these friends can play a vital role in shaping the different chapters of our lives.

Would we add or change anything to the list?

Naturally, we move on, or we change, for one or both parties the relationship has run its course. We reach a different phase in our lives, and that's okay; the relationship may fade away. Be sure to part on good terms, if possible, the friendship has run its course; they are not supposed to be in the next chapter of our lives.

> *"You will lose a lot of friends when you get serious about your life goals. That's why the Lamborghini has two seats, and a bus has 50!"* Warren Buffett

Relationships that become one-sided are hard work. Give people as much as they give us. Be mindful not to waste our 100% on people in exchange for their 10%. Relationships are about give and take, rather than the more we give, the less we receive. Surrounding ourselves with people who uplift and inspire us can make a world of difference.

Being in relationships with individuals who are further ahead in life, more experienced, and have bigger visions naturally push us to evolve and reach higher heights. Maybe their energy and mindset become contagious, encouraging us to step out of our comfort zone and expand our potential. It helps to be in spaces where we're being inspired, as we're striving to be the best version of ourselves.

Not everyone we lose is a loss.
If we don't have many friends, it's okay; choose quality over quantity. Sometimes, when we choose peace, it comes with a lot of goodbyes.

Surround ourselves with people whose eyes light up when they see us coming.

Harry Styles Lights Up ♫

I hope I don't settle for less ...

Meantimers

Meantimers serve their purpose – Temporary!

Dashboard The Green Light indicates: All Clear!
Sometimes in life we meet someone who does not meet our needs, but there's something about them that makes do for the time being with the intentions of hoping to meet the one. They are called Meantimers.
Meantimers are simply that, for a moment, or a season of convenience to fill a gap, while we wait for that 'significant other' to show up. However, it is important that we don't take our eyes off the ball, there will come a time when we need to show our 'Meantimers' the door before they have overstayed their welcome and their feet are firmly under the table.

I have encountered a variety of souls who, while they are spending their time being entertained by their Meantimers, let life pass them by. They become less sharp, and more comfortable or relaxed, when they say, they have let themselves go. They feel out of shape, and not as marketable as they once were. Hence, their confidence wanes, and energies get redirected to different priorities and distractions by which the temporary can seem more convenient than the 'permanent one.'

A relationship filled with dissatisfaction, frustration, resentment, and contingency plans will eventually dominate our lives. Over time, this "Meantimer" takes up all the space, leaving no room for 'The One'. The right person cannot knock on our door if Meantime holds the keys or owns the building. Don't settle for less simply because we're impatient to find the right person for ourselves. Do not settle for part-time love when we deserve full-time love. Do not settle for someone who doesn't treat us how we want to be treated. Mediocrity must go.
Find the courage to let go of the Meantimer once and for all, and communicate that the situation is over, no further contact is necessary. They have served their purpose, time's up! We are worthy of a great person; we do not have to put up with 'mediocre' because WE are a great person.
If we are lucky enough to find 'the one' and we finally dispose of our Meantimer, to stop any temptations, clean up that GPS, and don't leave a forwarding address!

   Consider changing to a different compound. Hard Tyre.

Eagles Desperado ♩

I hope I can connect with my feminine energy ...

The Power of Feminine Energy

We all have the potential to feel like a Queen

Dashboard The Green Light indicates: All Clear!
Women supporting other women is an example of a healthy relationship, a sense of sisterhood that raises each other up. We can't do it alone; each of us is finding our truth, our authentic selves, and helping other women to do the same for themselves. We're so much stronger together.

The power of the feminine encompasses our intuition and our inner knowing in finding our self-worth and our truth. We have both masculine and feminine energy. It is important that we tap into both in this fast-paced world in which we live in.

We're constantly stuck in our heads, doing and achieving, galloping from one task to the next, and we miss tuning into ourselves, our private intimate thoughts, emotions, beliefs, **spirituality** (260), and our internal world. This is the masculine energy that diverts us from our feminine energy. Feminine energy is seen as secondary and often denied, as it requires time, patience and practice. It is important that we are present, to rest, reflect, and receive, to be able to access and connect with our gut instinct, the feminine wisdom from within.

We hold the answers within to solve our problems, express our needs, and reconnect with our feminine energy each day.
Keep the crash and burnout away!

- Consider switching to a different compound. Wet Tyre.

Farafina Mousso Lubiana (Acoustic Version) ♫

I hope I can trust myself ...

Trust Thy Self

Once we Trust ourselves, we know How to Live!

Dashboard The Green Light indicates: All Clear!
Trusting ourselves is a key ingredient for success.
It takes confidence, and belief in our ability to face life's challenges. Without self-trust, our thoughts can scatter, leaving us in confusion and indecision.
Many people struggle with trusting themselves. Often creating toxic situations by depending on others to make our decisions. This weakens our boundaries, feeds self-doubt, and keeps us stuck in indecisiveness, Round and round in circles we go until we find ourselves in minestrone soup: a mess. Time to step back.

Self-trust requires independence and strong character for **decision-making** (202). We need self-awareness, knowing our morals, values, and boundaries, and the ability to say, *"enough is enough."* Trusting ourselves empowers us; it requires self-care and self-respect, along with faith in our ability to navigate life from within. This proves we are capable of overcoming obstacles. Each obstacle we overcome boosts our confidence and lessens the urge to compare. We grow more grounded and secure, and desperation keeps its distance. We feel more at ease knowing trust is available to us if we're obliged to lean into it. It's a strength to wholeheartedly trust ourselves, and others can sense that ease and confidence, making them feel more likely to trust us too. Knowing we can trust ourselves often comes from a range of experiences. Some that taught hard lessons or arose from painful situations that left us feeling disappointed. Sometimes things simply don't go to plan. We might fail, feel the sting of regret, and learn not to repeat the same mistake. Or, perhaps, we've hit rock bottom, only to rise, survive and thrive, earning the confidence to take risks, knowing we'll be okay, no matter what. These moments form the foundation of self-trust, shaping and defining who we become.

Through a range of life experiences, we build a deep belief in our own judgement and a responsibility to rely on it. Trusting ourselves takes courage and the willingness to look inward, especially in times of adversity.

Learning to trust ourselves requires self-awareness, **love** (191) and **compassion** (58). It means setting realistic, achievable goals, actively listen to

our inner voice, trusting our gut instincts, recognising our strengths and weaknesses, and following through on our promises. The worst, we might get it wrong, then we learn, begin again, and use the experience as a stepping stone.
Take a breath and start by making a choice.
We've got great instinct, use it!

Freddie McGreggor I was Born a Winner ♪

I hope I can turn change into a lasting habit ...

Change becomes Habits... Habits become Change

The Habits we choose will Decide our Future,

not us!

Dashboard The Green Light indicates: All Clear!
There are good habits and bad ones, and both play a vital role in shaping our future. Bad habits often form unconsciously and are easily welcomed, while good habits usually require deliberate effort and consistency. Ultimately, our habits determine whether we move forward a desired or undesired destination. They decide our future.

Let's focus on the good habits, the ones we truly want in our lives. These habits have the power to shape us and bring about meaningful change over time. This is how our journey unfolds.

> Changing small daily habits, compound into
> significant lasting change.

Making very small, microscopic changes to our daily habits will eventually compound over time and make difference happen.

For change to last, it needs a place in our lives, a consistent time in our daily routine where it can take root. Habits are formed through regular, intentional practice. When we create a schedule, and commit to a routine, a pattern begins to emerge, and overtime, it forms into a habit. Even though the changes may be small, their impact can be incredibly powerful. All the small changes come together and contribute to making a significant change.

For example, we begin with tiny steps before we make larger strides. Each small change opens new possibilities that once seemed out of reach, making the idea of self-improvement feel achievable.

Malachi. 31, struggled with moving forward in his life, explains.

Example 1. *"Aside from achieving studies, at school, I wanted to get into university. I went through a series of thoughts…"*

What kind of person do I need to be, or do, to get a place?

"I realised I'm not great at conversation, interviews, presenting myself isn't cool, my knowledge of the subject matter was poor, I knew I needed to improve."

What kind of person do I need to become to achieve this?

Malachi explains further,
"I wake up every morning and tell myself what I'm going to do to get things done. Every day I would start to affirm myself by talking to myself in the mirror, I started practicing conversational skills regularly, researched topics, spoke to teachers for more information, and worked on my fitness for my personal image.
All these little changes turned into my daily routine and gave me so much self confidence that when the interviewers arrived, I was ready and got ¾ offers."

Example 2. *"What do I want to achieve for my future?"*

As Malachi, 24, explains,
"Rediscover a social life, get out more, meet new people, rediscover my confidence again. To be healthy, strong and ripped again. I realised to make this happen, I needed to change a few things, and these changes involved self-discipline: getting good sleep in, being ruthless with my time, keeping my boundaries, saying "no" to distractions because I'm prioritising and doing me. Hitting the gym regularly, making sure I'm

getting good nutrition, not wasting time on social media. I booked a few solo trips, to meet the same like-minded people as me, and in no time, I had a new tribe of people that I connected with, it wasn't long before I was back on track.
I was in the best shape, I felt energised, in control of things, excited about my future. At first it feels insurmountable, all these little things add up that I gained traction from, the changes gave me more capacity to change other things and believe in myself, as the little things add up and I felt a sense of pride, all the things I used to avoid doing were actually crucial to enhancing my own life, that's why it's really important that you keep on top of your shit."

The small things are just as important as the big changes. Once we begin, we can build momentum and gain the traction needed to pick up speed and accelerate our progress.

The fastest way to reach the top of the mountain is by taking consistent small steps, towards the change we desire.

- Consider changing to a different compound. Medium Tyre.

Jungle Keep Moving ♫

All Clear!

Chapter 4

Move Over!

The Blue Flag chapter implies ...

Blue Flag

A faster car is going to overtake.
Move over.
We are about to be lapped.
Inform a driver leaving the pits that traffic is approaching.

This chapter refers to times in our lives when we are forced to look at the bigger picture; it enables us to assess the potential effects of our choices in a broader sense, rather than focusing on the minor details. We're not the fastest on the track right now, and that's okay. In life, this can represent times when we need to step aside, take a breath, and let others move forward. We can accept that we have our own pace and path.

This is a moment to assess!
Are we on the right track?
Are our goals aligned with our current actions?

89 **Our Expiry**

90 **Represent**

92 **Smug Spouses**

93 **Bereavement**

95 **Lessons**

I hope to accomplish my bucket list sometime ...

Our Expiry

We are all coasting towards Death

Dashboard The Purple Light indicates: Action Required! 🟣
Check Rear View Mirror!

If we thought we were dying, what would we do?

1) **Be unapologetically ourselves** – Drop the masks, embrace authenticity, and live freely.
2) **Love ourselves more** – Our overall well-being and happiness – grow, heal, and live authentically
3) **Pursue long-held dreams** – Finally write that book, paint that masterpiece, or start that passion project.
4) **Travel to bucket list destinations** – Visit places we've always longed to see.
5) **Spend quality time with family and friends** – Be fully present with the people who matter most.
6) **Say "yes" more often** – Embrace new opportunities, take risks, and step outside our comfort zone.
7) **Say "no" to things that don't serve us** – Cut out toxic relationships, jobs, or habits that drain us.
8) **Help others** – Give back, volunteer, or contribute to a cause close to our heart.
9) **Forgive ourselves and others** – Let go of guilt, regrets, and mistakes from the past.
10) **Prioritize our health and well-being** – Nourish our body, mind, and soul to feel our best.
11) **Conquer our fears** – Care less about what others think and embrace who we truly are.
12) **Embrace childlike wonder** – Play, explore, and find joy in simple pleasures.
13) **Experience something new** – Invest in experiences over things. Plan a staycation, skydive, road trip, join a group activity, go to a festival, learn a new language, or take up a new hobby.

14) **Work less, laugh more, stress less** – Find joy in the little things and let go of unnecessary stress.
15) **Love fiercely and fearlessly** – Express affection, hold hands, hug more, and cherish every moment.
16) **Make peace with our past** – Accept what was, embrace what is, and let go of what we can't change.
17) **Tell loved ones how much they mean to us** – Say "I love you" without hesitation. Express gratitude, love, and appreciation without holding back.
18) **Give ourselves a voice** – Speak our truth without fear of judgment. Live with honesty.
19) **Embrace our uniqueness** – Celebrate what makes us different, instead of fitting into someone else's mould.
20) **Be still enough to feel our hearts beating** – A reminder of the life and energy flowing through us. We're alive.

Life is short—so let's do it!

Don't wait until illness or age forces our hand. Chase our bucket list while we're healthy and full of life. Arrogance tells us there's time, yet none of us know how many summers we have left.
Time is too valuable to risk or waste.

> Consider changing to a different compound. Hard Tyre.

Bon Jovi It's My Life ♬

I hope I can speak for myself ...

Represent

Me, Myself and I

The way we express ourselves, through the words we choose olds real power. When we're connected to our feelings and speak from that place, our words carry weight, presence, and truth. However, when we speak in vague or abstract terms, we dilute the power. We distance ourselves not just from what we feel, also from those we're trying to connect with. Owning our emotions through language is a bridge to understanding, to closeness, and to being truly heard.

Speaking in abstract terms takes the potency and power away from our words of expression; not owning ourselves by distancing ourselves in our narrative from having a connection with others. This can be translated as keeping the person at a distance, not letting them be close. By speaking from an abstract position, we become inconsequential, insignificant, unimportant, or invisible. When owning and expressing ourselves,

"This is me ..."

Then we become seen, heard and accounted for.

Speaking in the third person tends to show objectivity, a way of disconnecting our emotions expressed from an observational 'detached' perspective. This creates emotional distance which can dilute the emotional impact of the story, and make a deeper connection with other more difficult. It can give the impression that we're talking about someone else rather than ourselves. describing ourselves as,

"he", "she", "they", "him", "her", "we", "us", or "you", and "them."

suggests that the first-person narrator is the actual character in the story being told.

As Charlie, 21, explains,

"...and then I was like, ahhhh maaaan, you just messed up, and then I said to myself, Yep, but whose stupid decision was this?"

It takes us out of the focal point, the frame of reference is of the speaker, implying that we won't become as personal with the character in our story. This creates an opportunity of getting 'missed' in the conversation by not discounting our feelings, and our feelings becoming overlooked.

It's beneficial to be seen and heard by speaking for ourselves.

Claim it and own the original script!

Keala Settle & The Greatest Showman Ensemble This Is Me ♫

I hope I'm not taking you for granted ...

Smug Spouses

Now we've Got them! Learn how to Keep them!

Complacency is the relationship killer.
Complacency often creeps into relationships when one or both parties become too comfortable. Gradually, motivation and effort start to decline, and we lose sight of what really matters. As a result, our partner becomes neglected.
In practice, I have encountered many couples, and what often emerges is the assumption that we know our partner so well we can read their minds, leading us to stop asking questions, stop being curious. Unwittingly, this breeds complacency.

We fall in love because of how we are treated, and just as easily, we can fall out of love for the same reason.

This often happens in relationships, contentment and routine can breed complacency, especially when one partner is overloaded and overstretched at work. We look to home as a refuge, a place to recharge. We want comfort and a soft place to fall, yet in seeking this, we may slip into a false sense of security, unaware of deficiencies that may have crept in because we've become too comfortable in the relationship. Consequently, we fall into complacency, taking shortcuts in the relationship, paying less attention to each other, making fewer thoughtful gestures, and planning fewer dates. The romance fades, and intimacy diminishes. For the neglected partner, this becomes a lonely and unfulfilling space, leading to feelings of resentment.
Over time, the relationship stagnates, breaks down, or one loses interest entirely.
It is about effort, unwavering respect, and the way we choose our partners over and over again. It requires open communication by expressing gratitude and appreciation to our partner, being present and proactive in the relationship to get it back on track, to bring the freshness back with new experiences shared together. Regular dating helps retrieve romance, win back intimacy, and improve our relationship.

Getting smug in a relationship means we've lost; trying to woo our partner is not over once the ring is on the finger. The courtship isn't over once we've married the love of our life. Now we've got them, we can relax.

Everyone's replaceable, so let's not get too comfortable as there will always be someone better who's more handsome, thinner, sexier, intelligent, charming, funny, prettier, taller, fitter, and smarter than us. Don't let the spark fade.

No one is irreplaceable!
Nurse the tyres!

Lil Wayne & Babyface Comfortable ♫

I hope I can get over my loss ...

Bereavement

Death comes to us all and remains the Uninvited Guest!

Dashboard The Purple Light indicates: Action Required! 🟣
Check Rear View Mirror!

Death is a natural part of life. A universal theme in people's lives is the death of a loved one, and when it hits us, we can feel like we're the only one in the world who is going through this.

There is a fifty- fifty chance in our lifetime we will become a widow/widower, and a hundred percent chance we will become parentless, it might be the loss of a loved one, a relationship, pregnancy, pet, job or way of life, other experiences could be losing connection, attachment with a 'living' person, or empty-nest syndrome or separation from family we need to grieve. Grief is a time in our lives when we look back after the event, and it's all blurry, with a few significant moments that will always stay with us. It isn't an episode in our lives we bypass, or conveniently schedule into our diaries; grief is very potent, and nothing can prepare us for loss when it arrives. Life will not be the same again.

We can't pretend to live our lives as though they are still here.

Grief can appear to be like an illness; we do not feel we are in control. It's exhausting and can affect our emotions, thoughts, behaviour, our sense of self and identity, as well as our relationships with others. Loss can leave us unable to make decisions and cause difficulty with our **sleep** (212). During grief, we lose hope, and the future can seem bleak and despairing. It's also not unusual to question our faith and beliefs as we search for answers and meaning from our loss. These are all perfectly normal to experience in grief. We skirt around talking about death, worried we might upset someone when we need to talk about the people we have loved and lost. Do talk about it, rather than hide away from our own grief. Nothing will ever be the same again, we will never see them again, or talk to them again. Death is final.

It is difficult to come to terms with grief, to accept they have gone,

it's okay to be okay with not feeling okay.

Allow ourselves to be with those uncomfortable feelings for a while; connecting with our feelings sets us free from pain, sorrow, and misery. This is not a time to compose ourselves. This is the right time to grieve. The time to release the pain, deep loss, and sorrow we're feeling. By swallowing our tears and not crying we keep the memory alive, leading us to believe they haven't left us because they remain of our emotional process. This prevents closure and leaves our sorrow incomplete. There is a different path. We can live with joy and happiness alongside deep sorrow; these feelings can co-exist. We can get through this time.

Naturally, everyone grieves differently, shaped by their unique bond with the deceased. The deeper the connection, the more intense the grief is likely to be.

Christmastime

Christmas is not always a season to be jolly, brimming with tinsel, sequins, and glitter.
Christmas, a time for family, can be unbearable for the bereaved. Their absence feels strongest, making the season especially challenging. Visiting the cemetery or a special place to remember a loved one becomes part of life, especially at Christmas.

There is an abundance of wreaths or flowers, with people visiting to pay their respects. Sometimes, listening to Christmas jingles, lighting a candle, or leaving a Christmas card expressing how we're feeling and how much we are missing them, or decorating their headstone with Christmas decorations of lights and tinsel. There are different ways of involving our deceased at Christmas; whatever helps to ease the pain of our loss makes a difference.

Unfortunately, death is a part of life; at some point, we will experience the loss of a loved one, often before turning forty. The older we become, the more loss we may experience. If we're fortunate enough to be free of loss at Christmastime, we should cherish every moment.

> *"Grief is the price we pay for love."*
> Queen Elizabeth II

- Consider changing to different compound. Intermediate Tyre.
- or Wet Tyre.

Rozni Wykonawcy John Williams: Schindler's List ♪

I hope I can afford to make the same mistake again ...

Lessons

Life's Exchange

Life gently teaches us who we are through every joy, challenge, and quiet moment in between. It shows us what we hold dear, which emotions we lean into or shy away from, how we view the world, and how we see ourselves within it. It's shaped by the choice we make, the lessons we gather and the people we allow to walk alongside us, or even take the wheel for a while.

Ever wonder why we sometimes feel stuck or stagnant in life?

Take Olivia, 29, for example. In therapy, she was struggling in romantic relationships, repeating patterns of failed connections that left her feeling rejected or abandoned. Once we delved into her past, we uncovered that she was often drawn to partners with personality traits like those of her parents. These partners were frequently unreliable and unavailable, often too consumed with work to meet promised parental visits. When they did show up, it was with gifts and apologies, temporarily making up for their absence.

Olivia was drawn to partners who let her down, making her feel like an afterthought, just as she felt with her parent. She recognised that past relationships mirrored unhealthy patterns she'd witnessed growing up. With this realisation, Olivia started to redefine what she needed in a relationship, moving away from what felt familiar and toward what was truly healthy and fulfilling for her.

**Nothing in life comes for free.
We pay to learn.**

Whether the lesson is positive or negative, there is always a lesson and a price to pay. If we don't learn from the lesson the first time, or even the tenth, the same lesson will show up again disguised slightly differently, the same partner disguised with a different name, job or situation. The same lesson will keep reappearing, coming down the conveyor belt of life, with our name written all over it, until we learn from it. Once we do, that's when we stop experiencing the same situations, and we move on to the next lesson.

Sometimes, we don't recognise the true cost of each lesson, as it depends on many factors, which can become costly. We often overlook the emotional toll of our bruised feelings and damaged self-esteem, or the time lost while being stuck in one place. Learning our lessons comes with a price tag, nothing is ever truly free.

Life has a bank account, and we're constantly making deposits and withdrawals in exchange for who we are!

What's our balance – are we in the red or black?

Villagers Courage ♪

iHope

Chapter 5

Slippery Surface!

The Red and Yellow Striped Flag is suggesting ...

Red and Yellow Striped Flag

> Slippery surface up ahead on track.
> Rain has rendered the service hazardous.

Slippery surfaces test our skill in maintaining control.
In life, moments of instability challenge our ability to stay composed, adapt to changing circumstances, and make sound decisions under pressure. These are the times when our emotional resilience is tested. Through this discomfort comes growth. We can emerge more grounded, and better equipped to navigate future storms.

We need to slow down and be careful through this section.

100 **Strictly Parenting**

101 **Energy**

104 **People can be Peoplely**

106 **Let's Face the Music and Dance**

109 **Listen without Prejudice**

111 **Loneliness**

112 **Relationship Outcomes**

113 **Shame**

I hope to raise my children with the highest standards ...

Strictly Parenting

Parents shape Tomorrow, not just today!

No one gives us a handbook on good parenting. Parenting is the most difficult job in the world, the most relentless, thankless, 24/7 job that exists, and we are expected to get it right. We have to discipline our children, teach them responsible behaviour, tolerance, and self-control.

Strict parenting can have its place, teaching our children to obey rules, and if rules are broken, there are heavy consequences and ramifications to endure. We teach children right from wrong, the way our parents raised us, to instil discipline. When overly rigid or abusive, it can cause deep childhood **trauma** (174) and lasting effects.

"It didn't do me any harm."

We may have suffered, but this doesn't mean we have to hand down our suffering. They don't need the burdens of our generation on their shoulders, it's not theirs to inherit. Strict disciplinarians create perfectionists in society, who are generally risk-averse and struggle to make decisions. They usually fear failing in life or become extreme workaholics.

In the short term, strict parenting may keep order. However, in the long run, it can leave an adult child feeling defeated, unable to attain our high standards and expectations believing,

"I'm not good enough." (184).

Some of the ancient, traditional family rules are outdated for today's generation.
It's not the consequences of rules that discipline our children. It is the depth of connection and intimacy we have together that bonds the relationship, which positively influences them.

In practice, an Asian client, Khalid, with a history of anxiety, and depression, aged 30.
"I didn't want to turn into him, my parents want to clone their identity onto me, to fit into this outdated

mould, the traditional, family comfort zone to serve the community. I realise I can't please everyone, I'll just stay miserable and depressed, even though he'll disapprove of me, or even disown me ..."

Our parents are our teachers; as role models, they teach us how we want to be or what we don't want to become. If our child feels a stranger to us, they will respect us as a stranger.

Our children don't need our past. They need our presence!
Nurse the tyres!

Micheal Kiwanuka Love & Hate ♫

I hope I've the power to ...

Energy

Rest. Sleep. Repeat

Dashboard The Purple Light indicates: Action Required! ●
Check Rear View Mirror!

Energy is our life force, when it's low, everything feels heavier.
Even the simplest action slow down: our blinking lags, facial expressions fade, our response becomes dull. We smile less. We struggle to stay present. These subtle signals are our bodies gentle plea for pause. A reminder that we are tired, and that it's okay to stop, breathe and rest.
It is that simple. Rest. Sleep. Do Nothing.

It can seem challenging at times, as much as we recognise that our bodies need to rest, our brains can refuse to switch off, our minds are constantly on the go.

In practice, Kiki, 36, a mother of two children under five, is struggling with fatigue and a constant lack of energy,
as Kiki tells us.

*"I should be doing this...I should be doing that...
I have a never-ending list of to-dos and worry that the list is going to accumulate more and more. If I rest more, I become more stressed. If I don't stop doing stuff, it will make my life harder in the long run."*

What takes the majority of our energies daily.

- **Work** – A lot of brain power, a lot of thinking, planning ahead.
- **Children** – Putting children to bed, especially when they are resisting going to bed.
- **Socialising** – Being around people a lot of the time, especially when we're hosting.
- **Emotions** – The constant worry, spikes of anxiety throughout the day.
- **Driving** – Takes up energy.
- **Partners** – Feeling we have to prove ourselves in the relationship.

"Sometimes I have feelings of frustration, feeling that the change that is meant to happen is down to me in the relationship, or what I want for myself and for the family and for the house, for those types of things to happen they are down to me.
Finding the energy to sort the children out and do a day's work sometimes feels like I'm setting myself up to fail."

If our train of thought is usually,
"I'm going to do the task first, then I can rest."

Somehow, we never get to rest, we're on a never-ending cycle, or treadmill of endless to-do lists, and rest becomes a treat, as though it's the pay-off for our hard work. We feel we need an excuse to rest.
It's vital to tune into our bodies and treat them with greater respect. To rest, starts with compromising with our minds for the sake of our bodies; for instance, our mind may say,

"Don't be silly, there's no reason why you would be tired now"
The compromise-
"Let me lie down for half an hour and see how that feels"

When we lie down for a short time, it can feel like charging ourselves like a **battery** (276), once we are recharged, then we are good to go again. Our minds can be an endless chatter in our heads, goading, seducing us to do stuff, and before we know it, we have a traffic jam. It is our minds that we must step out of to meet our bodies' needs.

We must take charge of our own minds to instruct our heads to be quiet, take a hike or simply shut up to have some relief.

Learning how to switch off can be taught in meditation, there are many apps to assist in creating some headspace, as Kiki explains,

"Now, after resting, sleeping, and doing nothing for a while, I have energy to do the daily tasks, they no longer feel laborious, I've started going to the gym to work out, and taking care of my skin, doing daily skin regimes, all of these take time and energy, but I recognised how much I was depriving myself of care because I had no energy left for me."

When we start to recognise the energy that we have to put out to meet our daily needs: walking to do the school run, running to catch the bus, doing the food shopping, cooking, washing, tidying, the bathtimes, putting children to bed, it all takes energy.
Without energy, we can't do anything. Everything will cease.

See, the options are, we either act on learning how to build our energy reserves, or we take a few more extra laps around life's circuit until we crash and burn.

We have a choice!

- Consider changing to different compound. Intermediate Tyre.
- or Wet Tyre.

Yung Wylin Good Energy ♫

I hope I can recognise my part in this ...

People can be Peopley

Nothing stranger than Folk!

Dashboard The Green Light indicates: All Clear!
The misery of our misses, our miss-demeanours, miss-takes and misjudgements can weigh heavily on us.

Each of us carries stories of injustices, navigating the pain and lessons from fallouts with friends, family and loved ones, all while walking our individual paths of healing and growth. Fallouts are testing for both parties. Our initial response to a disagreement or misunderstanding can be to react with feelings of anger, hurt and anxiety. These feelings are generally seen as negative; consequently, if something has upset us, we avoid circumstances that reignite those uncomfortable feelings. If the avoidance goes on for a long period, time will make it difficult to reconnect. The relationship has run its course.

Many of us make the mistake of judging the actions of others, by what they would do in certain situations and end up feeling disappointed as a result. They don't have the same morals or values as we do; therefore, they will have a different point of view from our own. Others can influence people's perception of events. As much as we try to navigate our world through our expectations, we end up feeling let down. Right or wrong, the bottom line is that their behaviour has more to do with their internal struggle than it ever had to do with us.

We all have a past, we all make mistakes, we all have preconceptions, expectations and we all have misunderstandings; we are only human. Those who are supposed to be in our lives will gather root, those who have tested and broken our moral code will hurt, and those who have fallen from grace, let them go.

The people that we think are in our corner don't always have the resources we hoped for. Whether they are friends or family, when things go sideways, there are three types of people (who symbolise features of a tree): leaves, branches, and roots. The people who represent the leaves of the tree will eventually fall off with the seasons. The people who personify the 'branches' can take a certain amount of weight before the branch snaps, and the people who depict the roots have proven their loyalty. The roots of a tree represent the 'tribe' we choose, they are deeply connected and well grounded, people who stick around in the stormy weathers of life. They are the strong relationships that have matured over time, their intentions come from the heart, they are the 3am people, who are our support network, our anchor, who inspire, protect, and love us for who we are. These are our people.

We do our best with good intentions. However, we can't be everyone's roots in life; sometimes that comes with disappointing others. We all have our place, however limited we might be, we all contribute to what makes a tree whole. Sometimes they are the leaves, branches or the roots through the seasons of our lives,

J.R.R.Tolkien wisely said,
"All that is gold does not glitter, not all those who wander are lost, the old that is strong does not wither, deep roots are not reached by the frost."

People's internal struggles will forge the leaves, branches or roots of our lives.

Alex Serra Human ♬

I hope we both stay sexually compatible ...

Let's Face the Music and Dance

Keep the Fires Burning

Dashboard The Purple Light indicates: Action Required!
Check Rear View Mirror!

When we meet 'the one', the chemistry is electric, the attraction is sizzling, and the sex is hot.

Imagine sex as a dance that requires a step-by-step approach. It doesn't start when we're lying horizontally in bed; by that point, it's too late, we've missed the train. The dance begins from the beginning of the week or the beginning of the day, steadily building up, with flirtatious behaviour. Engaging in intimate touch, squeezing their bum, spontaneous kisses, playful or lingering hugs, deep eye contact, cuddling, sensual stroking, or sending a flirty text helps keep the spark alive. To spice things up, leave a sexy note, leave an enticing voicemail, or a cheeky video, little gestures build anticipation. These are all signs of communicating to the other that they are desired; these actions help to encourage our partner to get in the mood for deeper intimacy or sex. This is the start of the dance; it warms each other up for the act of sex. Additionally, this is good, healthy feedback for any couple, to keep them interested, excited, and on their toes.

From Latin to ballroom, what is our preferred style of dance?
The waltz, the Argentinian Tango, the American Smooth, the Cha Cha Cha, the Rumba or the Jive?

It helps to know if we have the right dance partner, if our dance partner likes to dance the Salsa and we like to dance the Foxtrot, we can be compromised, and start to learn their style of step. They want to 'chasse' whilst we want to 'twerk', it's key that we match and we're both dancing to the same beat.

I have seen a variety of couples progressing to the next stage of living together. The dimensions change within the home, from one role in the relationship, we take up another when we live together. It's normal to have different roles and duties to help keep the home running smoothly, from emptying the dishwasher to putting out the dustbins, cleaning the bathroom, or cooking meals. Occasionally life gets in the way. Naturally, the dynamics of the relationship change. When we experience emotional crisis, bereavement, demanding work schedule, or take the big step and become parents, they all contribute to stress. When we are feeling stressed, it takes us longer to relax and be present enough to be aroused. To be aroused requires us getting out of our heads and into our bodies. If we are under pressure, we may struggle with other complications such as climaxing issues and self-confidence. **Stress** (164) can affect our sexual pleasure and weaken the potency of attraction in the relationship.

Here are some other examples: we start making their packed lunches, doing their laundry, buying their clothes, making decisions about the relationship on their behalf, and paying all the bills. We are treating them like a child, and if they are acting like a child, we are acting like a parent; we are no longer equal in the relationship. This behaviour is unhealthy and starts to become less attractive to the other partner.

How can we keep the home fires burning?

- **Quality Time** – Plan the event, make time for our partners.
- **Preferences** – Consider focusing on what makes them feel desired, special and loved.
- **Compliments and appreciation** – Share admiration.
- **De-stress** – Help them relax, so they can be present.
- **Intimacy beyond sex** – Longer foreplay.
- **Physical affection** – Holding them in our arms.
- **Experiment and explore** – Consider different sexual positions.
- **Surprise and spontaneity** – Practicing and introducing new sexual toys in the bedroom.

To keep the fires burning, it may help to consider how far we willing to meet our partner's sexual needs, or how far are we willing to sacrifice our own needs to meet our partner's sexual needs.
Do we take pleasure in satisfying our partner's sexual needs?

People in seasoned relationships, who schedule a 'date night' every Thursday, place unrealistically high expectations on both parties, the Russian roulette of 'being in the mood' to have sex. This turns up the pressure to perform, for a moment that all boils down to that one day in the week, the one occasion where they are expected to feel horny turned on, sexy; this can be a passion killer that's setting ourselves up to fail. If one party doesn't feel they want to have sex the pressure of communicating with the partner can trigger feelings of guilt, shame, **anger** (224), or **people pleasing** (182) to compensate for what is lacking, can become another additional stress factor in the relationship.

This can be a common theme that occurs in relationships, **not feeling good enough** (184).

As dancing partners, if we haven't kept up with the progression of the relationship either, one party is still in the honeymoon period and other has moved into the next phase, we will have different expectations. Our dancing partner has switched to a completely different dancing style. We may be Latin dancers, and they have become a ballroom dancer. We are no longer sexually compatible; one party has quickstepped off the dance floor. The attraction is gone.

Maintaining a healthy sex life is relies on transparency, and feeling secure enough to communicate openly about our desires. When we don't want sex, respond gently so it's not taken personally knowing how to turn them on, or let them down softly eases the pressure.

Keep our dances consistent whether we dance three times a week or three times a month; whatever is agreeable and works for both parties is healthy. When it comes to the dancefloor, deep and meaningful has its place, also keeping sex playful is key. It is the small consistent deeds that are the most potent in a relationship, like flirting, kissing, cuddling, staying physically close. Investing in intimacy, sending small gestures to the other, that shows appreciation, love, or desire that they fancy us that make us feel valued, seen and keep us young.

If we don't laugh during sex at least once, we might be with the wrong person! Sex is supposed to be fun, and playful, and not always so serious.
Keep the fires burning hot...

Put our best foot forward, or we'll seek a new upgrade!
Nurse the tyres!

Tony Bennet & Lady Gaga Let's Face the Music and Dance 🎵

I hope I'm not lonely ...

Loneliness

Enjoy the Company of Oneself

Dashboard The Purple Light indicates: Action Required! 🟣
Check Your Rear View Mirror!

We can be surrounded by people and still feel profoundly lonely. Loneliness is the experience of being alone with our own thoughts.

In a world filled with constant distractions, loneliness is often misunderstood and mistakenly equated with abandonment. Abandonment comes with a heavy emotional toll, shaped by past hurts, conjuring images of being left behind and isolated. It breeds feelings of rejection and stirs up sadness, confinement, and a sense of deprivation, all while intensifying the fear of missing out. Isn't that a heavy weight to bear?

Loneliness can be interpreted as a time for solitude to be with ourselves, a time to reconnect with our thoughts and our feelings without any distractions from others, a time to enjoy the company of ourselves. Some of us fear loneliness, and being alone with nothing but our thoughts can be scary, fearing what might reveal itself when we aren't distracted, keeping ourselves busy to avoid being with our truth.

"I can't be by myself, I'll be lonely."

If we have a very busy lifestyle and we're constantly on the move, we have no time to stop, or as I interpret, we are on the run from ourselves.
Loneliness generally comes from a disconnection from self. There's so much more of ourselves to explore, understand, and get to know; we stay focused on the external world that is full of things, rather than our internal worlds that we carry around with us all our lives.

If we take the time to connect with ourselves, we will find a whole world waiting for us. A world that will help us process, grow, and develop, to make sense of the meaning of things. Memories that enable us to reference and resolve **old baggage** (181), experience stillness instead of anxiety, and contentment instead of stress. Over time, with our attention, and some practice, stress, anxiety and fears will reduce, and our inner confidence will increase.

Loneliness is not an excuse to reconnect with toxic people. Just because were thirsty, doesn't mean we should drink poison. This is an opportunity to focus on nurturing ourselves instead of letting the fear of loneliness keep us running.

Take a few minutes, an afternoon, a day, or a weekend and check in with ourselves.

When we feel lonely, ask ourselves,
What am I withholding from myself that I need?
What am I lacking?
What am I suppressing?
What's missing of myself?

We have all the answers if we stay in moment long enough!

When we fail to meet our needs, to use our own resources to build a more intimate relationship with ourselves, we hold onto the fear.
How can we truly connect with someone and build a healthy relationship?

In practice, Jude, 31, after making some significant changes in his life, in making himself a priority, he realised,
"When we go through all the responsibilities, we need to do for ourselves first, and then see what else we have left for the day,
after we've cooked; cleaned, studied, hit the gym, then started to relax and unwind from our day through our Monday to Friday working week, there's no time left to be lonely."

Weekends are generally to be sociable, enjoying our activities, hobbies, spending time with our tribe, or recharging our batteries.
If we are working and living our life suitably in balance, and taking care of ourselves with high wellbeing, there's no time for loneliness. It's an advantage and a privilege to be with oneself.

Stop running, we've a private world and a best friend that's waiting to meet us!

- ◉ Consider switching to a different compound. Hard Tyre.
- ◉ or Intermediate Tyre.

Dua Lipa Scared to be Lonely (Acoustic Version) ♪

I hope I'm a good listener ...

Listen without Prejudice

Lost in Translation

At the core of human existence is communication.
As human beings we all need to communicate, to send and receive information through expressing our thoughts and feelings to one another to bond; to help, to play, to inform, to learn, to collaborate, resolve conflict, and to understand.

We express ourselves through language, nodding, winking, gesticulating, pointing, hand gestures, body movements, and so on. This area can have blurred edges, as we receive this type of communication based on our perception and interpret from our own experiences of what we believe to be accurate, which can be the cause of many disputes.
Most communication is non-verbal, body language comes first, then tone, and lastly words. Healthy relationships, rely on an exchange of talking and listening.

Do we listen to understand, or do we listen to reply?

Listening to reply is the easy option; simply waiting to get our own point of view across can be defensive, often leading to self-justification, whereas listening to understand takes active listening. Active listening involves our eyes, ears, heart and mind, to be actively engaged in processing what someone's saying to us. This takes observation, observing and responding to verbal and non-verbal messages, and giving the relevant feedback demonstrates we are actively listening.

To listen involves listening with our whole being!

Nurse the tyres!

Celeste Hear my Voice ♬

I hope I can change their minds …

Relationship Outcomes

As Above, So Below!

The early days of a relationship lay the groundwork for what's to come. When tensions arises early on with our partners family or friends, it can quietly strain the relationship. These connections often run deep, here before us and likely to remain long after, unless we've defied the odds, such early friction can steer the course of the relationship. Despite our hopes, many hearts remain broken when things don't work out. If we're involved with someone. Who's already in a relationship, expecting them to leave, the reality is that outcome is rare. If we fall for a philanderer, or charmer and believe we can change them, or that they'll treat us differently than their last affair, we may want to think twice.

Are we fooling ourselves?

I have seen countless hearts broken by situationships, getting entangled with someone who is already taken and emotionally unavailable. The disillusions, lies, deceit, and broken promises unfold at the beginning of the relationship. Whether the person leaves, or we end the relationship for them, there are no grounds for any healthy, respectful relationship to flourish. If a relationship materialises from the deceit; trust doesn't have a chance, trust supports our confidence, keeps suspicion and doubt away. This is when many have sought therapy, struggling with self-doubt, or lacking confidence, and **self-esteem** (144).

We cannot change anyone. If we come close and the person was not fully committed initially, it's likely that their hearts are not in it, they won't be giving their one hundred percent, and we won't be receiving all of them. When a relationship starts with one who doesn't seem fully invested, and the other party makes no decisions, or they are dominant and overbearing, and the other party is in love with their potential, hoping to change these qualities, the relationship is doomed. If one party is not fully invested initially, change is unlikely. This can feel like going down a one-way street that leads onto Resentment Lane.

People do not change for people; the only long-lasting change is changing for themselves.

If we want to know the ending, look at the beginning.

Time to do a U-Turn.
- ⚙ Consider changing to a different compound. Hard Tyre.

Thundercat & Tame Impala No More Lies 🎵

Slippery Surface!

I hope I don't feel ashamed ...

Shame

Not mine!

Dashboard The Orange Light Indicates: Caution! Slow Down! Rather than speak it out loud, we often hide it behind humour, sarcasm, passive aggression, defensiveness, or even anger. These responses are protective ways to shield the more vulnerable parts of ourselves, hoping to keep our deeper wounds unseen.

Shame stems from a childhood of abuse, neglect, scorn, and belittlement, which can leave lasting scars. Especially for men, this can breed rage, resentment, and the belief that we are never good enough, especially when we're not allowed to cry or express emotions. The constant pressure to perform or the expectation to "man up" only reinforces this emotional burden.

Shame is a toxic emotion that disables us and shuts us down. It thrives in secrecy, leading to isolation and emotional distance. It breeds feelings of inadequacy, unworthiness, and rejection, making us believe we are stupid, wrong, unloved, with the added weight of guilt fuelling shame. It is a powerful emotion, one that doesn't inherently belong to us; it is often imposed by external influences that take root when we fail to hold others accountable for their actions. This is particularly true for perfectionists who often carry deep shame, driven by the pressure to always get things right. If our childhoods have been shaped by a fear of failure and the need to avoid shame, this pattern will continue into adult life.

When we experience shame, we swallow untruths about ourselves, believing we are inherently wrong or bad. This can lead to deep feelings of guilt because we feel like we've done something wrong or failed in some way, reinforcing the belief that we are unworthy. Guilt is often tied to the belief that we have hurt others or that our actions don't align with our values. It keeps us trapped in self-blame, reinforcing the notion that we're inherently flawed. It's within this cycle that we abandon ourselves and fall off track. By embracing our vulnerability and sensitivity, we can confront and expose shame. With deeper wounds, we might initially feel scared and awkward about facing it. However, it takes bravery, courage, and persistence to reclaim our true selves and break free from the hold that shame has on us.

Here's a lighter, more relatable example of shame that most of us have felt at some point.

In practice, Elsie, 29, struggled with shame, anxiety, and stress, especially during presentations and interviews. Her feelings of shame started at a family gathering when she was mocked for not knowing quiz answers. Elsie used to sit nervously in interviews, fearing she would forget her words, stumble, or look foolish. After unpacking her experience and learning new techniques, she began approaching interviews differently. Before starting, she would acknowledge her nerves and give the interviewers a heads-up. By openly expressing her anxiety, she was confronting her shame triggers, and fear of shame, diminishing its power.

When we acknowledge our vulnerabilities and insecurities, we stop them from holding us hostage. In doing so, we reclaim our confidence, diminish the fear's grip, and regain control over our narrative. What once seemed intimidating becomes manageable, and we realize that shame only has power when we allow it to hide in the shadows.

> *"After that, I always mentioned it at interviews. It made me feel quite empowered not to let it win. It's more the sharing of it that I've found to be the powerful bit. "*

It takes real bravery, courage, and persistence to reclaim who we truly are, to break free from the grip of shame. Let's stop accepting the patterns that hold us back: hiding, shrinking, resentment, blame, and the fear of vulnerability. Shame is not ours to carry. It thrives in silence. so let's bring it into the light. Let's name it, face it, and release it. We owe it to ourselves, and to the next generation, these unhealthy patterns aren't ours to pass down. The cycle ends with us.

The Key Practices
- Recognising shame and understanding it's triggers
- Practice awareness of shame influences that drive shame
- Naming shame when it occurs

The unwanted identity we need to hand back!
Nurse the tyres!

Manic Street Preachers If You Tolerate This Then Your Children Will Be Next ♫

iHope

Chapter 6

Stop the Race!

The Red Flag chapter is insisting ...

Red Flag

Signal to stop.
The race has now stopped in the interest of safety.
Reduce our speed and proceed back to the pit lane.
Line up at the exit and await instructions.

Next, we'll explore those 'red flag' moments in our lives, when we reach the point of having had enough.

Before we lose any more of ourselves, engage the emergency brake and stop! Immediate action is required; these destructive behaviours will cost us the race.

118 **Comfort Zone**
120 **The Trust Factor**
122 **Self-Sabotage**
124 **Emotionless Parents**
125 **Indebted to Debt**
127 **Dirrty Thoughts**

I hope I can keep my comforts ...

Comfort Zone is Poison!

The Betrayal of the Century!

Dashboard The Red Light Indicates: Stop! 🔴
Engage the emergency brake!

R.I.P to the opportunities we lost by clinging to
cosy stale comfort.

The comfort zone can feel like a safe companion that's familiar, predictable, even soothing; until we realise it has been our enemy the entire time. Intentionally distracting us with familiarity, keeping us stuck in one place and isolated from the world of new opportunities, our comfort zones control our lives without us knowing.

The 'comfort zone' is poison; the whole intention is to stop us from progressing in life, to stifle our freedom, and restrict us from living a full, wholesome, independent life. The comfort zone constantly confirms and affirms all our insecurities about who we think we are:

I'm not good enough.
What's the point?
I can't ...
I won't...

It robs us of our self-worth, confidence, joy, energy, curiosity, creativity, self-belief, motivation, optimism, and spontaneity in exchange for fear, sadness, and hurt. Ageing is the aggressive pursuit of comfort; the more we seek comfort the faster we age.

Why accept a lifetime of disappointment when we have the chance to take a risk and pursue what we truly want?

Anything too comfortable for too long is not our friend. Our comfort zone keeps us hidden and cocooned from the world, stepping out of the box and into something that will challenge our perception, expectation, fears, and hurts from the past, isn't appealing to us. It's the past that's been controlling us all along and stopping us from moving forward. We become passengers in our own car, while our past comfortably takes the driver's seat, steering us down a dead-end cul-de-sac in life.

When we stop taking risks in life, it shrinks who we are and slowly builds walls around us and isolates us from reality. If we allow ourselves to step into a bigger world that's not poisoned by fears of the past; whatever's holding us back will never be bigger than us, or more powerful than us, or more adaptable and resilient than our spirits can be. When we step out of our comfort zone, it will change our life in exchange for a future we can control.

For **high wellbeing** (272), it's fundamental that we step out of our comfort zone by doing something different and trying something new for the **first** (51) time. We can afford to challenge ourselves; we owe it to ourselves to have fun, check out new things, have a laugh, and enjoy the rewards of growing, or feeling exhilarated and alive. Stepping out of our comfort zone may cause discomfort at first, however take note, there's no growth without a little discomfort. Being out of our comfort zone is likely to bring challenges, more power and responsibility, lessons, and some redirections in life. These are key to a journey of progression, towards different experiences, independence, maturity, and self-confidence.

Discovering who we are and what drives us in our 20's may look very different in our 30's 40's, 50's or 60's. This is where transformation begins. Sometimes the magic happens when we stop worrying if things will work out. If we have to take our hands off the wheel, let go of control, and take a different ride to do something we've never done before to get a different result. Stepping out of our comfort zone is where the good things happen.

DIS-COMFORT = GROWTH

Consider a year we say "**Yes**" to everything rather than "**No**" to get out of that poisonous zone, it's a slow burner, a silent killer.

Step out of the back seat and throw that 'comfort zone' out the window!
It's time to take the wheel of our lives. and set the satnav to a place called 'Transformation'.

Strap ourselves in, turn the key in the ignition, put our foot on the throttle and go.

    🌐 Consider changing to a different compound. Intermediate Tyre.

Scissor Sisters Comfortably Numb 🎵

I hope I can take a chance and trust ...

The Trust Factor

Actions speak Louder than words!

Dashboard The Red Light Indicates: Stop! 🔴
Engage the emergency brake!

Trust comes on foot but leaves on horseback!

Trust is the bedrock of any successful, healthy relationship.
We cannot trust someone a little bit. It's like a person being a little bit pregnant. They can't be a little bit pregnant; they are pregnant, Trust is the same principle. Trust is whole; trust is a process that is complete. The power of love in a relationship allows us to become our best selves, because of trusting each other. Trust is an asset in any relationship, it's the fundamental building block that reinforces stability. Most would argue that without trust, there is no relationship, trust matters. There are various kinds of trust in relationships; take leadership which depends heavily on trust.

Healthy relationships are a partnership, a collaboration of hearts and minds, however, it helps if one can lead:

- If we don't have a vision of the future, we can't lead.
- If we don't know where we're going, we can't lead.
- If we don't carry our weight financially, we can't lead.
- If we can't communicate, we can't lead.

Sometimes, we need to trust our partners enough so that we can take a back seat and let them take the lead. Oxytocin is the hormone associated with love and trust. It is the bonding hormone in relationships. What becomes problematic in a relationship is when the oxytocin levels aren't mutual; they are at different levels between each partner. One partner is more bonded than the other, giving and being more physical, whilst the other is less physical, losing connection. This provokes an urgency to fix things because they are less physical, which leads to contempt. These are the first signs of trust beginning to deteriorate. Trust is also shown through our actions. Trust in romantic relationships is built over time. We either, trust the other straight away to confirm our trust or we seek proof to substantiate our trust. The honeymoon period is a time to test and challenge each other's **boundaries** (215) to discover who we are; once established, a deeper sense of commitment and trust is formed.

To earn trust, we require a moral code that refers to core principles that guide how both parties behave, interact, and make decisions in the relationship. **These core principles are centred on consistency, transparency, honesty and fidelity.**

These principles support how we treat each other and negotiate trust in the relationship.

The Key Practices

1. Effective communication and reliability.
2. Keeping our promises.
3. Following through on our commitments by way of actions.
4. Openly admitting mistakes or errors that have occurred by showing vulnerability and empathy.
5. Agreeing to set clear boundaries that are realistic to maintain.

Trust is an ongoing exchange that builds strong bonds. Once broken, it is rarely the same again, we don't give enough space for them to tell the truth; they lie out of fear. Lying generally starts with good intentions, not to disappoint or hurt the other, until the lies manifest into something uglier, and we find ourselves trapped. Many who have experienced their trust shattered struggle, they change. Their behaviour may change, acting on feelings of insecurity, e.g. putting up a wall for self-preservation by becoming on edge or hyperalert, and after they've put themselves through hoops, then what? Sometimes they may be unable to go back, back to what it once was. This means that the relationship is very close to being dead in the water.

Some couples can survive infidelity; there needs to be a period where we rebuild the trust for it to be earned back. We need to decide what it will take to regain the trust. It's the actions of the other party that will determine whether we can bring our partner back or not. We need to get real, show up for them every day. Be our authentic selves that our partners want; be selective with our words; words are powerful. It takes time to get to a place together, where the relationship becomes something of value to both parties.

As humans, we make mistakes. If there is goodwill, trust can be rebuilt after a betrayal, requiring forgiveness and time. Trust like a crumpled piece of paper, may heal, however the marks remain. It's vital in every relationship, including with ourselves.

Without trust, a relationship cannot truly exist!

⚙ Consider changing to a different compound: Hard Tyre.

Nitefreak, Imad & Clubhouse (Black Coffee) Not the Same ♫

I hope I can avoid becoming my own obstacle …

Self-Sabotage

Obstacle on the Track!

Dashboard The Red Light Indicates: Stop!
Engage the emergency brake!

We all have a negative committee chattering away in our heads that diverts us off track with criticism and commands to take us back to the past, to what feels familiar to us.

"I'm not good enough."

Self-sabotage usually stems from deep-rooted feelings of **not being good enough** (184). These self-beliefs encourage us not to have independent thoughts, to believe we are 'not important' enough, or we 'don't belong', and many more old perceptions that prevent us from succeeding or living autonomous lives. These negative thoughts can happen consciously and unconsciously, deliberately blocking and damaging and impairing ourselves from success or accomplishing our goals, ultimately preventing us from getting what we want. Self-sabotaging behaviours can affect our professional and personal lives, especially our mental health.

We must become aware of self-sabotaging mindsets or patterns to break them. Generally, self-sabotage happens when our values do not align with our behaviour, or what we really want, so we do something that doesn't get us to that destination. Emotions such as fear or anger, anxiety, and **stress** (164), will have us falling into avoidant behaviour. Naturally we will start to shy away from what feels bad.

Who turned you so against you?

I have experienced a variety of souls, whether they are a perfectionist striving for a flawless finish, we spend too much time and miss the deadline, and many more.

The Key Takeaways
- Procrastinate on a decision long enough for the decision to be taken out of our hands.

- We are given the answers, yet we disregard them, or change the subject.
- We go out on a bender with our friends and break our leg.
- The day before our interview, when we know that we're so close and we think we have it in the bag, we put ourselves in temptation's way.
- We ease up and take our foot off the gas, just before exam time.

We struggle with moderation and prefer a 'go hard or go home' mindset. We often find ourselves lacking **boundaries** (215), overstretching ourselves, at work or the gym, and end up with nothing left in the tank. Sabotage is likely to be contributing to blocking our pathway to success. Whether it's behaviours such as staying up too late, making us late for work, or less productive at work in the morning, **people pleasing** (218), and ignoring or neglecting our own needs, or we're procrastinators, preventing ourselves from reaching our goals; self-sabotage is present.

To overcome self-defeating behaviour, it is essential to:
- Have self-awareness, notice unhelpful thought patterns and self-sabotaging behaviours.
- Treat our struggle with compassion, not contempt.
- Understand the emotions that are associated with the behaviour.
- Identify and label the negative thoughts and beliefs that cause the emotion.
- Change our behaviour, emotions, and thoughts.
- Start small and develop self-supporting behaviours.

It is essential that we starve these voices, be aware of these bullies at all times, and take control of the steering wheel by keeping focus on ourselves. Words are powerful, and our thoughts can be the worst bullies we will ever encounter.

Time to take charge and take back control in giving ourselves choice and permission to travel down the road less travelled, signposted 'autonomy'.

Our minds can become our best friend or our worst enemy.
Make our mind up!

49ᵗʰ & Main Self Sabotage ♫

I hope I can share my feelings ...

Emotionless Parents

Sharing a problem wouldn't be Halving it,
it would be Doubling it!

Dashboard The Red Light Indicates: Stop! 🔴
Engage the emergency brake!

The first and most important relationship for a child is the relationship with their parents. This relationship becomes the template that is replayed in different ways and reverberates throughout our lives until we are consciously aware or healed.

Parents who habitually avoid and reject their own feelings are not likely to have the capacity to connect and empathise with the feelings of others, especially their children. They may struggle with emotions, how to process, express, and communicate emotions appropriately with themselves and others, creating distance rather than emotional closeness and intimacy in relationships.

Children who are neglected by their parents often become adults who emotionally neglect themselves. All of us learned a way of surviving at home, we weren't allowed to feel or express 'inconvenient' emotions' at home, for instance,

"Don't cry" typically used for boys.
"Don't be angry" typically used for girls.

As children, we hid our sadness to protect our parents, as they had taught us. Later, we realized they did the same, burying emotions instead of addressing them. As a result, we learned to conceal our own feelings.

In practice, Scarlet, 36, suffers because both parents raised her without expressing any 'difficult' emotions.

"I'd fallen unintentionally into a language that would keep me under the radar and at a distance so no one would notice, people would just skim over my feelings. Because I was taught not to express my emotions, I would naturally learn to avoid feelings by using abstract terms that keeps me 'below the parapet', just chit chat, small talk, or gossip about others. No one would notice me because I didn't want to upset my parents,

believing that they wouldn't be able to help, so things would get shoved under the carpet, or buried down below, doesn't get processed, recognised or acknowledged. Always believing the result of sharing a problem wouldn't be halving a problem it would be doubling it, because I never saw emotional problems confronted and dealt with.
We don't share, we deal with them ourselves! Learning that 'you're on your own.......by becoming very independent and doing things for myself, a very lonely place to be."

A classic example of a grown adult reflecting on their childhood, realising the consequences of emotions that weren't accepted at home. To prevent this from becoming generational, we need to embrace emotions, starting by learning to feel, communicate and take responsibility for them.
What we don't heal, we repeat!

We must apply the emergency brakes!

Joan Armatrading Show Some Emotion ♫

I hope I can be intentional when choosing my partner ...

Indebted to Debt

I Take you....... to Have and to Hold..

Dashboard The Purple Light indicates: Action Required! ●
Check Rear View Mirror!

After the honeymoon and we've stopped counting the many ways we say,
"I love you."
We take the honeymoon specs off and begin to recognise more flaws in one another. If the flaw is financial, we are now attached, signed up, contracted, obliged, we are bonded to the debt.

Debt is seen as a form of embarrassment for us, especially in relationships. It is super important to check out our partners' financial hygiene to know our potential partners are financially responsible; their habits, the way they treat their money, their emotional connection, their relationship with their money, whether they gamble or have regular spending sprees, or are actively deceitful with their money. Additionally, it is wise to be mindful of each other's backgrounds regarding money; different backgrounds produce different morals, as their value of money may speak a different language to ours.

The Key Questions
- Is buying gifts their love language, to impress others?
- Is money always on tap from mummy or daddy?
- How well do they prioritise bills over impulsive spending?
- Have they faced hardship, and learned to make ends meet?
- How do they conceptualise money?

"Money is bad!"
"Don't think about money! "
"Money is evil!"

If they have inherited the concept of money is not good, by nature they will want to get rid of it, relying on the next paycheque. It is vital that we view money positively; money is a tool for security and freedom, not constraint. It helps to be financially fit to maintain healthy money habits, or money will make us worse and amplify all our unhealthy habits.

Healthy practice requires discipline and regular attention to.
- Ability to master debt management – Focus on debts with the highest interest rate.
- Understand our cash flow – how much is coming in, where is it spent, and create a budget.
- Building emergency funds – high-interest savings accounts or set up automatic transfers.
- Maintain good credit. – timely payments, or one-time payments, show we're trustworthy.

If a married couple hits a bumpy road financially, it's likely to have implications; we are both committed emotionally, mentally, and financially to the relationship, regardless of living together, sharing a mortgage, or having children together. Finance is an important factor to acknowledge when considering a potential partner, numbers are never ending.
Whatever the number…what is mine is yours and what is yours is mine!

Engage the emergency brake!

Radiohead Reckoner ♫

I hope I don't succumb to my thoughts ...

Dirrty Thoughts

Lead us off Track

Dashboard The Red Light Indicates: Stop!

Leave your door and your back door open.
Let thoughts come and go. Just don't serve them tea!
Shunryu Suzuki

Our minds are powerful, intricate, and beautifully complex, capable of great insight, but also prone to noise. Sometimes that inner dialogue fills with doubts and fears with of limiting stories of "should" and "don't". When left unchecked, these thoughts can become like quiet saboteurs holding us back from who we truly are like, weapons of our minds. They can be very persuasive by seducing us into a false sense of security, believing our thoughts are true. The truth is our thoughts are not based on facts, but stories from our past that tend to become disorderly.

If we've struggled in life, not feeling we are a confident person, guaranteed, some dirrty thoughts have been lurking around feeding our insecurities, running riot in our heads, and, to add insult to injury, they rent enough space in our heads to become an endless loop of dishing the dirt.

There are different levels of dirrty thoughts, some are more harmful than others. Most thoughts come from tales relating to perspective, judgement, an opinion, an attitude from a frame of reference that is not ours to own, and untruth. Dirrty thoughts are toxic, they form and reshape how we see ourselves. Imagine a 'dirrty' thought being a taxi that can escort us down a journey of fear. Causing 'inaction' or 'indecision', like: **'comfort zone'** (118), **ego** (152), **people pleasing** (182), or vulnerability, **self-sabotage** (122), self-harm, self-loathing and many other forms of psychological abuse.

These thoughts can progress and grow roots, becoming that toxic voice in our heads. For instance, we might be busy getting ready, minding our own business, and suddenly, some dirt pops up.

"What are you wearing that for?"

and without hesitation, we put the dress back and choose something else. Some of these troubles are commonplace in therapy especially in difficult and dysfunctional relationships with our parents or authoritative figures.

The parents who didn't raise us with unconditional love can create deep-rooted feelings connected to feeling 'not good enough' in life. We may not be in regular contact, or live on the other side of the world, but, somehow, they are still with us in our head, that critical voice chattering or shouting at us. It is important that we resolve and dissolve these dirrty thoughts, whether they are alive or deceased.

Here are a few typical examples of dirrty thoughts.

>"You're just like your father..."
>
>"You never do anything right!"
>
>"You'll never get anywhere in life with that attitude!"
>
>"Eat all your dinner, there are starving children in Africa"
>
>"Stop whinging and moaning, no one's listening."
>
>"Why can't you be more like your brother?"
>
>"Stop crying or I'll give you something to cry for."
>
>"Who do you think you are?"
>
>"You're a waste of time!"
>
>"You should know your place!"
>
>"I am too busy to play with you. "
>
>"That's ridiculous, there's nothing to be upset about."

Words like these can instantly stop us in our tracks, silence us, suppress our feelings, and limit our potential by holding us back from living authentically.

Are we living for our parents or for ourselves?

Many of us whose parents have passed away may still be having daily conversations, obeying their instructions. The critical voice of our parents becomes an echo in our heads even when they are no longer with us. Let's not be misled into believing a parent 'can't rule from the grave' so to speak; they can. We can't tell them to shush, and this is where professional help (i.e. therapy) is required.

Living our lives under the pressure of fulfilling our parents' expectations can negatively impact our lives and be all-consuming and burdensome. Most of us want to make our parents happy, which might mean doing as we are told, not getting too above our station for that glass ceiling to prevail. Dirrty thoughts simply seduce us into believing,

"I can't do it..."

If we haven't experienced, we wouldn't know we can't do it; it is not a fact, it is not real until we do it. Don't let these dirrty thoughts define us and choose wisely which taxi we jump into.

One way we can view our thoughts, imagine they are like taxis. They will come and go; take control and allow them to pass us by. Defuse those thoughts by disarming them, through means of:

The Key Practices

- **Distraction** – Take a dirrty thought and replace it with something positive and accurate, to ground and allow us to be fully present.
- **Journaling** – Check in, monitor or challenge our thoughts to assess if they come from an authentic place or if they are dirrty.
- **Silence** – Our silence can reveal what our busy minds have overlooked. Let's silence the noise and allow the truth about who we are to rise to the surface.

Let's not fight the thoughts, let them pass. We are not our thoughts, our authentic selves lie beneath the criticism and judgements of others, so when we see a 'dirrty' taxi coming, let it pass us by and bid it farewell.

Adios, Adieu. Laters!!!

We must apply the emergency brakes!
- Consider changing to a different compound. Wet Tyre.

Utah Saints My Mind Must be Free ♪

Stop the Race!

Chapter 7

Danger!

The yellow flag is indicating ...

Yellow Flag

Danger.
There is a hazard on the track.
Overtaking is prohibited.
Approach with caution.

Drive within our limits; we cannot overtake and must be prepared to change direction. It must be evident that a driver has reduced their speed during the relevant sectors.
Slow down considerably. It is often used when marshals are on track.
Double wave yellow flag means slow down and be prepared to stop!!

When we are experiencing 'yellow flag' moments, we encounter difficulties that are troubling, not yet critical. These situations have the potential to become complex if left unaddressed. Rushing through a yellow flag situation is not only reckless, but it also leads to further complications. In life, this might look like taking on too much during a stressful period or ignoring the need for self-care. The yellow flag signals that we need to be prepared for sudden changes, prompting us to adjust our course or even stop entirely. This mirrors life's unpredictability, where obstacles may demand quick thinking and adaptability.

It is time to slow down and make the appropriate changes to progress in the race.

- 133 **Social Media**
- 135 **Procrastination**
- 137 **Careful what You Wish For**
- 138 **Mental Load**
- 140 **Family Feuds**
- 141 **Friends for Sale**
- 143 **The Misconception of Female Ambition**
- 144 **Self-Esteem**
- 145 **The Art of Picking a Partner**

I hope I can look after my mental health …

Social Media

Put the Gun Down!

Double wave Yellow flag!
Slow down and be prepared to stop!!

"Don't be fooled by the internet. It's cool, to get on the computer, but don't let the computer get on you. It's cool to use the computer, but don't let the computer use you. You saw the matrix. There's a war going on with the battlefields in the mind and the prize is the soul, so just be careful." Prince (1999).

When social media first arrived, we thought it was our best friend, now it seems it's turning out to be our enemy, the genie we can't put back in the bottle. The posts that we see are like a trailer for a film, simply clips that don't tell the full version of our lives. As for Artificial Intelligence, we may need reminding AI is a machine imitating life.

Most of the posts are not real, making us feel ugly worthless, causing stress, anxiety, and depression; it can become a tool for abuse from others as well as ourselves. It relentlessly demands constant attention and steals the most precious asset we have, called time.

Today, social media is reminiscent of an 'all you can eat buffet', that never closes, we can be served up some good stuff, but also an unpalatable amount of garbage. Many use social media for networking when they simply want to be social. We find ourselves in a 'meat market', openly allowing people we do not know, who do not know us, in other words, strangers, to critique who we are, and our world.

Social media has a lot to answer for. In my practice, I have observed a variety of souls wounded and scarred from their experience of social media, the abuse, the trolls, and the questioning of their self-worth. It encourages us to compare our worlds can only lead to despair. For souls that aren't so thick-skinned, the only answer is to take a break and remove the app. Agree with our circle to support one another by taking a break from social media every month or season to help regulate phone use. Life is passing us by, with our heads stuck in our phones. Being on our phones distracts us from being with our own thoughts.

There are some positives, social media can provide great connections, and can be entertaining from time to time. However, it also brings an infinite loop of distractions. These distractions pose a threat to our health. If we imagine social media is the gun, then distractions are the bullets. Now, more than ever, we are we are exposed to current affairs, and news, with the option to observe horrific content (e.g. war) in graphic detail, like never before. We are bombarded with a sensory overload that distorts our reality. 'Doom scrolling', compulsively reading negative news, along with deliberately addictive algorithms, can lead us down rabbit holes. The impact of this kind of scrolling is contributing to an epidemic of mental health problems, particularly among young people.

We're constantly on our phones afraid of missing out, continually seeking validation based on how many likes we receive. The modern world is hyper-stimulated, expecting us to be alert, switched on, and engaged at all times., This creates new challenges for our physiology, the inability to disconnect causes our stress levels to rise. Our brains are fried from overstimulation. As overstimulation becomes normalised, we increase the stimulation just to feel the same level of sensation, sending our anxiety levels off sky high. These guns are addictive.

How often do we find ourselves unnecessarily picking up our phones throughout the day?

To help to disconnect from our phones, consider.

The Key Practices

- Monitoring how long we spend on our phones. Set screen time limits, to see how often we pick them up.
- Limit our phone use after a set time, e.g. 8pm.
- Turn notifications on or off – whichever helps to reduce our urge to constantly check.
- Make our phones less attractive by switching them to greyscale, turning the screen black and white.
- Download the 'Forest' app and try to grow a virtual forest by staying off our phones.
- 'Barebacking' -commute without any digital distractions. e.g. - no phone, Air Pod, Kindle.

Having a break from our phones improves our sleep quality. Our mood lifts and we're no longer slave to our devices. If we consume too much trivial, meaningless content for too long, we risk developing 'brain rot'. We physically can't be in two places at the same time, or all the places all the time. Take some time out and put the gun down before we cause ourselves harm. Consider setting a daily limit on social media.

It's cool to use social media, just don't let social media get up on us. Moderation is our best friend; excess is the enemy.

Try not to pull the trigger!

I hope I can just do it ...

Procrastination

Just Do it......If we're not First, we're Last!

Procrastination is a warning light
Indicates: Caution. Slow Down!

Procrastination is a mental tug of war, a battle between intention and delay. We may dilly-dally around, putting off today what we can do tomorrow. Thinking our decision making will be better in the future rather than the present, only to find ourselves on the field of 'last minute dot com'.

Procrastination happens when we are challenged with negative feelings. We develop a way of avoiding unpleasant feelings, which in turn becomes an open invitation to fear and anxiety of not overcoming the task. If we want to make an easy task seem harder and keep delaying and putting it off, anxiety will find a place to stay.

Recognising the word "*try*" in our vocabulary can be a powerful step towards breaking through mental barriers. Phrases like *"I'll try and do that.."* are often signals of inaction. Psychologically, "*try*" reflects hesitation, fear of failure, a lack of commitment, or avoidance. This implies we're not fully invested, or that we're seeking an excuse not to act. This tendency to procrastinate often stems from a deeper feeling of **not being good enough** (184), creating a cycle of excuses that prevent us from acting and moving forward.

We know the thing we need to do, yet we have an inability to act, feeling trapped or frozen, absent-minded, indecisive, or passive with decision making. Whatever the excuse, however big or small the dither. If procrastination is part of our process; the good news is that we can make our time of procrastination smaller if we become aware of our fears and overthinking.

In practice, Samara, 29, had this history, and her procrastination became an issue at university, as she struggled to complete deadlines and was unable to complete her coursework. Unfortunately, she didn't inform her tutors that she was struggling. Consequently, she began to spiral, her fears of failing modules and inevitably the exams were becoming a reality. We explored her story and to overcome her issues, rather than the symptom of procrastination, we explored the pressure of expectations from herself and others and the negative emotions that became her obstacles.

Nike – Just Do It! ✔

Nike has the most effective strapline, with simple, clear instruction.
Once we understand why we procrastinate, then we can start to tackle our behavioural stuff, whether it's starting to exercise, moving house, or a new regime. It is a clear instruction when life is demanding there's no time to procrastinate, we must DO it anyway. If we keep to that approach, we will be winning.

Do one task at a time.

Start with the hardest task first, it adds the most value. Completing it will boost our confidence, makes us feel proud and motivated to complete the rest.. Putting things off, only creates stress.
When we have a focal point, to ensure we stay on track and keep distractions out, we act, without allowing our overthinking to get the better of us, we take action. Step out of our heads. Step out of our emotions...It's time to take ACTION. Just do it!

Don't think about it. Don't sit on our laurels.
Get up and... Just Do it!

Gwen Stefani What You Waiting For?
(Jacques Lu Cont's TWD Mix) ♫

I hope I can have the best career ...

Careful what You Wish For

Desire meets Reality

They say, "Be careful what you wish for."
Sometimes the things we long for the most, can feel different, it isn't quite what we imagined once it arrives. In practice, Xavier, 35, passionately and proudly loved his career as a doctor, he believed this career was his calling. Finally, after dreaming of becoming a doctor, and enduring the hard slog of training, he did it, he qualified as a doctor. He had arrived.

He wished that he could become the best doctor he could be, wanting to heal and cure as many patients as possible. As time progressed, Xavier moved up the ladder and opened his own practice. Life was rewarding them accordingly, he thought his wish had come true.

As time went by, he recognised that he was slowly running out of gas, regularly hitting high levels of exhaustion. He began to question his position in life and assess his situation only to discover that there was no one there, no one for him. He was on his own.

His career became a barrier for every other area in his life. He had spent all his years focused on becoming a doctor; he was so proud of himself, so consumed that he forgot about himself. There was no balance in his life, no life after work, just work. He had no more energy left to give for anything else.

He could not maintain relationships because he didn't have the capacity to be consistent enough to hold down a relationship. He couldn't spread himself any thinner; he wasn't emotionally available to himself, let alone others.
His career had consumed all his **energy** (101), he wasn't able to do anything else - activities, hobbies, holidays, family, even friendships, he was married to his job.
In the end, his wish had blocked every other area in his life.

Sprinkle a touch of reality onto our dreams and consider the bigger picture.

- Consider switching to a different compound. Hard Tyre.

I hope I won't burnout …

Mental Load

The endless To-Do List in our Heads

Double Wave Yellow Flag
Slow down and be prepared to stop!!

Mental load is the invisible weight we carry.
It's all the background stresses, the running to-do list in our minds, the emotional and logistical labour of keeping life organised, especially at home. It's the planning, remembering, and anticipating that often goes unnoticed yet never truly stops. It's the constant, behind-the-scenes thinking including the mental and emotional admin required to keep a household running smoothly. From, managing family life to handling responsibilities at work, the mental load can quietly pile up. When we reach the limits of what our minds can process, it becomes overwhelming, especially for single parents who often juggle it all alone.

Mental load requires meeting the needs of family members, such as meal planning, keeping food and items regularly stocked, writing shopping lists, scheduling everyone's diaries, dentist, doctor or vet appointments, events, anniversaries, birthdays, family gatherings, meeting school requests, exams, packing lunch boxes, remembering cards, presents, to RSVPs, clean, and tidy the house, kitchen, bedrooms, car, windows, laundry, walk the dog, empty the bins, book holidays, pay bills; and manage others' feelings, opinions, distress, grief, from losing the dog to the overwhelm of homework, leisure activities, and so on. The tasks accumulate and start to stack up as the load gets heavy.

Abiola, 42, a mother of two, was experiencing symptoms of burnout, and recalls her partner explaining the cupboard saying to their son,

"This is the 'magic' cupboard, it's always got our favourite things in here, it never runs out. "
"That 'magic' cupboard is me, constantly making sure they are stocked up. I'm the only one in the house that thinks of these things.
That remembers to ask the parents if their children have any food allergies for my son's birthday party,
or remembers to buy them gift bags for the children to take home. It's me. Miss Reliable."

Danger!

Our mental load can feel burdensome and potentially lead to burnout. To avoid burnout, we need to let go. To let go of "my way is the best way" or the idea of perfection, the family will not be able to do this as well as we can because we aren't giving them the opportunity to have a go, to practice these skills.

Here are some tips to lessen the mental load:

The Key Practices

1. Ask for **help** (283). Talk to our partners to share the load.
2. Take the stress of remembering everything out of our heads and onto paper.
3. Make a list of priorities, rank the chores in order, and start to delegate the tasks; the children can pitch in.
4. Give everyone a role that has their own task to maintain.
5. Set **boundaries** (215) in the house – tasks completed on certain days.
6. Prioritise self-care. Learn to reduce the stress levels by avoiding multi-tasking and focus on improving sleep and introducing relaxing pursuits into our weekly routine, such as yoga, meditation, and massage.
7. 'The Fair Play Deck' – Putting the fun back into domestic chores and taking the responsibility out of our hands. This offers a family or couples, a strategy for evening out domestic duties by way of using a pack of cards with one hundred different household responsibilities. This method offers a practical way of levelling out the load and helps reduce our anxiety by supporting families to share responsibility. Simply by drawing a card, no need for delegation or conflict. This gamified system keeps score and fairly distributes the tasks.
8. **Spiritual Hygiene** (260) - Practice cleansing our spiritual energies.

We can't do it all.
It's time to free up our mental capacity and shift the responsibility at home. Give the family members access to the list to encourage volunteers.

Mental Load leaves no room for us, only burn out!

> 🛞 Consider switching to a different compound. Intermediate Tyre.

Jamiroquai White Knuckle Ride (Monachy Remix) ♫

I hope we can resolve ...

Family Feuds

Trust. Respect. Power.

It is healthy to have people who don't care about what we do, who love, respect, and treat us all the same. The people we love the most and who care the least about our status outside of the family circle, this may seem like an ideal notion about family. However, some families are different, not all share the same sentiment, or standpoint. It is common to have tension amongst family members that can last for years or generations, so patience is key.

We may agree to meet but there's no progression. These may be small wins that take time, sometimes we need to break everything down to its foundation so we can rebuild a solid structure and become stronger.
When families are fractured, arguments are generally about three areas:

Trust. Respect. Power.

These three areas may also intertwine with the traditional toxic 'sibling rivalry', and there we have a classic recipe for a family feud.
If we won't agree to disagree, can't trust, or are not prepared to listen to family members, or if the family will not agree to disagree, struggles to trust, or is not prepared to listen to us, then it is time to take our power elsewhere and move on!

If we are all on the same page, it is essential to start with small regular discussions, whether weekly, monthly or seasonal meetings, or we can consider starting online first, leading to in-person meetings.

- **Communication** – recognise we are all singing from the same hymn sheet, to make change, to start the process, and to heal rifts.
- **Focus on getting to the root cause** of the disagreement, rather than hovering around the issues.
- **A Mediator** present can help in case we reach a stalemate. Someone neutral, who is outside of the family loop can help to keep focus and stay on track when emotions are heightened. Unlock the door to the beauty of forgiveness!

Danger!

If all else fails, it is key to remember we can't force feed our family members. Sometimes we have personalities that have become more anxious, or more resilient to the situation, we may love them and not like them. What is important is to focus on our own expectations. Consider letting go of any expectations we have of others. Once we terminate expectation, we take our power back, by removing their power to hurt us. Self-preservation is key.

When it comes to family, it's important to acknowledge what came before us, and for some, that's where it ends. Don't get caught up in settling for family members that expect us to do nothing more than repeat old dysfunctional cycles for gain. Sometimes honesty and loyalty come with solitude.

To meet, or not to meet, is a family effort, not solo.
Stay true to ourselves and fly free!

Fleetwood Mac The Chain ♫

I hope they will change …

Friends for Sale

Beware of Syrupy smiles, for Jealousy lurks Beneath!

Dashboard The Green Light indicates: All Clear!

Our friends can become the family we choose; we let them into our world and entrust them to share and support one another as we progress in life. It's natural to have a tinge of jealousy about their achievements, new car, great holiday, or an incredible job. Nonetheless, some friends have ulterior motives given that their motivation comes from a place of desire.

If we notice they are overly competitive, fail to openly celebrate our achievements, but celebrating our downfalls, they don't have our best interests at heart. They may have their own agenda.

Not everyone wants or thrives on being different.
Jealousy comes from comparison. They want something that we have and their fear of losing in the competition overrides the friendship. They perceive

our successes, whether in relationships or possessions as threats, and so they react and respond accordingly.

In practice, Isobel, 39 explains,

> *"I had a 'green-eyed monster' friend that was very envious of me, it got in the way of the relationship when she made a pass at my ex, I let her go, and we lost contact, I bumped into her ten years later and hoped they had changed, matured for the better, to give both of us another chance for new friendship. She hadn't changed.*
> *At the time her jealousy was focused on my dating life, and relationships. However, when we reunited, her jealousy shifted towards my career. It became a constant comparison, like a sense of entitlement, secretly she built her own business trying to compete and outdo me. She seemed focused on my blessings and disregarded her own blessings."*

The stronger, brighter, happier, and more successful we become, the more envy grows, disguised behind syrupy smiles. We can't change this, having awareness gives us a degree of strength. Frenemies might keep us on our toes; however, their intentions can be mean and insincere. Their negative behaviour prevents relationships from growing, and in turn, increases our suspicions, doubts and mistrust. It's a one-sided relationship.

We can do nothing about green-eyed folk, jealousy is not becoming of a true friend. No matter how lonely our journey gets, never reinvite toxic people back into our life!

There's no reason to settle for those who do nothing but weigh us down.
Zen Shin wisely said,

> *"A flower does not think to compete with the flower next to it, it just blooms."*

Our fortune, their envy.
Our misfortune, their relief!

Wish them well.

Bob Marley Who the Cap Fit ♫

I hope I can have it all ...

Misconception of Female Ambition

Women can't have it all

Double wave Yellow flag!
Slow down and be prepared to stop!!

I'm not talking about a queen, goddess, being a size 10, or maintaining model looks, which counts for little when it's our tenacity and vibrancy that capture people's attention, not the rest of the aesthetics that pressure women today. Women of the nineties were a generation who believed they could have it all and do just as well, if not better than a man. Over time, my thoughts changed. I believe feminism has misled women; it has gone too far, disillusioning women with unrealistic notions in believing that we can have it all. Balancing three roles successfully, being a life partner, an attentive mother, maintaining a ruthless, successful career or business is no longer realistic nowadays. One of those roles will give way. It is a myth that we can juggle all those roles successfully and strike a balance while maintaining our own high level of **wellbeing** (272).

The world has changed dramatically, demanding more of us. For relationships to survive these days, they require 100%, not 50/50. Motherhood requires 100%, our careers and wellbeing requires 100%, and looking after everyone's feelings demands another 100%. There's nothing left of us to give to ourselves! Yet we are still sold the conventional, unrealistic dream of falling in love, getting married, becoming a mother, having a career. It would be beneficial if girls were properly informed at school age, rather than being set up with fairytales. It is an unrealistic dream choose one or two roles and focus on our happiness, whether to be a mum, or have a career and a partner. This is our life.

Women fall short on starting a family because they have been focused on their careers, or they struggle to meet an adequate mate. Dating is brutal out there, plus, it's another full-time job given the time we invest in getting to know each other. I encourage us to take that pivotal life step earlier, to give ourselves the opportunity before Mother Nature takes away the option.
Women have come into my practice crushed by the myths of motherhood and unrealistic expectations of women, being misled into buying into the fairytale.
Choose wisely.

Raye & Hans Zimmer Mother Nature ♪

I hope I can understand why I'm lacking ...

Self-Esteem's Out of Steam

Seek and we Shall Find!

Dashboard The Purple Light indicates: Action Required! 🟣
Check Rear View Mirror!

Self-esteem quietly shapes how we see ourselves and how we show up on the world. When it's low, it can gently pull us back, making us question our worth, shrink in social spaces, and retreat from connection. We may start to feel uneasy in social settings, struggle to form meaningful connections, find it hard to make friends, and gradually withdraw.

Interactions with others may leave us feeling insulted, rejected, criticised, not good enough, bruised, belittled, or unloved. Low self-esteem often stems from the belief that we are **not good enough** (184). This pain we're feeling reflects what we are lacking within ourselves. These emotional responses highlight the areas we need to heal and grow; we are being shown we need to work on ourselves. Relying on others for approval or validation to legitimise our existence is unhealthy and unsustainable. It cannot fill the emptiness within us. Depending on someone else to fill our emotional voids will never truly heal us. Seeking approval from others may temporarily soothe our wounds, but it only addresses the surface, not the deeper issues. These unmet needs will resurface, again and again, under different circumstances or relationships, offering only fleeting relief. Patching emotional "holes" with external validation is like treating the branches of a damaged tree while ignoring its weakened trunk and roots. To feel worthy, self-assured, confident, and capable of standing strong on our own, we must nurture our inner selves. Taking charge of our own emotional "vehicle" ensures the path leads to fulfilment, not to further disconnection. True fulfilment comes from addressing and strengthening our sense of self-worth. Our most important relationship is with ourselves.

The Key Practices

- Start by setting small, realistic goals to achieve in a week.
- Discover more about ourselves by joining a therapy group.
- List our goals and focus on achieving one.
- Join a group sport activity.
- Focus on high wellbeing.

Danger!

- Choose a role model.
- Practice mirror work.
- Watch out for our inner critic, keep it positive.
- Practice journaling and meditation.

A clear sign that we've done the inner work, and our self-esteem is thriving is when we can confidently check in with ourselves and say,

"I'm fully safe within myself."
"I'm fully loved within myself."
"I'm fully enough within myself."

This sense of safety comes from self-trust, self-acceptance, and the assurance that we can navigate life challenges without relying on external validation. It reflects deep inner strength and the ability to stand tall, knowing our worth comes from within.

Fall in love with the reflection in the mirror!

○ Consider switching to a different compound. Wet Tyre.

Cat Burns Live More and Love More ♪

I hope I find someone like mum or dad …

The Art of Picking a Partner

Mum or Dad?

Double-Wave Yellow Flag!
Slow down and be prepared to stop!!

In relationships, we choose what's familiar. We are either influenced by our mother or father. Each parent has characteristics that are familiar to us, whether positive or negative. For many, these familiar traits feel like home, even if they don't meet our needs.

Choose a partner based on the positive qualities that feel like home, rather than defaulting to negative or toxic traits.

For example, did we grow up with a...

- Controlling father?
- Mother who was emotionally neglectful?
- Narcissistic mother?
- Distant and introverted dad?
- A mother who craves attention?
- Supportive compassionate dad?
- Workaholic father?
- Unambitious, irresponsible mother?
- Strong minded, responsible and protective father?

And so much more. After all, our parents are our first role models.

Do they share characteristics with our current partner?

Maybe we see those traits as love, because they feel like home.
In practice, Boadicea, 37, would subconsciously choose men of a competitive nature. Her father was a narcissist, at the top of his game in a particular sport; he naturally competed to win and believed he was always right. Her partner was very opinionated. He believed his views were superior to hers and always insisted he was right. The theme of competition ran deep in competition, there are only winners and losers, rather than mutual participants. Patterns often follow familiar themes and recurring dynamics, so I enquired about how competitive the men in her life seemed to be. As a result of parenting, attachment styles often show up in interpersonal relationships shaping how we relate to our inner world. These can be fearful and critical, disorganised and unaware, secure and accepting, or avoidant and dismissive.

The people we choose to have intimate relationships with usually convey some level of familiarity for us that we recognise and associate with home. That's often linked to our mum or dad. Whether we are raised by a toxic parent, a narcissist, or a controlling figure, these dynamics are familiar Their traits, such a can unconsciously draw us ins how our parent responded to our feelings or made us feel as children, can unconsciously draw us in. These are often red flags.
Once we recognise the parent we've subconsciously chosen, it's time to tear up the script and start again, choose wisely. It's not wise to choose a partner to please our parents. It's not wise to choose a partner that enhances our image. We must choose a partner who is genuinely good for us.

Choose YOU!

Khalid & Disclosure Know Your Worth ♫

Danger!

iHope

Chapter 8

Unsportsmanlike Behaviour!

The Black and White Flag chapter is assisting ...

Black and White Diagonal Flag

Warning!
Unsportsmanlike behaviour.

What is coming next relates to the 'black and white flag' moments in our lives. Those times when we feel worn out, defeated and overwhelmed. This symbolises moments when emotional struggles extend beyond us influencing our actions and words in ways that may harm others or ourselves, either through direct behaviour or neglect of responsibilities.

Our self-worth and self-esteem may be at a low point, and our actions can unintentionally hinder both our own progress and the well-being of those around us. Unchecked behaviour can escalate if left unaddressed. However, adversity can also spark positive transformation if we choose to learn from it, make amends, and work toward restoration.

Slow down and nurse our tyres.

150 **You Complete Me**

152 **Ego**

154 **Competition and Comparison**

155 **Hurt People**

157 **Legacy**

158 **Listen Up**

159 **Prelude to a Stranger**

I hope my significant other has what I need ...

You Complete Me

Only We have the Privilege to Complete Ourselves!

Dashboard The Orange Light Indicates: Caution! Slow Down!

In practice, many have often wondered, including Lubiana, 31,
"Why am I always attracting the ones who leave?"
"What's missing? Why can't I keep them...?"

This may require exploration.
Write down all the qualities we are seeking in a partner,
 such as,

- Ambition.
- Confidence.
- Loving.

...Now, apply these requirements to ourselves first!

The type of partner we choose often reflects our own self-worth. We are often drawn to qualities in others that we admire, desire, or have yet to develop within ourselves. If we're pretending to be someone else to compensate for insecurities won't create a healthy relationship. Eventually, the façade will crack, our vulnerabilities will show, the relationship breaks down, and they will leave.

True **self-esteem** (144) isn't found in a romantic connection; it comes from within. We must first fall in love with ourselves – me, myself and I, to build the foundation for a fulfilling life, independent of external validation.

Self-love and self-acceptance are essential. Our unloved self often prefers a relationship with someone else rather than being in a relationship with our ourselves. We often seek a relationship with someone else to avoid facing our own unresolved emotional needs.

> **We settle for less because we come from less!**

We believe we are worth less, and become attached to someone else, relying on them to feel validated, to feel love within ourselves, to validate our self-worth. This isn't love; this is dependency. A relationship that is rooted in co-dependency, a reliance on someone else to fill emotional gaps, which can only be filled from within.

This dynamic creates a fragile foundation, propping up a co-dependent attachment rather than encouraging real love. Constantly seeking approval, acceptance, or compliments from our partner gives away our power and creates vulnerability. Depending on someone else to build us up can lead to unhealthy dynamics, as the same validation can be withheld, breaking us down. This is a known as a codependent relationship, an unhealthy cycle of dependence and external validation.

To attract the partner of our dreams, we must first become the version of ourselves that aligns with the person we seek. This requires us to meet our own deeper emotional and psychological needs by practicing and embodying the qualities that support our own wellbeing.

Once we reflect these qualities, we may find that our preferences shift, we will naturally be drawn to partners who align with our authentic selves. Not the version of ourselves that was shaped by our insecurities or fear.

We overlook the truth that we are already whole; we simply need to do the work to realise it. Healing isn't about becoming someone new; it is about uncovering who we've always been beneath our hurts and insecurities. Ultimately, for lasting happiness, the most important relationship is the one we build with ourselves. This is the foundation for everything else in our lives, including the love we seek.

… Now, match and attract what we've become through our efforts!

Alexis Jordan Happiness ♪

I hope I can stay humble ...

Ego

Everything we Need is on the Other side of Ego!

Ego is a warning light on our dashboard indicating:
Caution Slow Down!

Denzel Washington shared these words with Will Smith after he assaulted Chris Rock at the Oscars,

*"At your highest moment, be careful.
That's when the devil comes for you."*

Most believe Denzel was implying that at our highest moments, we are also the most vulnerable, prone to reacting impulsively. Success can sometimes bring on unexpected burdens. When people finally reach their moment of triumph, the pressure, the fear, or unresolved emotions can lead them to act in ways that jeopardise everything they've worked for. In Will's case, assaulting Chris Rock may have stemmed from many reasons, but the moment was a stark reminder of how quickly things can unravel.

From my experience as a therapist, I have seen many stories similar to Will's. We unknowingly create obstacles for ourselves just when we're about to achieve something great: They work tirelessly, enduring the toughest climb of their life. Every detail is accounted for, all their ducks are in a row, all the boxes are ticked, every 'i' is dotted and every 't' is crossed. Then, just as they reach success, standing at the edge of their greatest achievement, they unexpectedly derail themselves. I call this self-sabotage.

We see it often; **self-sabotage** (122) appears in many different forms. However, it leads to the same outcome. We ease up just before reaching the summit, believing success is certain. We stop pushing, convinced we've done enough, even when there's still five per cent left to go, and something shifts; we become the ones who change the outcome.

Many of us wonder, what is the 'ego'?

Many relate to the ego being the voice in our head. The ego is our inner critic that we all have all inherited from our past. Those old tapes that we keep

replaying daily, forming a non-stop narrative that chases us out of bed in the morning.
Our ego persists in criticising us and everyone else in our world. It constantly wants, judges and compares telling us we are not good enough. Our ego hooks into our 'FOMO' (fear of missing out), it creates imposter syndrome, continually sabotaging us by keeping us forced on the past or the future instead of being present and grounded in the now.

If our ego is on the prowl, another way of deciphering is to check out the 'seven deadly sins' derived from Catholic theology. The sins are seen as the behaviours and feelings that inspire further sin. We'll often find ego deeply entwined with one of the seven sins: sloth, pride, greed, envy, lust, gluttony, and wrath. Gluttony could be defined as self-sabotage. Sloth can be equated to wasted ability or time wasting. Wrath can be defined as hatred or resentment. Lust may lead to adultery. Pride, greed, and envy can all be linked to self-sabotage and ego. This is not to suggest we become Catholic. This is simply a helpful checklist to reflect on whether our ego is running riot.

I've seen many who have had good intentions, good prospects, a chance to make a positive difference in their lives, and at the most crucial time, they sabotage the opportunity.
There are so many reasons why we sabotage ourselves: worthlessness, self-esteem, self-hatred, fear of success, or the belief that we're not good enough, or will never succeed.

We are all self-sabotaging in some form or another: **procrastination** (135), perfectionism, comparisons, infidelity, criticism, emotional unavailability, and many more. It depends on how severe the setback. We all have the urge to protect ourselves, logic doesn't apply, survival does!

Ours may not be as steep as Will Smith's lesson. This is an example we can all learn from: never be too complacent, or our self-sabotage will come for us.

Keep the ego in check!

The Ego light on the dashboard is flashing.

- Consider switching to a different compound. Intermediate Tyre.

Ezra Collective Ego Killah ♪

I hope I don't undermine my self-esteem, and fuel my anxiety ...

Competition and Comparison

Compare only Breeds Despair!

Dashboard The Purple Light indicates: Action Required!
Check Rear View Mirror!

In the absence of security, we often compare ourselves to others, cheer ourselves up artificially, or seek approval or permission to get a measure of where we are in life; this rarely makes us feel better, often, it makes us feel worse. Everything happens on the inside first, and then the outside. We're at an unfair advantage from the start, not aware that we are comparing how we feel with what we covet, to make ourselves feel better. Comparing our insides with other people's outsides puts us in a 'lose/lose' situation. The nature of competition implies that one party wins or loses. In making comparisons with others, we are gambling with ourselves.

Comparing ourselves to strangers often stems from feeling **not good enough** (184). When we make comparisons, we are comparing our feelings with their performance, the 'end job.' Whatever has happened to them, whatever experience the person has encountered, it starts from the inside and then translates externally to the outside.

In practice, Lucia, 41, had this history of constantly comparing her life to her friends believing,

> *"Something's wrong with me, I should be doing better than this, I can't seem to do all the things that she does and have a tidy house and children in order, she's lost all her baby weight and looks amazing..."*

Not knowing that her friend had a cleaner for the house, extra support from both her parents and the in-laws, and she had an eating disorder, everyone has their own battles.

Should

Lucia expresses , *"... I should be doing better."*

> *"It isn't the mountains ahead that wear you out, it's the pebble in your shoe."* Muhammad Ali

'Should' is a word with shackles and restrictions attached; it comes with conditions which imply obligation, conformity, and comparison, a measure of what we are trying to match up to. If we use the word 'should', we know that we are making these comparisons.

Or we catch ourselves 'shoulding' all over everything!

We must be careful about what we are limiting ourselves to. Burdening ourselves with endless expectations and unhelpful self-judgement. It's beneficial to focus and get stuck into our own goals and dreams to fill our lives with them. There would be no time to compare our lives with others.
It's unwise to compare our hearts with style and design. What feels normal to one person can seem weird to another. In competition, there are winners and losers, but when we shift our focus, we become participants, not rivals. Until we realise, we are enough just as we are, we will keep seeking validation from others. Instead, its' healthier to compete only with our own potential and capabilities, striving for personal growth rather than external approval.

Self-sabotage usually stems from deep-rooted feelings of **not being good enough** (184). It's better not to judge ourselves by measuring our internal struggles against someone else's external presentation.

● Consider changing to a different compound. Intermediate Tyre.

I hope that my own pain doesn't spill onto others ...

Hurt People, Hurt People!

Accountability stops the Hurting

Dashboard The Red Light Indicates: Stop! ●
Engage the emergency brake!

Over the years, we've acquired many experiences, some good, some bad. Imagine the memories are like tape cassettes; when the bad memory feels too much, it gets archived, with no attention for recovery or healing, just pushed as far to the back of our minds as possible.
These hurts that we've suffered in our lives might originate from an experience with our ex-partner, and as a result, we end up hurt, and that then

becomes a taped experience. Our wounds are the consequence of that experience, so we decide never to return to that moment again. The tape gets archived, we put our foot down on the throttle, and don't look back. Subsequently, we reach a good place in our lives with a new partner and take a chance on love again. The relationship will naturally be tested, maybe our values or boundaries, our buttons get pushed, triggering us enough for that tape to float to the surface of our minds at our most vulnerable times. It's replayed in our heads reminding us:

I'm not good enough.
I'm unlovable.
I'm stupid.
I don't belong.

And so on. See, we inappropriately react to the current partner as though they are the ex-partner. The problem is that the current partner has no knowledge of this tape or that we've been triggered.

Our way of coping is to remedy the old situation in the present time is to put some distance between us and the tape, so we act hastily and quickly abandon the relationship and start running, putting our foot down on the throttle again so the tape gets archived once more. At the same time, we've hurt an innocent soul while protecting our own hurts.

Until we confront, address, heal, and recover, we will continue to replay thoughts, feelings, and behaviours associated with that tape, with an innocent soul.

People get hurt from our old hurts.

We can't keep running from ourselves. The tape will continue to control life until we seek professional help. Make a different decision to free ourselves from old wounds and past hurts.
They don't deserve our crumbs!

Tyres are falling off the cliff. We're losing performance.
   🎱 Consider switching to a different compound. Intermediate Tyre.

Christina Aguliera Hurt 🎵

I hope to be the great parent we remember ...

Legacy

What happens in the Dark always comes to the Light

Dashboard The Red Light Indicates: Stop! 🔴

Some men chose to be loyal, and some choose not to.

"Some men are only as faithful as their options."

This reflects Chris Rock's often candid and comedic approach to discussing relationships and infidelity. It plays into the idea that people's loyalty or fidelity can depend on available options. For someone like James Bond, the 007s of the world, their commitment might fluctuate with circumstances. The consequences, emotional toil, and impact on loved ones can be significant. The repercussions aren't just personal; they can ripple through relationships.

In practice, Florence, 48, shared that her father had taken his own life:

"I had the best dad when he was alive, he was a very loving, caring, supportive, encouraging, protective and celebratory father, his love was unconditional, but a lousy philanderer of a husband to my mother. He was a beautiful, handsome, charismatic, masculine, alpha male that had endless options. He led a secret life and lived up to his nickname, Cassa short for the character, Casanova, and with all his good intentions, the philandering ways of Casanova caught up with him and he took his own life, he couldn't cope with the reality of his ways being exposed, when he checked out, he passed on the burden for others to inherit."

It's not merely the responsibility of the existing parent to consider, the responsibility of their legacy matters too. Depending on the circumstances, the legacy of the deceased parent can overshadow or override the memories of the surviving parent'; their actions will impact their loved ones. Being a parent holds the highest privilege of responsibility life has to offer, not only for the living, but also when they have departed.

Our past catches up with us, however, it is for us to bear the cost, not our children.

Take care of our legacy.

Tyres are falling off the cliff.
Engage the emergency brake!
- Consider changing to a different compound. Intermediate Tyre.

Jill Scott Comes to light (Everything) ♫

I hope I can get away with not doing right by ...

Listen Up

We Reap what we Sow

Dashboard The Red Light Indicates: Stop!
Engage the emergency brake!

After spending time speaking with many men, particularly middle-aged men, I asked what advice they would've wanted to receive when they were younger, DC explains.

"Don't break a heart deliberately!"
"Sometimes our carnal urges can blur our visions and override our sensible heads. Don't dabble with a woman you know that is not compatible for you, and you have
no intention of hanging around.
You can maintain civility if you split up but
when children are involved, it's messy."

It's time to move differently. Our decisions about a short-lived casual fling can have lifelong ramifications. Life changes completely when we become single parents.

"Things come to roost!"
"Make decisions about who we lie down with because the ramifications of our desires can have high consequences. And, the ripple effect of a every man's action adheres to trauma of generations to come."

They're making a valid point here, we all must be responsible for our actions, and show respect and consideration for others' feelings. Some men might think I'm just speaking to them, there are some women out there who act irresponsibly too, it takes two.

A moment in bed can become a lifetime in the head!

Losing traction.
Engage the emergency brake!

> 🎱   Consider changing to a different compound. Intermediate Tyre.

George Michael Let Her Down Easy ♫

I hope I can be open to getting to know ...

Prelude to a Stranger

Mirror Mirror

"If you hate a person, you hate something in him that is part of yourself. What isn't part of ourselves doesn't disturb us." Hermann Hesse

Throughout our lives, we cross paths with many different souls.
When we meet one another, we are communicating without even knowing it. A considerable proportion of our communication is non-verbal, based on what we see and on how our body language interacts. Sometimes, when we meet someone for the first time, their presence, character, attitude, body language, or appearance shapes our perception of them. We instinctively judge and interpret their world based on surface impressions.

On meeting, there will be something that draws us to the stranger or repels us from them. Without knowing any information about them, we simply can't put our finger on why. This is called 'mirroring; they're innocently mirror something back to us, reflecting some part of ourselves that we don't want to see or accept. There is no reason to take it personally; it may feel deliberate, yet these strangers are blameless.
They are innocently wanting to get to know us.

Wherever we are in life, whoever we meet, both parties will be unconsciously mirroring either their own strengths or weaknesses to each other. Our insecurities about what we're lacking or concealing from others can feel threatening as one of us sees something within the other that we're seeking, and vice versa. Deep down, we feel like we are doing ourselves a disservice by not utilising all the joy that life offers us.

We may sometimes experience an unexplainable reaction, undesirable feelings that stir us uncomfortably, irritate us, or make us feel vulnerable. We might even take an instant dislike to someone without being able to pinpoint the reason. It could be their attitude, character, tone of voice, laughter, gestures, or even their swagger that reminds us of someone we've encountered before. This response often stems from an unconscious association, where the stranger exhibits traits or behaviours that mirror those of someone from our past, evoking familiar yet unwelcome emotions.

In practice, Nimah, 42,explains,
"Mr West was a schoolteacher who we disliked because he made us feel small in class."

If a stranger's laughter sounds just like his, our brain instinctively links the two, bringing back old emotions. To protect us from a past negative experience, our mind replaces the stranger with the image of Mr West laughing. As a result, we subconsciously associate the stranger with Mr West, reacting as if they were the same person. This happens because their shared traits trigger emotions like those we once felt toward Mr West. This is a chance to pause, reflect, and begin healing unresolved emotional baggage, leading to personal growth and self-awareness.

On the other hand, as Erin Essenmacher wisely said,
"Our light may irritate a lot of unhealed people."

So be it, shine anyway!
Tyres are falling off the cliff; we're losing performance.

Seal Get it Together ♫

iHope

Chapter 9

Mechanical Problem!

The Black and Orange Flag chapter is instructing ...

Black and Orange Flag

> The car has a mechanical problem.
> We are in danger to ourselves.
> We must stop at our own pit on the next lap.
> Box, Box.

The car may return to the track if the chief scrutineer is satisfied that the issues have been resolved. Penalties for infringing the warning flags or speeding in and out of pit lane can be costly in championship points and positions in the race.

These different aspects we may experience are the 'black and orange flag' moments in our lives. These talking points will highlight the threat we come up against with our mental, physical, and emotional health.

It's not the end of the race, this is a chance to ensure we can finish stronger and safer by heeding this warning, trusting our team, and taking the time to repair. Let's give our full attention to these serious issues and act with urgency. We can return to the track ready to push forward with renewed energy and purpose.

164 **Stress**

167 **Life's Options**

169 **Solitary Isolation**

170 **High Achiever Vs. Over-Achiever**

172 **Burnout**

174 **Trauma**

176 **Addiction**

I hope I don't get stressed ...

Stress

The Modern-day Silent Assassin!

Stress is a warning light on our dashboard. Indicates Stop!

Stress has become an increasingly significant influence on our mental and physical health.
Most of us experience some level of stress daily. We are all trying to do more, work harder, and be better. Stress has become an inherent part of our everyday modern life. Whether it's work-related, financial pressure, or personal relationships, everything contributes to a stressful lifestyle. Often, we describe ourselves as 'stressed' when we feel worried and overloaded, fearful and anxious, with everyday symptoms that include not being able to relax or suffering from insomnia, panic attacks, suffering headaches, or upset stomachs, or becoming short-tempered.

Stress is designed to keep us safe by alerting us to danger; however, our stress responses are no longer being activated by wild predators anymore. If we're still in denial about living a stressful life and simply believe,

"it's just the way life is now"

Let's break it down a little further. Our stress comes from daily life: overstimulation from social media, endless emails, caring for children, long commutes, moving away from loved ones, relationship breakups, weekend binge drinking, demanding lifestyles, and juggling jobs with countless responsibilities and obligations. It's exhausting, even before factoring in notoriously high-stress careers. We constantly feel the need to put out as many fires throughout the day as possible, which put us in a state of hypervigilance, continually searching for the next problem to solve. Stress negatively impacts our mental health and contributes to a shorter lifespan.

The modern-day silent assassin is stress, a slow burner that manifests into poor health and becomes the cause of many illnesses, diseases, and conditions. Stress is the cause of many deaths today. It is time to recognise that stress is our emotions feeding into our health. Stress invites cancers, heart attacks, strokes, high blood pressure, anxiety, conditions, personality disorders, cardiovascular disease, depression, and many other illnesses. We must do all we can to stop accepting stress as a way of life.

Our reactions can become habitual, how we would react in our childhood, becoming overwhelmed, withdrawing, or freaking out and running for the hills. Stress often stems from **not feeling good enough** (184) not knowing when to stop, to multi-tasking, overstimulation, unrealistic expectations, childhood insecurities and inadequacies. Sleep-deprived constantly flooded with cortisol are the bullets that load the gun. It's about how we respond or react to pressure. We can put our minds in order by focusing on one thing at a time. Think about our energy resource, can we afford to multi-task?
We may only have energy for one task at a time without increasing our stress increasing.

Combating and confronting our daily stresses begins with being aware of a stressful lifestyle, taking accountability, and consciously starting to make small changes throughout our day. The goal is to erase or replace stressful lifestyle elements to enhance our lives and reframe our day with less stress. We can resist stress by finding something to focus on to stop our minds from racing. Micro changes in our daily lives are just as important as the big adjustments to keep us in the here and now. Here are some examples that are preventative and help safeguard us from highly stressed lifestyles.

The Key Practices

- We may have to commute to work. Consider an uplifting playlist or podcast to listen to, distracting us from anticipating what is going to happen at work.
- Escape into the world of fiction and listen to an audiobook to take our minds off stress of the day.
- Cold water therapy reduces stress, triggers endorphins, and enhances our mood.
- Escape to a quiet place or walk in nature during lunch breaks to reduce stress.
- Breathwork reduces our cortisol levels (stress hormone) by managing our breath to slowing our heart rate.
- Exercise – Yoga – lowers our cortisol levels and reduces stress.
- Saunas and steam rooms lower stress.
- Sleep, siestas, power naps, snoozes, and consistent 'shut eye' reduce stress.

Breathwork

Breathwork can be a powerful tool for emotional release and reducing stress.

To experience breathwork, we need to lie comfortably flat on the floor, fully clothed. Floors are very unforgiving, to use a yoga mat or bed for comfort. Most lie on their backs. Close our eyes, allow our body to flop into position and relax. Focus on our breath, the mind will eventually follow the body. Allow our minds to switch off and our body to take over and relax. We will be taken through different breathing techniques that help reconnect with our body. Deep breathing helps release endorphins, create shifts in the nervous system, and reduce cortisol levels. This has a positive impact on heart rate variability, which measures how resilient we are to stress.

When we are less stressed, we have more energy and recover more quickly from cortisol spikes. This will likely improve sleep quality and encourage deeper sleep, particularly slow-wave sleep. Slow wave sleep (SWS), the third stage of (REM) rapid eye movement sleep, also known as deep sleep.

Stress is about our body and our mind. Sleep is essential for reducing stress as well as being physically fit enough to have the capacity to manage stress. Sleep well every night. Whatever we repress becomes stress. So, schedule some time each week to release it until it becomes a routine. Take up a cardiovascular sport to sweat out cortisol. Flow-type activities are also helpful for calm and relaxation, whatever takes us out of our heads, such as Tai Chi, Pilates, or Qigong. Or something creative, such as knitting, painting, or jigsaws., writing, playing an instrument, model making, or photography. Journaling helps us to connect, express, and release thoughts from our minds onto paper instead.

Humming helps us de-stress by sending signals to our vagus nerve, which is connected to our nervous system and helps calm our body down.

We can't always control the pressures of life; nevertheless, finding small wins counts. Stop sweating the small stuff, stop worrying whether things will work out, and raise our standards of care for ourselves. It will help to improve our well-being.

Managing stress is the key to being happier and healthier. The higher our stress, the less clearly we think, and the harder it becomes to make sound decisions.

Stress will not go away until we decide it no longer has a place in our lives!

The higher our standards, the lower our pressure!
The car is losing performance and starting to aquaplane.
Box, Box.
- Consider switching to a different compound. Wet Tyre.

A Tribe Called Quest Stressed Out ♫

Mechanical Problem!

I hope I can acknowledge my options ...

Life's Options

Warning Signs

Dashboard The Orange Light Indicates: Caution! Slow Down!

Life has a way of getting in the way of our plans and expectations. Nonetheless, when we are in the midst of situations, life will offer us warning signs when it's time to take action, make a decision, exit a situation, or stop certain habits, and so on. It's our choice whether to act on the warning signs or not, knowing they could lead to a cul-de-sac, a road to nowhere on our journey.

When life is letting us know, time and time again, that change is around the corner and something isn't working, we need to act, make a decision, or do something different. For example, we might find ourselves in a relationship with an expiry date, or with a sense that our partner is not faithful. Sometimes we find ourselves hanging on for reasons that just don't make sense. It might be because we're too scared to be alone for the first time in our lives, or we hold on to prove a point to others. Either way, the relationship is expiring, and no matter what we do or say, the relationship is dead in the water, on its way out.

Life will show warning signs that things are not improving but instead, getting worse. These are cues, hints, indications that we're being prompted to act on the situation.
I often liken it to the weather.

Imagine we are walking down life's pathway. Naturally, we like to be protected and prepared, deciding whether to turn back for a coat, or umbrella, or simply to wait it out.

Imagine we're walking down the road of life, and life sends our first warning sign, for instance, a few raindrops on our head. We take our chances and keep walking. Then we receive another sign: it starts to drizzle, but we disregard it and keep walking. Life sends us another clue, it starts raining, yet we ignore the rain. Then, small pebbles start falling out of the sky as another sign to alert us that we need to act. We pay no attention and keep walking, until finally, bricks fall, forcing us to stop and realise we need to take action now.

With each step we continue to take, we reduce our options or choices to manage the situation and diminish our chances of a swift recovery. When the bricks start to land, we find ourselves cornered, and our options have dried up. We ignored life's indications, so our story concludes with no option other than to suck it up.

Here's an example or a typical situation, in stages:

A relationship dilemma:

1. **Raindrops** – they seem distant, less intimate, regularly tired, and frequent headaches.
2. **Drizzle** – constantly losing their phone, or always on it, they seem unpredictable and difficult to contact.
3. **Rain** – making more effort with their appearance when they go out without us.
4. **Pebbles** – spending less time together, they're at the gym more, with friends more, working more.
5. **Bricks** – a friend tells us they've seen them romantically with someone else.

Until we learn our lessons, and accept total responsibility for our lives, our lives will keep sending us experiences to get our attention.

Don't wait for the bricks to knock us out, when we can all recover from the drizzle!

We're losing traction.
Box, Box.

> 🏁 Consider changing to a different compound. Intermediate Tyre.

Coldplay Warning Sign ♫

I hope I can cope being on my own ...

Solitary Isolation

Childhood can be a Resource to Fall back on

Dashboard The Purple Light indicates: Action Required!
Check Rear View Mirror!

A client, Angelo, 56, was experiencing social isolation. His partner had died, his friendship circle was very small and didn't live close by; he had retired and lost contact with his co-workers. He had withdrawn from the world and found himself chronically alone and isolated.,

*"Feels like the world is closing in on me
and I don't know what to do..."*

He had become vulnerable to loneliness and isolation. When we met, he was depressed and emotionally distressed.

Some personality types, especially the introverted types, enjoy their own company, and tend to take much fulfilment from their own thoughts, ideas and reflections. They genuinely feel comfortable and need to spend time with themselves to regroup. However, if we have experienced many significant losses of friends or family in a short space of time, or we become housebound due to an unexpected illness, we may find ourselves vulnerable to loneliness and isolation.

Loneliness (109) slowly leads to isolation. Isolation and loneliness remind us of the different people we no longer have in our lives, or the people we may have lost through disappointment, disagreement, or conflict. Either way, we need to make sure that we don't drift into isolation.

As an intervention, I would encourage exploration into our childhood, when we were teenagers, and dreamed of doing this or that. When we grow into adulthood, we tend to lose all of that dreaming.

What dreams did we once have that we never achieved?

If we make a list of ten things we've always fancied doing but never had the courage to pursue, let's start with number ten. It's about extending the palette and trying new colours. Join groups of our interest. If we were not introduced to a variety of different activities in our childhood, we may have a very limited palette to draw on when we get older. There's no guarantee that we'll like it, but if we try it once and we don't, at least we know, and we can move on to the next one. Eventually, we'll have a list of things that really float our boats, and we can meet new people with shared interests.

Social Isolation can be associated with adverse health consequences, such as depression, cognitive decline, poor cardiovascular function, impaired immunity, increased risk of dementia, poor sleep quality, obesity, high blood pressure, and premature death. Staying remote for too long can take a toll. We need connection and communication for our wellbeing.

When "remote" overstays its welcome, it's time to reconnect and revive our childhood dreams!

The tyres are falling off the cliff.
Box, Box.
    ◉ Consider switching to a different tyre. Intermediate Tyre.

The Police So Lonely ♫

I hope I can be enough ...

High Achiever Vs. Overachiever

Too much Meat in the Pot!

Dashboard The Orange Light Indicates: Caution! Slow Down!

Knowing when to push for excellence and when 'good enough' is sufficient is the key to maintaining balance. However, for all the overachievers, it's time to exhale.

The 'go hard or go home' attitude keeps us on the relentless treadmill in pursuit of success. Hard work and achieving seem to be much easier for an overachiever because we have been training from a young age to perform better, being very busy people, who are busy doing and achieving in life. It's empowering to recognise we have the ability and a little more determination than others; we tend to work harder, work longer, and go above and beyond what is expected of us. Work is rarely separate from our personal lives; it's not unusual to find we are 'married to our job'. This is a fine reward to receive for most humans from the outside looking in; it is admirable.

It's healthy for us to experience success and be high achievers; it's healthy to want to strive in life, progress, achieve, and even enjoy a little competition along the way. That's all good, unless our self-worth is defined by achievement. To overachieve, we sabotage ourselves with excessive behaviour that sends us into overdrive.
We put too much meat in the pot!

If achieving success is at the risk of our health, we must dial it back. Most of us are in hot pursuit of success, in high-performance mode, continually searching for the next accomplishment. We tend to overlap achievements while swiftly shifting onto the next mission with no reward for completion. We are the crusaders who keep on running. Overachieving often stems from feeling **not good enough** (184).

I have seen perfectionists put themselves at high risk for burnout by avoiding risks due to a fear of failure. As a result, they aren't challenged enough by life, leading to stagnation and a failure to grow, or evolve to meet life's demands. Instead of striving for a perfect ten, we need to take the pressure off. Perfectionism often breeds procrastination, and we are our harshest critics. What we see as a seven, someone else might see as a perfect ten.

Our 7/10 is good enough!

In practice, Austin, 31, had a history of over-achieving, it was vital for him to recognise that he wasn't in control of his life. We explored who sat in his driving seat, and who was associated with his feelings of shame, for him to get behind the steering wheel of his life.

Who's in our driving seat?

We are defined by our achievements, yet beneath the trophies of success, who are we? It's essential to recognise who is truly in the driver's seat of our lives, and to realise that it may not have been us all along.
Focus on who we are, not what we do.

It's healthy to want to achieve, we may find room to "go hard," however, self-sabotage must go home!

Tyres are falling off the cliff. We're losing performance.
Box, Box.

- Consider changing to a different compound. Intermediate Tyre.

I hope I can avoid burnout ...

Burnout

Nothing left in the Tank!

Burnout is a warning light on our dashboard. Indicating Stop!

Beware of burnout. It's a creeper that sneaks up on us quietly when we least expect it. At first it may feel like being tired or overwhelmed, over time it chips away at our energy, focus, and joy.

It's like holding a foggy champagne glass; we can't see the bubbles anymore. it distorts our emotions, clouds our thinking and feeds negativity, making even the small task seem heavy. It disconnects us from ourselves and others, often leaving us emotionally drained and needing real time to heal. We need time to rediscover who we were before it took hold to recognise early signs to protect our wellbeing.

When we're burnt out, we might seem fine on the outside, and get through the day appearing okay, yet inside, we're physically, emotionally, and mentally exhausted. We're not just running on empty, we are empty.

Murphy, 27, a client struggling with burnout, explained.
"When we're constantly trying to upgrade ourselves to better our profile, and improve what we do to get our numbers up online, the pressure to perform, to keep raising the bar becomes all-consuming and too much."

Through a prolonged time of stress, there are some classic symptoms to be aware of.
The feelings listed below include:
- Feeling overwhelmed.
- Depleted.
- Stress, and a lack of energy and motivation.
- Creeping self-doubt or negative thought patterns.

We feel physically tired, sleep deprived, suffer from muscle aches, headaches, and our immune system becomes run down. As a result, we become more susceptible to colds and viruses.

Burnout often stems from **not feeling good enough** (184). If no action is taken, we may go on to develop further mental health conditions such as anxiety, depression, or even experience a nervous breakdown. Burnout is serious!

Signs to identify burnout early:

1. Emotional exhaustion – long periods of constant stress cause irritation over small things, apathy, lack of motivation, poor sleep, cynicism or pessimism.
2. Disconnection – from people around us, we feel too tired to connect with our partner, friends or children.
3. Lack of creativity at home or work.
4. Struggle to keep structure and order at home.
5. Inability to stay on top of things.
6. Neglecting self-care – we know what is good for us, yet we're struggling to exercise, consequently we go to bed late, comfort eat, or drink more alcohol.
7. Physical exhaustion – when extreme tiredness causes deep exhaustion, and leaves us completely drained.

If we leave burnout for too long, we may lose ourselves, and struggle to bounce back to our former selves.

The Key Practices

- Eliminate the stressor.
- Move our body and exercise.
- Sleep well.
- Take outdoor walks in nature.
- Limit alcohol.
- Eat healthily.
- Talk to a trusted friend.
- Take a break.
- Do something we love.
- Practise mindfulness.
- Set our boundaries and learn to say 'No'.
- Seek professional help to understand why we're experiencing burnout, and ensure it's not repeated in future.

We can't avoid being human!

Burnout is a bona fide condition, recognised by the World Health Organisation.

We are losing traction! The car starts to aquaplane.
Box, Box.
◉   Consider changing to a different compound. Wet Tyre.

Faithless Salva Mea 🎵

I hope I can have the courage to heal my wounds …

Trauma

The Body keeps Score!

Trauma is a warning light on our dashboard, indicates: Stop!

Trauma occurs when we have experienced very distressing, disturbing, or terrifying events that are out of our control and difficult to manage.

Many of us spend our lives running from trauma. From being fat-shamed at school; or shamed for receiving free school meals, called 'stupid' in class, witnessing our mum being physically hurt, watching our dad die of cancer, discovering a partner's infidelity, or our dad suddenly stopped his weekend visits, right through to being bullied as a child, these moments leave a mark. We have all experienced some level of trauma in our lives. These significant moments have a ripple effect that can dictate the rest of our lives if we allow them.

When we've experienced trauma, we often try to outrun it, like a stamped memory we're desperate not to relive.

Most of us are running from something or running towards something. Can we imagine how different our lives would be if we stopped running, and stopped allowing that experience to control our lives?
For instance, if someone who discovered their partner's infidelity could recognise that the betrayal came from the partner's insecurities, not their own flaws, they might come to realise they are still worthy of love and respect.

The 'stupid' kids could recognise they are intelligent and more than good enough, or the teenagers bullied at school, who realise they don't deserve to be abused, could stand up for themselves and give themselves a voice. Life becomes very different when we are free of that lived experience.

**No matter what we watch, listen to, experience, or do,
the body keeps score.**

We may believe the trauma is in our heads; however, it is physically remembered by storing the trauma in our bodies, believing it is still in danger, and responding whenever we are triggered.
Our brains and bodies want to protect us from danger by releasing a stress hormone that keeps circulating, keeping us on high alert. This shows itself in various ways: through our heart rate increasing, sweaty palms, a sick feeling in the gut where we feel trapped in a life-or-death situation, feeling numbness, dissociation, confusion, anxiety, agitation, and exhaustion. We can also experience recurrent nightmares from experiences that belong in the past, yet keep being replayed in the present until the trauma is resolved.

If we choose not to resolve the trauma, it will manifest into something further, weakening our immune systems, creating an imbalance in our body that brings about conditions like PTSD, allergies, and dis-ease that will affect our health, unless we can become aware of it, to change and heal.

I understand that, for some of us, this might seem unimaginable. We may be hesitant to go back to that crime scene or episode in our lives, believing that it might be too big a price to pay for change if we were to disclose our traumatic experiences in our relationships, leave our job, or end a friendship, believing it's too expensive. However, the cost of remaining in fear might turn out to be a bigger a price to pay for our health, where we are left with little or no choice.
With support and help, having the courage to resolve and put a stop to the trauma ruining us. We're worth it!

Seek professional help if we're experiencing trauma of any kind, such as PTSD.

The tyres are falling off the cliff; the car starts to aquaplane.
Box, Box.
   🎧   Consider changing to a different compound. Intermediate Tyre.

Folly and The Hunter Lose that Light ♬

I hope this helps me escape those bad feelings...

Addictions

One is too many, Ten is never Enough!

Dashboard The Orange Light Indicates: Caution! Slow Down!

Sometimes, when we experience those unthinkable, challenging, or traumatic times in our lives, our spirits have a way of looking after us by managing how we process those experiences.

They give us manageable portions or recall just enough, allowing us to filter through, manage and cope. The rest gets parked in a 'waiting bay'. Eventually, we reach a point in our lives where there's space, and that's when buried feelings catch up with us, demanding to be felt in the present moment.

If we lack self-awareness, this can take us by surprise, and down the well-travelled road of addiction. Some people who are less aware will put their foot on the gas pedal for a quick fix, to temporarily wipe out that unwelcome feeling or memory, in search of instant gratification. However temporary it might be, so long as it brings instant relief, it helps them feel better and in control.

Addiction wants us on our own.

These coping mechanisms come in different styles and methods, such as overeating, shopping excessively, gaming, porn, drugs, alcohol or sex. Some have become the 'new socially acceptable' forms of self-harm, such as tattooing, piercings and other behaviours done to excess. This is called self-medicating. All regular self-medicating becomes our little secret, nonetheless, it is our behaviour that will keep us isolated and on the run from ourselves, usually until we hit rock bottom.

Reaching our rock bottom helps us get back on track.
Believe in ourselves and figure out that we are worth saving.

The tyres are falling off the cliff; we're losing performance.
Box, Box.
- Consider switching to a different compound. Intermediate Tyre.

Marvin Gaye Got to Give it Up. Pt1 ♪

iHope

Chapter 10

Immediately Return to the Pit!

The Black Flag chapter is announcing ...

Black Flag

> Warning! Immediately return to the pit.
> We are in trouble, make sure we recognise the situation.
> To disqualify a driver, return to the pit immediately.
> This flag is only waived based on the decision of the stewards.
> Disqualification.
> Box, Box.

The 'black flag' serves as a powerful symbol, representing moments in our lives when we feel overwhelmed, stretched too thin, or disconnected from ourselves. It forces us to face the serious consequences of our actions, choices, or circumstances. It signals a critical moment for reflection, intervention, and realignment, urging immediate action to prevent further harm and regain control.

180 **Distorted Relationships**

181 **Unresolved Baggage**

182 **People Pleasing**

184 **Not Good Enough**

I hope I can be what they want me to be ...

Distorted Relationships

Bent out of Shape!

Dashboard The Orange Light Indicates: Caution! Slow Down! 🌕

Life's challenges can sometimes push us to lose our shape.
The minute we accept less of who we are, we start to bend ourselves out of shape, distort our truth, and lose touch with our authentic selves.

In my experience, many people twist themselves out of shape to please their partners, parents, family, lover, or a friend, seeking validation, acceptance, survival, love, and many more reasons.

Originally, we each had our own unique shape, which is true to ourselves; the quality of being authentic is at the core of who we genuinely are.

Sometimes, in our lives, our shapes are challenged. We give more of ourselves, and for whatever reason, we overstretch ourselves, Our values are overlooked, and our **boundaries** (215) are stepped over. That challenges every fibre of our being just to reach the finishing line, tick a box, be accepted, comply or fit in, and it keeps on happening until it becomes a regular pattern. Routine becomes habit, and we realise the things that we're doing aren't serving us. We've lost ourselves. We're bent out of shape! This frequently happens in a relationship when it's expired, when the other wants out and we can't accept it. So, we hang on and sacrifice our morals, values, or trade away our boundaries to convince or persuade them to stay. When the relationship eventually ends, we find ourselves lost and bent out of shape.

Reclaiming ourselves takes time, to rediscover our truth, invest in our well-being, place ourselves at the top of the list, reconnect with what truly matters, realign with our values, and moral compass, and reforge our sense of sisterhood or brotherhood.

Never give consent to being bent out of shape.
Tyres are falling off the cliff; we're losing performance. Box, Box.
　　　⚫ Consider switching to a different compound. Intermediate Tyre.

Brandon Flowers I Can Change 🎵

Immediately Return to the Pit!

I hope I can just forget about it and move on ...

Unresolved Baggage

Feelings Wait for Us!

Dashboard The Orange Light Indicates: Caution! Slow Down!

Sometimes we choose to forget painful times in our lives, or, for some reason, we mentally can't remember the experience. That doesn't mean our body has forgotten the experience; our bodies remember, and our spirit waits.

Consider, a single woman seeking security in a relationship. Melita, 33, was experiencing a happy time in her life when the unexpected happened.

> *"When I've been trying to just keep my head above water, to keep going in life, I couldn't afford to take my foot off the pedal or my eye off the ball because I couldn't afford to crumble, I was afraid of falling to pieces for everything I had built to come crashing down, so I kept holding my breath, I kept going. Then I met Mr Right, finally a time to exhale for the first time in my life, I felt secure, no more fighting,*
> *no more barricades, no more defending, my gloves were off,*
> *and I'd switched off my 'worrier' mode.*
> *Finally, this was a wonderful time to celebrate and be happy in my new life, to then find myself unexpectedly overwhelmed with a mixture of unwelcome emotions of disappointment, grief, sadness,*
> *hurt, or anger, that weren't connected to my new life.*
> *I felt swamped with emotions, confused, scared, and I couldn't make sense of why I was feeling this way."*

Melita had forgotten the hurts of the past, her old, unresolved baggage. The old experience, and the thoughts and emotions attached to that time, are unprocessed and waiting to catch up with us. The painful memories that we've pushed to the back of our minds, the feelings that have been too intense, the overwhelm that felt like it could threaten to take us off track or into a head-on collision are still here. They didn't dissolve; we just buried them with deflection and distraction.

Our feelings have been waiting for us to create space free of drama, a time where we are able to hold space for ourselves, to acknowledge and process them for closure.

Now is the time to surrender to ourselves and BE. Go there. Process it. Acknowledge the experience. Once we do, the overwhelm, intensity, confusion, and fear will fade, and those old feelings will disappear.
Only our spirit knows what we endure.

Tyres are falling off the cliff.
Box, Box.

> Consider changing to a different compound. Intermediate Tyre.

Pearl Jam Rearviewmirror ♪

I hope I can make them happy …

People Pleasing

Pleasing everyone pleases No one!

Dashboard The Orange Light Indicates: Caution! Slow Down!

You can't be everyone's cup of tea,
otherwise you'd be a mug!

Unnecessary expectations create pressures that can seem overwhelming and burdensome, especially if we believe we were born to live up to other people's expectations.

The need to please at the expense of ourselves is a high price to pay, yet the feeling inside holds no option when we are striving to feel loved, valued, to be enough, to feel accepted or to find a place where we belong. I have noticed that people-pleasing often arises from a sense of inadequacy, from **not feeling good enough** (184). The bottom line is that the sacrifice is too high a price to pay, and the long-term costs are too expensive. It takes a lot of energy, hope, and time to put our hearts in the hands of others with little or no guarantee of happiness or validation. If we don't know who we are, we find ourselves playing a role, or becoming pigeonholed into what others expect of us, and we become bent out of shape. It is our choice if we buy into pleasing, being fully focused on the permissions and approvals of another, at the price of knowing less of who we are.

Getting to know ourselves is a 'sooner or later' option, and a privilege that allows us to have a good crack at life authentically. As adults, we have a new contract with society: we are equals, we are equal to every other adult, and we have the same rights. They are not here to live up to our expectations, and we are not in this world to live up to theirs. We have no reason to feel trapped or live in constant fear or a chronic state of anxiety to please others and do things we really do not want to do. Despite having good intentions, we don't have to tell little white lies, out of fear of disappointment or worry. Adults can handle such feelings of disappointment; they will get over it in time. Whether we struggle with having to visit unlikable relatives at Christmas or maintain the same predictable boring sex life with our partners, we can give ourselves a voice.

We can hold integrity in our truth and offer an alternative option or decline, simply say "No". Imagine if we gave up lying and stopped doing the things we don't want to do?

Imagine how it could transform our lives!

We need to care less about others' opinions to unlock our potential, focus on our strengths, and value our own needs and desires, rather than fearing rejection. Freedom comes from learning to accept that we are enough. The more we love and value ourselves, the more we care less about what others think of us. That is when the pressure to please subsides.

We can never do enough to please others or make them happy.
Instead, focus on what makes us happy.

Do what feels right. Do as we please!

Our job isn't to make people like us, it's to like ourselves. That's the real path to happiness, anyone who's on board with that, welcome!

People pleasing is too expensive for our souls!

We're losing performance.
Box, Box.

> 🎧 Consider switching to a different compound. Intermediate Tyre.
> **Lola Young** Messy ♪

I hope I can feel worthy and confident of being enough...

Not Good Enough

The obstacle to Peace and Self-acceptance

Dashboard The Orange Light Indicates: Caution! Slow Down!

Being raised with the belief that we're not good enough can profoundly shape our adult lives in many ways. This deep-rooted sense of inadequacy often begins in childhood, yet it doesn't remain confined to those early years. It extends into our adult experiences, affecting how we perceive ourselves, relate to others, and navigate the world.

I've seen many who have felt 'not good enough'; they often experience a nagging voice inside that tells them they're not enough, not achieving enough, or not deserving of success or love.

It's the inner critic that amplifies mistakes and diminishes successes, as Bruce explains:

"I felt huge discomfort in being vulnerable, feeling unsafe to show my true self, feeling like being vulnerable would reveal that I'm unworthy or inadequate. I kept putting up walls and avoiding intimate connections or fearing commitment in relationships and the pressure to prove myself was immense. I constantly felt a need to achieve more, to be more, do more just to feel normal. Even though when I did accomplish it, it was never enough to get rid of that inner voice telling me "I'm not good enough". With all the recognition in the world, I still felt empty and unsatisfied, it's like trying to fill a bucket with holes, it's never truly full. Looking back, no matter how I did, there was always something missing, cos I never focused on my worth. I stayed trapped in the vicious cycle kept me chasing, blaming, judging, distracting, and stimulating, but never finding peace... "

As we get older, we try to outrun failure and toxic emotions like shame by chasing approval and validation. This mindset drives us to believe we must do more, achieve more, and demand more of ourselves and others. We seek control, fear the future, and chase perfection, to fill the void, allowing us to feel okay. This cycle can leave us exhausted and keep us from finding true peace and self-acceptance.

Here are some of the impacts of this belief:

- **Perfectionism and Overachievers:** This belief of not being good enough can drive us to constantly strive for perfection. We may feel like we must **overachieve** (170), to prove our worth to others. This can lead to **burnout** (172), chronic **stress** (164), and a constant feeling of never being "enough," no matter how much we accomplish.
- **People Pleasing and Fear of Rejection:** To gain acceptance or acceptance from others, we might excessively try to please those around us, often at the expense of our own needs and desires. This can result in unhealthy relationships and a lack of authentic self-expression.
- **Low Self-Esteem and Self-Worth:** If we internalise the belief that we are not good enough, we may struggle with low **self-esteem** (144). We might constantly seek external validation to feel worthy, which can leave us feel empty and disconnected from our true selves.
- **Difficulty setting Boundaries:** People who believe they're not good enough may struggle to set healthy **boundaries** (215).
They might fear being rejected or unworthy of love, so they allow others to overstep or take advantage of them. This can lead to toxic relationships and an inability to prioritise self-care.
- **Self-Sabotage:** Deep down, we may feel like we don't deserve success or happiness, so we subconsciously **self-sabotage** (122) by avoiding opportunities, **procrastinating** (135), or undermining ourselves when we get close to achieving something meaningful.
- **Perpetual Comparison:** Believing we're not enough often leads to constant **comparisons** (154) with others. We might feel jealous or inadequate when we see others succeed or do things, we wish we could, which only reinforces our sense of inferiority.
- **Chronic Anxiety or Depression:** This belief can fuel **anxiety** (220), depression, or feelings of worthlessness. We may fear failure, rejection, or making mistakes because we feel like these things confirm our inadequacy. Over time, this can weigh heavily on mental health.
- **Difficulty Accepting Compliments or Success:** If we feel like we're not good enough, it may be hard to accept compliments or acknowledge our achievements. We may brush off praise or downplay our success because we don't feel we truly deserve it.

Ultimately, the belief of "not being good enough" can become a deeply ingrained narrative that affects how we see ourselves, our relationships, and the choices we make.

A common theme that often arises in relationships is the feeling of not being good enough. This feeling can influence how we interact with others, shaping our confidence, communication, and even how we show up for social situations. Feeling unworthy can create barriers to authentic connection, preventing us from fully embracing the moment and enjoying relationships to their fullest.

Healing (75) these beliefs involve challenging the thought patterns that reinforce them, practicing self-compassion, and learning to recognize our intrinsic worth beyond external achievements or validation.

For these patterns to cease, we must separate who we are from what we do, block **self-sabotage** (122), and break the grip of perfectionism. The key to healing is awareness. When we become aware of the times this belief arises, we can begin to observe it without judgment. Notice the thoughts and the feelings that trigger it, and instead of reacting impulsively to its demands, like seeking approval, overworking, validation, or avoiding vulnerability. We sit with it, feel it, and breathe through it. It's okay to pause.

It's okay to simply be. It's okay.

Box, Box.

- ◉ Consider switching to a different compound. Wet Tyre.

James Vincent McMorrow Higher Love ♪

iHope

Chapter 11

End of Racing!

The Chequered Flag chapter declares ...

Chequered Flag

> End of race.
> Symbol of victory.
> Life Hacks to help us achieve our iHope and cross the finish line.

The chequered flag stands as a powerful symbol of triumph over adversity, signalling not just the end of the race, but the close of a challenging chapter and the start of a new one, filled with hope, purpose and renewed direction. This chapter invites us to reflect on our progress, celebrate our victories, and put into action the strategies and smart solutions that lead to lasting transformation.

We focus on practical tools to carry us across the finish line with life hacks that help us navigate change even in the face of hardship, struggle and setbacks. Finishing the race isn't just about speed; it's about strategy, preparation, and knowing when to push our limits. It calls for time management, problem-solving, healthy routines and embracing *iHope*, our vision for meaningful change.

Now is the time to reduce drag, pick up speed and drive on the limit. Press the DRS button. Go full throttle, those hot laps will carry us to the finish line. Don't stop until we reach the chequered flag.

Embrace the journey and look forward to change!

DRS Enabled

191	**Self-Love**	208	**Winning at Life**
193	**Change**	210	**Self-FULL**
195	**Success**	212	**Shut Eye**
197	**Failure**	215	**Boundaries**
199	**Winning Formula**	218	**On the Pulse of the Morning**
201	**Best Friend**	220	**Anxiety**
202	**Decisions Decisions**	222	**Fear**
204	**Emotions**	224	**Anger**
207	**Science = Cause + Effect**	226	**Right Here, Right Now**

229	**M.O.T**	291	**Celebration**
235	**Liquid Truth**	292	**Marriage Sabbatical**
237	**Process**	293	**Meditation**
238	**Exercise**	295	**Self-Love Languages**
240	**Positive Mindset**	296	**Menopause**
242	**Time**	300	**Screaming**
244	**Rock Bottom**	301	**Zen**
246	**Breathing**	302	**Talk-in-Trifle**
248	**Financially Faithful**	304	**Confidence is Power**
251	**Playful Story Wheel**	307	**Happy Ever After**
252	**Our Condolences**	309	**Dear Unfinished Business**
254	**Medicine Vs. Medication**	311	**Hugs**
257	**Fruit Bowl**	313	**Nature Walking**
258	**Break-Ups not for Make-Ups**	315	**The Survivors of Bullying**
260	**Spiritual Hygiene**	316	**Life Changing Goals**
262	**The Owl and the Lark**	317	**Relationship Ding Dongs**
265	**To Grieve our Loved Ones**	320	**Manifesting**
267	**Who Are You Vs. Who am I?**	321	**Role Models**
269	**The GQ Collective**	322	**Me Dates**
271	**Royalty**	324	**I'm Home**
272	**High Wellbeing**	325	**Celebrate Life**
274	**Circadian Clock**	326	**Gratitude**
276	**Recharge our Battery**	328	**At the Strike of 12**
278	**Hormonal Cycles**	330	**Yearly Reflections**
279	**Dating**	332	**New Year, New Vision**
283	**Help**	334	**Memory Jar**
284	**Therapy**	335	**Gong Baths**
286	**Chemical Romance**	336	**Faith**
289	**The Climb**	338	**Ode to Joy**
290	**Journaling**		

I hope I can learn how to love myself ...

Self-Love

Turns the Key in the Ignition

Dashboard The Green Light indicates: All Clear!

We all strive to improve and become better versions of ourselves.

To thrive and flourish, we must pour into ourselves to fill our cup.

Self-love is about embracing compassion and care, tuning into positive affirmations, and quieting our inner critics.

If we can't love ourselves, how can we love others?

Without self-love, we can't give what we don't have to our friends, family, and partner. For meaningful connections and personal growth, we must invest in ourselves.

What is Self-Love?

Self-love stems from the relationship we cultivate with ourselves. Giving ourselves more love and attention results in a stronger relationship with who we are. By giving ourselves attention, we strengthen self-love; neglecting ourselves weakens it. To truly love ourselves, we must invest more time and energy into strengthening our relationship with ourselves. In learning to accept ourselves, we may realise we love who we are, even if we don't always like certain aspects of ourselves. There's inner work to be done, to reconnect with our true selves and heal our inner child.

In practice, Makena, 38, after working on self-love, felt empowered in embracing her authentic self. She had a pivotal moment, where she recognised that:

"I don't have to like everybody, and everybody doesn't have to like me. I don't have to like everyone or need their approval or opinion. I'm not expecting to be everyone's cup of tea either, there's no malice, just the way it is sometimes."

And that's okay.

Loving ourselves means we accept responsibility for all our strengths, and weaknesses, as part of our self-development to improve. We practice, apply, refine, and tweak what we need for our health and happiness. Improving our self-development takes self-discipline, which requires making promises to ourselves as an act of love. Discipline is challenging for any soul to have to lean into discomfort and visit there on a regular basis to achieve the outcomes we want.

Let's consider relationships, and all those qualities we want to receive from a relationship: to love, cherish, honour, respect, and care. We must learn how to love, cherish, honour, respect, and care for ourselves first, so we know the currency of what each quality means personally, and can recognise if they measure up to our own standards or expectations.

How can we receive love if we don't know how to love?

We can start by learning how to give love to ourselves, by learning our **love languages** (295), and how to really take care of ourselves. **High wellbeing** (272) requires consistency; learning how to love ourselves requires being non-judgmental, accepting of who we are. Learning self-respect requires setting **boundaries** (215), learning how to trust in ourselves requires self-belief, keeping our promises, and so on. These qualities require character and discipline; they are the bedrock to sustaining a healthy relationship with us and then with others.

Once we connect with ourselves, loneliness and desperation fade. When 'lonely' or 'desperate' no longer reside with us, they will not allow us to fall for unhealthy relationships. It helps to recognise our inner child. Reparenting our inner child, who is so in need of attention and love, who is thirsty to be acknowledged and loved unconditionally, is essential. To fill those voids that we feel in our souls, to find out what truly makes us happy or content, we must consistently invest in ourselves. Not just at the weekend, or during the holiday season. It is vital that we actively listen, **eavesdrop** (55) and respond to the needs of our inner child. These are reasons we can never make someone else responsible for our own happiness. They'll never get it right. Waiting until we find "the one" to counterbalance our own shortcomings is not the answer.

We must represent all that we are, starting with ourselves.

True empowerment comes when we reach self-assurance and become resilient to judgment, where no one can shake our inner peace.

"If you don't like me, that's your problem, because I like me. Period!"

Recognise that love, care, and attention to ourselves get us over the finishing line, when we pull over into the pits and refuel ourselves to go back on track.

Time to change to fresher rubber to gain an advantage for the undercut.
- Consider changing to a different compound. Hard Tyre.

Set the fastest lap at butt clenching speed!

Mike Cruz Most Precious Love ♫

I hope I can change ...

Change

Superpower of `Transmission: Shift Gears to Accelerate

Dashboard The Green Light indicates: All Clear!

The only guarantees in life are death, taxes, and change!
Everything else is temporary, and as creatures of habit, we often resist change or struggle to keep up with the times. Yet change is inevitable; without it, we risk being left behind.
The power of changing our minds is often underestimated. It's not always the strongest, smartest, or most experienced who survive, those who are more adaptable to change often do. Change is a superpower that enables people to create the life they want to live.

In my experience, we often choose to invest in ourselves for one reason: Change. We want to be or do better, whether it's to resolve issues, learn, let go, accept, forgive, or anything else that requires doing things differently, the goal is always growth. Sometimes, we find ourselves in situations where it feels like,

It's not us, it's them!

As difficult as it may be to accept, the truth is that we can't make someone do something they don't want to do.

The only person we can change is ourselves!

Our own actions and mindset are the only things we can truly control. Sometimes, the shift we need is in our own approach to a situation or relationship, which may mean changing ourselves, not the other person. There's no need to worry, it's our responsibility to change someone else. It never works; in the long run, it only breeds resentment. Even if it seems to work, the change is often temporary.

Change is a natural part of life, and it's our right to redirect our course whenever we choose. Change gives us the opportunity to let go of outdated thoughts and habits, reframe our mindset into a **positive mindset** (240) and upgrade our goals and aspirations, ensuring we don't get left behind. Even those of us who are most resistant to change. When the pain of staying in our **comfort zone** (118) becomes greater than the discomfort of change, we must embrace doing things differently. Continuing to do what we've always done will only give us what we've always had.

Old ways won't open new doors!

Accepting Change

Accepting change is about flexibility and adapting. It is not simply about changing when things go right. It's also about being prepared to change to prevent things from going wrong. It's not about being rigid, with our thoughts, beliefs, and values. It's about holding them lightly, allowing space to change our attitude and perspective. We must embrace the new and flow with the times to keep moving forward.

Before we can effectively create change in our lives, we must first believe that we are worthy of a better experience.

The Key Questions

- Will it enhance our lives?
- How would we have to change as a person to achieve it?
- What lengths would we go to achieve it?
- Are we ready for change?
- Visualise how we will spend our time once we have achieved or changed.

◉ Consider changing to a different compound. Soft Tyre.
Shift gears at lightning speed to accelerate progress!
We've gone purple and set the fastest lap.

Maze Changing Times ♫

I hope I can be successful ...

Success

Optimism breeds Resilience – YES, We Can!

Dashboard The Green Light indicates: All Clear!

Most of us strive to do better, to be better, and for that reason, to have success in balancing love, family, career, and health. However, success doesn't care about what we believe we deserve. If we cannot master our own minds, we cannot master anything. We can only be as good as our thoughts, as successful as our mental patterns, as progressive as our resilience and options.

Our thoughts shape our success, yet many of us struggle due to limiting beliefs that keep us motionless, preventing us from reaching the chequered flag.

So, what's the secret behind successful people?

They maintain a **positive mindset** (240), resilience, and curiosity. They **dream big** (334), take risks, and adapt when things don't go as planned. They view failure, mistakes, and struggles as opportunities for growth. Instead of being derailed, they stay focused on creating a life they love. With confidence and clear plans, embracing risk opens new doors that lead to new opportunities which propel them forward.

From my experience, optimistic people are often **high achievers** (170), driven by hope and resilience; they refuse to let setbacks define them. Failure doesn't intimidate them. Instead, it fuels growth, learning, and smarter decisions.

Go with Our Gut

Success also comes from trusting our instincts. We've all hesitated in moments of opportunity, only to regret not acting later. According to Mel Robbins' Five Second Rule, we have only five seconds to seize an opportunity before our brain talks us out of it. Our minds are hardwired for safety, keeping us trapped in a comfort zone filled with limiting beliefs, like a computer virus or a faulty program preventing growth. Our brain won't naturally push us toward bold decisions, success, or progress.

To progress in life or business, we must step beyond comfort and trust our intuition. When that inner voice whispers,

"Go for it...", we have 5, 4, 3, 2, 1...

seconds before hesitation and doubt creep in. The key is listening to our internal guidance system and acting before hesitation takes over.

Along the way, the right teammates can make a difference. When life throws challenge our way, and our *iHope* is tested, supportive partners remind us of who we are and encourage us to keep our dreams alive. They become part of the solution, not the problem. Choose wisely.

To succeed, we must envision success with all our senses—smelling, tasting, seeing, hearing, and feeling it in our minds.

Visualizing where we want to be given us a focal point of reference. This process involves our senses, engaging our creativity and imagination, which can lead to favourable outcomes. When we imagine each step of an occasion, we are preparing our entire being to take those steps in real life. Wasting energy on negative thinking or focusing on what we don't want holds us back.

Everything starts with a thought, instead of thinking, "I don't want to fail again." Consider an alternative thought,

"I embrace every opportunity to learn and achieve success."

Our thoughts create our world, what we focus on grows, hence, the more we practice a positive mindset, the better we become.

Visualisations

Relax, close our eyes and breathe deeply. Imagine we have travelled into the future one year from now. Take all the lessons we have learned, and imagine it's our best year yet. Take our time until the vision is crystal clear, and vividly picture ourselves in the desired situation, paying attention to the details.

- What's changed in our personal lives?
- What's changed in our professional lives?
- What happened to our relationships?
- How is our mental and physical health?
- How do we feel?

Hold and savour the moment.

Revisit this visual every day. When we focus on these matters each day, we are likely to bring them into reality. When we visualise, we are telling our brain,

"This is the reality!"

Allow imagery to harness the power of our mind to focus and generate powerful positive feelings.

...**Because We Can!!**

Time to load up tyres, set the satnav and drive!
- Consider switching to a different compound. Soft Tyre.

Des'ree You Gotta Be 🎵

I hope I don't fail ...

Failure

Tough times forge Character and Resilience

Dashboard The Green Light indicates: All Clear!

"If you're going to succeed, you need to know about failure." Alan Yentob

Anyone who has not made a mistake in life has not lived life properly! Everyone worries about making mistakes and failing at some point in their lives. Failure is unattractive to most of us. We tend to associate failure with feelings of shame or inadequacy, which can affect our confidence. Consequently, we build a picture of what failure looks and feels like as a result, which makes us reluctant to try again. To redefine failure, it helps to understand what failure means to us and overcome our fears to move forward. To move forward, logic tells us we must overcome these hurdles in order to grow so we can develop and progress.

Failures and mistakes are inevitable; they mark the beginning of growth, development, and progress. Failure is the starting point of every journey towards resilience and **success** (195). It's through not giving up that we build that resilience muscle to succeed. Learning often comes through trial and error, and there are valuable lessons in every venture, whether a success or a failure. Failing teaches us what not to do, guiding us towards success. Failure is an essential part of any **process** (237), adding fulfilment and meaning to life. Learning to fail is learning how to succeed more effectively.

There's no point in putting the inevitable off to avoid unsuccessful outcomes. It's a part of life to make mistakes. To obtain something that we've never had, we must do something that we have never done in order to have the guts to take a chance on failure being an option. We need to have the courage to fail; without failure, we haven't tried. There are no mistakes in life, only opportunities to thrive and grow. All mistakes teach us something valuable. Failure is part of success; there isn't an entrepreneur who has not failed. Failures are simply feedback, allowing us to evaluate, measure, and monitor ourselves, too. Feedback to learn what we need more or less of, to check, tweak, and retune to turn it into an opportunity that works for us. We don't have to be the best, just do our best. The best approach is to set ourselves some goals with the permission that we're open to failing at some of them, to consent to thinking.

It's OK to fail.

This helps to make us thick-skinned and builds resilience, not fear. We won't win every time, but each setback offers a lesson, and that's OK. When we zoom out, we realise failure can become a redirection, not defeat. Each failure has the potential to become a stepping-stone to the good stuff in life. A mistake is just a 'miss-take' and a great opportunity to learn that every "no" leads us closer to a "yes".

Micheal Waltrip wisely said,

"Typically, you learn more when you lose than when you win."

Do not despair; this is not a time to throw in the towel and throw our hands up in the air. This is a time to roll our sleeves up.
Let's go again!!

Time to slipstream downhill to a 90* bend.
- Consider changing to a different compound. Soft Tyre.

Foo Fighters Wheels ♬

End of Racing!

I hope I have a strategy to achieve this life-changing task ...

Winning Formula

Design a Blueprint for Success

Dashboard The Green Light indicates: All Clear!

This is a serious, sober, and 'no messing' time!
This isn't a time to wait for something to happen. If we don't turn the keys in the ignition and put our foot on the throttle, nothing will happen. We must give ourselves the chance for opportunity to happen, keep looking and keep moving; they won't come to us.
It's crucial to take the time to program ourselves for the life that we want to have. No disturbance or distractions. Close the door to toxicity and negativity. We must be unapologetically **self-full** (210). No alcohol, no drugs, no sugar.

When we are presented with the opportunity to **change** (193) our lives for the better, with our name all over it, we give ourselves the best shot at winning. To win we must possess the drive and passion for our new venture. Whatever venture we choose to take on, our passion will eventually be challenged and tested, enough for any rational person to give up, so we have to love it, enjoy it, or we will give up on it. Choose wisely.

Events occur one at a time until the process is complete. Devoting a little of ourselves to too many goals dilutes our efforts; we take our eyes off the ball and spread ourselves too thin, only to find we have committed a great deal of ourselves to nothing. To accomplish the task requires an approach of consistency, hard work, balanced with relaxation. It is beneficial to take advantage of the time of day to harness our energy, to be most productive, perform, and excel. That time depends on what creatures we are, **lark or owl** (262). Give ourselves enough time to wind down daily, preferably around two to three hours before bedtime. Whatever we use to wind down from our day, to relax and prepare ourselves to sleep, will allow us space to clear our minds, maintain our energies and reset for the next day.

Our pillars for a healthy lifestyle are simply to eat well, drink well, and sleep well, aiming for around eight hours of rest each night. It is vital for us to eat healthily and sleep well so we can function to optimise our mental and physical wellbeing to attain our goals. Do whatever we can to feed our brains because we're asking for more, e.g. learn more material and retain the information.

Our **brain** (72) controls everything we do, talk, walk, think, see, hear, feel taste, sit up, and even move our eyeballs. Now we're asking it to retain vast amounts of information at an intense level, consistently, over extended periods of time. As a result, we need to provide it with extra resources to perform at its best. A high-protein diet is recommended for studying of any kind. Protein and fats feeds our brain cells and keeps us awake and alert longer. Whatever our preference, graze on proteins, such as nuts, tofu, or chicken pieces whilst studying. Drink more water than usual, two litres. The brain can survive for a longer period deprived of food than deprived of water. Water helps brain function; water also helps our energy levels and concentration, so drink up.

Sleep is paramount to everything; it is our freest medicine, and sleep is the only time our body repairs itself. Sleep has many benefits: regenerating parts of our brain needed to function normally, improving our mental health, concentration, and memory, as well as reducing our stress and anxiety. If we do not get enough sleep, it can affect our behaviour and harm our performance. Make sure to get our zzz's. These pillars will keep us on our feet.

This temporary period in our lives requires time, so create extra time, reduce chores to the bare minimum. This does not mean introducing chaos; instead, if there's no time to go shopping, go online instead. Batch cook once a week, at the weekend, less everyday cooking. If someone can help with the batch cooking, laundry, tidying and cleaning, let them. If not, spend the minimum amount of time on these chores for this period. Remember, this is temporary. When we consider the above, it's clear that we must eliminate certain habits and distractions, and **procrastination** (135), to prioritise, focus and achieve our goals and ambitions. We must be focused, following our vision of what we want to accomplish. Manifest it. When we can see it, we can feel each piece of the puzzle come together as we get closer to the finishing line.

Do remember; we are not Ai, we are human beings who require maintenance for our physical, mental, and emotional health to get the best out of ourselves. This is not a time of self-neglect. This time in our lives requires **self-love** (191) and balance.

Like a postage stamp, focus on one task at a time
until we reach our destination!

Time to gain traction and get some hot laps in. DRS is open, overtake. Set the satnav, put our foot on the throttle, and drive!

- Consider changing to a different compound tyre. Soft Tyre.

Eminem Lose Yourself ♪

End of Racing!

I hope I can enjoy my own company ...

Best Friend

We need Ourselves more than We need them!

Dashboard The Green Light indicates: All Clear!

The most important thing in life is our relationship with ourselves.
No one will truly understand our journey or walk in our shoes. Life can be so much easier when we can depend on and trust ourselves to make life decisions and take action. Ultimately, no one can give us more than we're willing to give ourselves.

It is essential for us to connect deeply with ourselves, to be our own best friend. We must build and develop a healthy, responsible relationship with ourselves. Being responsible is how we respond to what really matters in our lives, and being accountable for our health, ourselves, and our lives. Hold on to our integrity; it is shown in our thoughts, feelings, and actions aligned with the words we speak to ourselves and the way we interact with others.

No one knows what we are feeling all the time, and no one understands us better than we understand ourselves. We are the ones who meet our own needs, feed ourselves, dress ourselves, take care of our wellbeing, and stand by our side. Ultimately, we know ourselves better than anyone else. If we find ourselves feeling lost and not truly knowing who we are, it's essential to take the time to discover our true selves, as we'll spend a lifetime together. We must accept, respect, and honour our strengths and weaknesses, even our peccadilloes. Our strength and authentic power lie in embracing who we are in our entirety, loving ourselves, and knowing we can rely on ourselves. No one else can lift our self-esteem, boost our self-worth, or give us hope better than we can. This builds our confidence, opens more opportunities, and lessens our fears. The loneliness we feel will gradually become less of a threat and more of a distant stranger. When we look externally, expecting others to understand us better than we understand ourselves, we set ourselves up to be disappointed and hurt by others.

Our relationship with ourselves is crucial to being true to who we are, enabling us to make autonomous decisions and navigate our lives authentically. This is the moment to trust our body, embrace our feelings, observe our thoughts, and treat ourselves with kindness.
Even if we are in prison, if we are true to ourselves, we are free!

Keep to the racing lines and hammer the throttle.
- Consider switching to a different compound. Hard Tyre.

Brandy Best Friend ♬

I hope I can make my mind up ...

Decisions Decisions

Decisions Drive Progression

Dashboard The Orange Light Indicates: Caution! Slow Down!

Decisions shape our lives, bringing resolution to our dilemmas. Only we can create our own options by making a decision.

Decision-making is fundamental to life. Decisions have the power to change our lives indefinitely, for better or worse. We make them personally, professionally, or in relationships.

Decision-making is one of the most important tools we have. With decisions comes action and change, which can generate progression opportunity, support us in leadership and self-development. It can be a stress buster, end the misery or suffering, give us a voice, meet our needs, boost our confidence, and even save our lives, among many other benefits. Along with decisions, there may be consequences, or repercussions that may fall in our favour, or they may not, at least we are in charge. Decisions, which require responsibility and accountability, are what make the difference between an adult and a child. A child does not have to consider these duties.

To live a healthy life, adults must make decisions.

In practice, Kingsley, 34, was great at making decisions in his professional roles. Decisions at work are supported by frameworks, rules regulations, and governed by logic, a timeframe, staff, budget, experience, knowledge, talent and skills. Professional decisions often rely on gut instinct, which can sometimes be distorted by emotions, expectations, and fears. Personal decisions, however, posed a different challenge. They were shaped by his attachments to people, his expectations, emotions, and assumptions, often without a clear timeframe or direction. This lack of structure led to overthinking and self-sabotage, which held him hostage; he felt trapped.

We cannot lead our lives, or lead others, if we avoid making decisions.

Choosing not to make a decision means allowing everyone else to control our lives, instead of taking charge ourselves. The world keeps turning and, naturally, push will come to shove. Eventually, circumstances will force our hand driven by life's natural ebb and flow. In the end, life and time will make the decisions for us. If that's the decision we choose, fair play to us, but here's the tricky part:

Not making a decision is a decision!

In relationships, decisions can create significant outcomes, especially if we're struggling to agree to disagree, or compromise. If we leave our partners to make all the decisions in our relationships, the balance shifts, and it stops being a true partnership.

From my experience in couples therapy, here are a few common scenarios that create distance between partners or push them apart: One person becomes tired, bored, and disengaged; an affair ensues, or abuse occurs. Abusive, coercive relationships often encourage this dynamic, where control and dominance prevail. In these situations, our thoughts and feelings are dismissed, and we lose our voice. Choosing the right time is crucial when it comes to making a decision. If we find ourselves confronted with an overwhelming situation that requires a decision. Try not to make permanent decisions based on new feelings that are likely to be temporary. Making permanent decisions based on temporary feelings rarely lead to the best outcome Give things time to settle so the mind can clear.

Decisions will put us firmly in control, and back in the driver's seat of life. Expect that there may be a few tweaks, adjustments, and changes along the way to help guide us on our path towards reaching our *iHope*.

The decision-making process involves prioritising.
Here are a few tips to consider:

- List in order of 'urgent' and 'significant', say 'yes'.
- List 'significant' and have no urgency, delegate.
- List 'insignificant' and 'not urgent', 'No'.

The rest of the list can be delayed, put on hold, and scheduled for another time.

A choice is different from a decision; a decision is backed by reasons, while a choice is simply an option. Choose to be responsible, to have a voice, to be accountable, and to make decisions that are right for us.

We always have a choice – "YES" or "NO."

We're gaining traction!
- Consider changing to a different compound. Intermediate Tyre.

Heatwave Mind Blowing Decisions ♪

I hope I can let the feelings slide ...

Emotions

Travel Lightly

Dashboard The Green Light indicates: All Clear!

The emotions are like warning lights on our dashboard. All the emotions are classified in groups represented by different colours: green, red, orange, purple, yellow, and blue.

Our emotions can be carried, accepted, analysed, transformed, learned from, or even suffered through. In a single day, we might feel happy, sad, anxious, or angry; that's the nature of life, how life is supposed to be. To experience a range of emotions fluidly, our feelings are not good or bad; they simply are.

No matter what we do or how enlightened we are, sometimes fear, self-criticism, judgement and anxiety will present themselves. Our emotions are here to guide our lives rather than control them; they are there to protect us, speaking with us all the time. There are advantages and disadvantages, our feelings are temporary; nothing lasts forever. If we're feeling on top of the world, it's temporary, if we are devastated and in despair, know it's temporary. We don't need to change or get rid of negative thoughts and feelings, simply recognise they're temporary.

Emotional intelligence is awareness.

To get along with our emotions, we need to be aware, mindful and compassionate with ourselves. Going through **self-enquiry** (65) is useful to identify things are not working for us. We can trust that our emotions are doing their best to protect us. Some emotions can be the result of the past, such as sadness, while fear is what's projected into the future.

Our feelings aren't harmful to us. They won't kill us, at worst, they may bring us to our knees, even so, we'll still be okay. Letting go of old, toxic feelings will free us and lighten our load. Let's recognise what we're carrying; we are always carrying around the same unprocessed feelings. Like a car, if the load is too heavy, the car will require more fuel, which in turn means more of our energy to lug around, day in day out, twenty-four seven, our old baggage when we can simply travel light.

It's healthy for our feelings to address the problem within the same season. Of course, we may need a moment to reset our thoughts and emotions, giving us the space to process and to rationalize the experience.

Feelings are like visitors; they come and go.

Imagine our soul as a home, and we've got some unexpected visitors, forgotten feelings we've been avoiding and running from, showing up at our front door. They've formed an orderly queue depending on how deeply they've impacted us, or how recent they are. Open the door, let them in, feel them, acknowledge them, and they will eventually pass through and leave.

By embracing our emotions, we tap into the superpower of vulnerability, giving us strength, bravery and courage.

Being busy with family, children, or our careers, can distract us from being in touch with our emotions and understanding what we're truly feeling.

As a form of self-preservation, we abstain from vulnerability and keep ourselves busy instead of feeling. When we lose connection with our emotions, we begin to lose our way in life, disconnect from ourselves and strain our relationships, especially romantic relationships. If we have a '**ding dong**' (317), focusing on our feelings helps us to make clearer **decisions** (202) and manage conflict more effectively. By identifying our emotions, we can understand ourselves, and our significant other better. Then we can work towards a compromise and resolution.

Stuck

At times, we emotionally get stuck. This means we haven't acknowledged that there's another feeling present, alongside anger, or fear. Once we become aware and the other emotion is revealed, the sensation of feeling stuck releases.

Many of us choose to avoid uncomfortable feelings by doing the opposite; yet by avoiding uncomfortable feelings, we are holding onto them, which allows them to ferment, manifest and deepen.

Until there comes a day, after months or years, when we're settled, and all is well in our lives. Out of the blue, perhaps at an inappropriate time, our feelings come to the surface and, start knocking on our door, waiting to be acknowledged. Yet we can't remember; we've pushed that time so far to the back of our minds that we may have forgotten the situation. Consequently, we are unable to make sense of what's happening to us.

I've heard many stories in my practice, where clients have shared,

> *"My life's great, the best it's ever been. I've a good job, partner, friends, life is good, but I feel sad, I can't stop crying."*

With time, we can open the door and unpack the baggage to obtain what we need to heal. We are entitled to honour what we feel; whatever we repress will become distressing and stressful.

> Be a welcome host and let them pass through and leave out the back door.

Feelings wait for us!

- Consider changing to a different compound. Intermediate Tyre.

Time to get some purple sectors in using DRS.

I Virtuosi Italiani & Daniel Hope Experience 🎵

End of Racing!

I hope I will get the outcome I'm looking for ...

Science = Cause + Effect

Intention = Outcome

Dashboard The Green Light indicates: All Clear!

There is a science to baking. When baking a cake, we choose a recipe, use the appropriate ingredients, and select the correct temperature to ensure the cake rises. If the cake is not baked in the correct climate, there will likely be no rise, only a fall. Every aspect of baking is essential to achieve the desired result.

There is no difference when it comes to making decisions. We can apply the same concept. With every decision we make, we hope the strategy gives us the expected outcome. If we aren't using genuine constituents, the result will likely be unpredictable or unwanted; we cannot bake a cake with toxic ingredients and expect it to rise or be palatable.

How we feel can play a part in determining the outcome. When deciding, check what emotions are being provoked. If they are negative, acknowledge that our approach is likely to reflect how we feel. Therefore, the outcome will be negative. If our desired outcomes rarely materialise, we might require further thought, and consider a different approach. Consider that the same thought patterns lead to the same choices, the same choices lead to the same behaviours, and the same behaviours lead to the same experiences which lead to the same emotions... and so on.

Our thoughts are powerful, and our emotions are influential. It's crucial to have a level of emotional intelligence to ensure that the same outcome does not keep occurring. To ensure that we have a different outcome, it is essential that we account for our thoughts and feelings. Healthy decision making can require working things out in reverse. Start by deciding what outcome we desire, and then consider an appropriate approach that supports our desired outcome. Consider any consequences before making the decision, and beware of what emotions are driving our intentions, keeping in mind the desired effect that we are seeking.

It is scientifically proven that cause and effect tells us that the cause is directly responsible for the effect, by demonstrating what is related, in accordance with how it changes.

If we match our behaviour with our intentions and actions to equal our thoughts, and our mind and body to work together in harmony, we can acquire a new, positive experience.

With intention, determines the outcome.

Our **emotions** (204) may be in our driver's seat, driving our intention right off track!

⚫ Consider changing to a different compound. Hard Tyre. Gaining Traction.

Pharrell Williams Piece by Piece ♬

I hope I can find my way on the right side of life …

Winning at Life

Positive Mindset

Dashboard The Green Light indicates: All Clear!

To be winning at life requires having a healthy and positive outlook on our perspective of life, and positive thoughts about ourselves.

When we have a vision or an idea, the only thing that will stop it from happening is ourselves. What we think about ourselves tells us what we believe about ourselves, influences the choices we make and the outcomes from those decisions.

- If we believe we're unlovable, it's no surprise we may end up alone.
- If we belief we're invisible and unheard, it's no wonder we feel helpless and depressed.
- Thinking were not good enough, might explain why we overwork and run on empty.
- If we see ourselves powerless, it could be why we end up in toxic relationships.

What we think about ourselves holds power.

Winners don't just think about winning; they have a vision that they're working towards and imagine what success might feel like. To make it happen, we need to see, hear, and feel success in order to truly believe it's possible.

Winning and losing come with momentum. If we're on a 'winning streak' we're gaining traction and momentum. If we aren't achieving, we're gaining traction in the opposite direction. When we lose hope and momentum, things start to compound against us, and we can spiral due to our decreasing serotonin, dopamine, and oxytocin levels. This can affect our motivation, and lead to self-doubt and low self-esteem creeping in.

Behavioural activities, such as exercise, sleep, and nutrition, make a difference to our quality of life. These elements impact the chemical make-up in our brains. Scientifically, they create chemicals, such as serotonin or dopamine, which are our happy chemicals. This chemical process helps us feel optimistic and good about ourselves, and in turn lifts our vibrations. They're similar to the conductor of an orchestra. We're left with a melodic symphony in our brains, which we call a chemical balance.

A **positive mindset** (240) takes the position in our driver's seat of life and will take us far.

Consider being our own cheerleader in life, rather than acting as judge and jury, or we're likely to face a life sentence!

- Consider changing to a different compound. Soft Tyre.

Time to load up the tyres and hammer the throttle.
We can get a fastest lap in.

Radiohead Airbag ♪

I hope I can learn to put myself first ...

Self-FULL

Make time for Wellness, or we're Forced to make time for Illness

Dashboard The Green Light indicates: All Clear!

It is not selfish to love ourselves!
It is not selfish to take care of oneself and one's wellbeing.
Prioritising ourselves and preserving the essence of who we are is about being self-FULL. It's not about luxury or indulgence. It's about being proactive in meeting our needs. It is an act of survival; it means actively tending to our mind, body, and spirit with purpose and care.

When we fly on an airplane, the flight attendant instructs us to 'put our oxygen masks on first", before helping others. This is seen as an act of survival. If we run out of oxygen for ourselves; we can't help anyone else. In life, this is no different. We must prioritise ourselves; we must come first.

Being self-FULL requires making tough decisions that meet our needs for our physical, spiritual, and mental health. This requires setting **boundaries** (215) that protect, respect, and maintain our values and who we are, to ensure toxic experiences do not repeat themselves.

Most of us worry about being labelled as 'selfish' if we are seen to be prioritising ourselves. Putting ourselves first and being self-full neither selfish, self-centred nor self-absorbed, it is a responsibility we owe to ourselves, and in turn, to others, to be self-FULL.

Burnout (172) is commonplace nowadays. We live highly stimulated, chaotic lives; we find that life is busy running us. We become tangled up in a culture that promotes fatigue or exhaustion. This lifestyle is simply wearing us out. It's expected, accepted, and seen as being okay, allowing us to be rewarded for self-neglect. We are seen as 'good people' when we put others first and ourselves at the bottom of the list. If we choose not to put ourselves first, we may have little choice later.

In practice, I've experienced many who understand that we must look after ourselves and care for ourselves first, whatever our circumstances, before we can help others. To look after others, we need be the best of ourselves, and in return, others will get the best of us, too. Additionally, it is good practice for our children to see and respect the importance of being self-full. We are entitled.

Being self-full requires us to fall in love with ourselves; to care for ourselves, accept ourselves, and take the time for ourselves to develop our emotional intelligence and awareness. A process that is a journey and requires time and practice to learn how to give to ourselves. Being kind to oneself allows self-compassion to develop and establish a place in our inner world. Self-compassion is a skill to acknowledge and enjoy the good in ourselves whilst having the courage to release the stuff that holds us down.

Looking after ourselves is not a task or an achievement, but a privilege to practice good mental, physical, and spiritual hygiene and feel the benefits of high wellbeing and good health. Being self-full is a practice of prevention, not cure. It requires consistency and commitment that becomes a part of our daily or weekly routine as a way of self-preservation. This is not a temporary fix for emergency procedures only.

We must come first!

We need value ourselves, our process, our esteem, our confidence, our emotions, our voice, our femininity, our masculinity, our social batteries, our difference, our body clocks, our thoughts, our healing, our energy, and our time, in order to be able to give fully to ourselves, our friendships, our relationships, our spouse, our children, and our lives, with the ability to both give, and receive fullness.
This is what we deserve.

Self matters!

🎱   Consider changing to a different compound. Soft Tyre.
Time to use DRS and get the fastest lap in.

Terri Walker Fearless 🎵

I hope I can rest, recharge, and renew my soul …

Shut Eye

Our Freest Medicine with No Side Effects

Dashboard The Green Light indicates: All Clear!

Sleep is more important than work, we cannot survive without sleep!

Sleep is the foundation of emotional, physical, mental, and spiritual health. As human beings, we need the full performance of sleep. Seventy-five per cent of us are not getting an average of eight hours of sleep at night, and then there are others, whether we have babies or we're doing shift work, who find it difficult to sustain regular sleep.

We aren't all the same; we all live very hectic and complex lives that may contribute to sleep difficulties. Poor sleep can be detrimental to our health. It impacts our physical, mental, emotional, and spiritual wellbeing. Sleep deprivation affects every process and organ in the body; it impacts our sex drive, increases risks of dementia and heart disease, obesity, diabetes, stroke, some forms of cancer, and even lowers our life expectancy.

Sleep is essential. When we think about a healthy lifestyle, we focus on diet, nutrition, and exercise, yet sleep is as important as exercise and nutrition. The only time our bodies repair is when we are asleep; our bodies have many clocks, and sleep supports them ticking over smoothly. When we sleep, our bodies are busy taking care of us, preparing for tomorrow to wake up feeling refreshed, ready to start a new day. It is crucial for our health to get good quality sleep.

Generally, from 10 p.m. to 2 a.m., our bodies will go through a process to repair our physical being, and from 2 a.m. to 6 a.m. our bodies will go through a process of repairing our psychological being. Our short-term memory gets moved into long-term memory, and toxins get washed out of our brain. When we are in REM (rapid eye movement) sleep, we are dreaming, which is when we come up with the most creative and original ideas during the night.

When we suffer from persistent chronic poor sleep, the next day we can feel irritable, short-tempered, low in energy and mood, with poor concentration. We're less likely to exercise, our appetites increase, we tend to turn to foods high in sugar and the wrong kinds of fat, and subsequently, our weight increases. Midnight munchies are a 'No, No!' Emotional eating late at night hinders our chances of getting a good night's sleep; our body needs time to digest food, it's not ready to unwind and relax for bed, and our bodies are on a mission to digest our food intake before we can sleep soundly.

Our **brains** (72) like routine; it's essential that we keep our bedtime regular, which includes our weekends. Waking up and going to bed at the same time as we do on a school night helps; disrupting our routine doesn't help our sleep even if it's the weekend.

If possible, avoid obsessing about our poor sleeping habits when we go to bed; our troublesome thoughts are likely to keep waking us up. The more we worry, the less likely we can switch off, and we're caught in a vicious cycle. If we wake up in the middle of the night, avoid tossing and turning. Get out of bed and find whatever distracts us from rest. Find a cool, dark room to empty our brain by physically writing down whatever's on our mind. Put the distractions onto paper, take that list out of our heads.

Once we've dumped our thoughts, do whatever we like with the paper, as long as we don't re-read it before going back to bed. If it's useless stuff, trash it. If our thoughts aren't troubling, we do some boring stuff, read a book, nothing too over-stimulating for the brain, and go back to bed when we feel tired again.

The bedroom should serve just two purposes:
Intimacy and sleep.

We can teach our brain to associate our bedroom with sleep. We might have to get rid of anything else in the bedroom that isn't about sex or sleep. The bedroom is not an entertainment centre for blue light gremlins that trick our body into thinking that it's daytime. This includes all devices; TV, videos, gaming, phones, computers, laptops, they must go. Additionally, our bedrooms are not offices; if we work in the same room we sleep in, a loud and resounding, **"No."**

If a separate room isn't an option, create distinct zones within the space, one for work and one for rest. Keep our bed solely for sleeping and avoid working in or on it. Maintaining this separation is essential for balancing productivity and relaxation.

Considering the creatures we are, especially teenagers and young people can be night owls. Early morning light is imperative to resetting our internal clocks. Take an early morning walk to help regulate our circadian clocks. The sunlight sends a direct signal to the brain to wake us up, giving us a better mood and daytime focus and alertness throughout the day. The process of being outside with sunlight at the beginning of our day sets a timer for when our bodies are ready to sleep. Owls always have difficulty trying to manage their own body clock. Of course, owls will have less exposure to the sun, which causes our melatonin levels to decrease.

Our 24-hour clock is governed by light, so taking an early morning walk helps put our clock in check and persuades our clocks to start ticking earlier so that we can sleep earlier and enjoy much deeper sleep. We must turn this practice into a regular routine for it to be long-lasting. If we expect less sleep because of work patterns, as we are leading up to a shift, it might be worthwhile to 'sleep bank'; we sleep more and accumulate extra hours leading up to the occasion to ensure we don't get into sleep debt. On the other hand, as a matter of urgency, a quick solution would be a nap, a power nap. Sleep no more than 21 minutes per interval. Naps can help us to step out of the red by depositing naps to level up our e-balance.

Exercise (238) is one of sleep's 'little helpers', a workout will tire us out and encourage rest at the end of the day. Exercising during the day, especially outdoors, has two advantages: it keeps our circadian clock ticking smoothly and helps us to sleep better. There are many different approaches to getting sleep; one way doesn't always suit all, depending on lifestyle or age, if we find ourselves out of the red, some sleep is far better than no sleep at all.

Beware!!
Side effects of sleep are feeling refreshed, alert and energized.

Time to load up the tyres and hammer the throttle at butt clenching speed, we can get a fastest lap in.

- ◎ Consider changing to a different compound. Wet Tyre.

Flawed Mangoes Somniferous ♪

I hope I can stop being taken advantage of ...

Boundaries

Teach people How to Treat us!

Dashboard The Green Light indicates: All Clear!

Without boundaries, a healthy successful life isn't possible.

Boundaries are compulsory.
Boundaries are healthy, normal and protect our peace, never feel guilty for having them.
Nothing is real unless we have a contract that is personal to us. That contract is called a boundary; it is vital for supporting our self-care and acts as a shield of honour. Boundaries are used to protect our needs. Saying "no" to others is saying "yes" to ourselves, making ourselves a priority, and giving ourselves a voice. Boundaries contribute to self-discipline, self-control and self-respect.

Taking someone to their limit is never positive or attractive; it can be unhealthy and even toxic. Understandably, we all make mistakes the first time; however, if the error is repeated more than once, it becomes a choice. Boundaries look like,

> "Don't do it again, or if you do it again there are consequences and repercussions."

Options must be clear and concise. If boundaries are not adhered to, it can hinder our wellbeing, create a distance; and invite more drama, encouraging tiring confrontations, that may lead to a breakdown in the relationship. The alternative is to accept the other's boundaries, based on respect and trust. When we don't establish boundaries, we can turn a well-meaning partner into a bully. With boundaries in place, we can trust ourselves to ensure no one can enter our lives and treat us badly.

> "We are entitled to set boundaries, whether people like them or not!"

To set boundaries, we must consider our emotions and know our worth. It takes integrity and maturity to have the courage to set boundaries, along with emotional intelligence to communicate healthily for a favourable outcome, it's worth it. Boundaries can save relationships, even lives. They are essential to earning respect and being respected as an individual.

In practice. Chanel, 28, had struggled with setting boundaries in her life. She lived with her family, had no privacy at home, she ran a beauty business, her diary was dictated by her clients, Chanel would work the hours they suggested, often until 10.p.m. She felt heartbroken, experienced numerous relationships, and felt used, neglected, and unappreciated. Her last partner cheated on her. She was fatigued, angry, hurt, and depressed, lacking self-esteem and almost no sense of self-worth. Her mental health and wellbeing started to improve once we put boundaries in place in every area of her life: work, home, romantic relationships. She learned to say 'No' to others.

A lack of boundaries invites a lack of respect.

Lacking boundaries often stems from deep rooted feelings of **not being good enough** (184). When we don't believe in our own worth, we leave ourselves wide open to being mistreated, taken for granted, or exploited by public services, family, colleagues, or friends. We might struggle to assert ourselves or say "No", fearing rejection or conflict. Struggling to take ownership of our feelings for the sake of others, all because we don't prioritise ourselves, permits us to be imposed upon or victimised, leaving us feeling powerless.

When we set a boundary, it will be tested. People will recognise we're changing, and they will naturally try to pull us back to what's familiar for them. Keep reinforcing our boundary, whether they like it or not. We can't oversee everyone else, we can only be in charge of ourselves. Everyone who comes into our life must keep to our standards.

We have the resources to assert ourselves appropriately and own our authority. Before setting a boundary, we must consider the significance the significance of the matter, whether it requires priority, or urgency, whether we can delegate, before deciding to decline. To justify and support "No", add a little context or softness.

Here are a few examples of how to say, **"No"**

1. Be honest and explain the situation.
2. Sympathise without agreeing to anything:
   "So sorry to hear, maybe next time, all the best with...."

3. Make an excuse: *"I'd love too. If only I hadn't booked with XXXX I would've been able to come.", or "Unfortunately I can't this time. I'm skint."*
4. Offer alternatives without saying 'No'.
   "Absolutely not...", By no means....", "No way...", "Under no circumstances...", Never..."
5. Give feedback: *"I had a blast last time, but I need to slow down, some me-time."*
6. Let them down gently: *"If only you'd have given me more notice, I would have been able to make it, let me know next time."*
7. The American "No" *We'd love to see you at the wedding...",* or
   "We think you're great, and you'd fit well in this company."
   In fact, we never invite them.
8. *"I'm afraid this doesn't feel right for me this time...*
   "I've had a really busy week, I'm super tired".
9. *"I wish I could ...but there's no chance, my weeks full. "*
   "As much as I love you, I love myself more, I've reached my limit!"
10. *"No"* with a smile.

Additionally, it helps to focus on goals and avoid distractions:
- List our tasks and prioritise them.
- Set a boundary by focussing on our top three.
- Let go of or say "No" to the rest.

We are not Ai machines or robots. We are human, we have our limitations.

"No" is a full sentence!

- Consider switching to a different compound. Hard Tyre.
- or Wet Tyre.

Time to hit the throttle at butt clenching speed, to get some hot laps in. DRS.

Mahalia Terms and Conditions ♪
Franky Wah Boundaries 🎵

I hope I have a moment to myself before ...

On the Pulse of the Morning

Carpe Diem!

When we wake up, we are in a peaceful and vulnerable state, whether alone, or lying next to another soul. Those initial few moments, when no one knows we're awake, belong solely to us. They offer an ideal opportunity to steal some me-time, to listen to our spirit which often speaks the loudest, before the day's demands begin to weigh us down or before innocent little souls hijack and hold our peace hostage. In those quiet moments, it's best to avoid external influences like news feed; podcasts, reports, or emails as these can trigger anxiety, stress, guilt, and sadness that lingers throughout the day. This time is precious, a window to identify our authentic emotions. It may be the only moment we truly have to ourselves, and it has the potential to shape the rest of our day.

Our spectacles may not be as spectacular as we believe.
We each view the world through our own subjective lenses, shaped by our beliefs and life experiences. Some of these lenses are empowering, while others may be limiting. They colour how we interpret the world, sometimes distorting reality in subtle, unconscious ways.
For example, the emotion we are feel upon waking can influence the persona we present to the world, potentially setting the tone or disrupting the rest of the day.

"Sorry, I woke up on the wrong side of the bed this morning."

We've all experienced mornings clouded by being in a bad mood for no apparent reason. Similarly, if we believe deep down that we are unlovable, that belief may manifest in our external world, perhaps explaining why we remain single.
Fortunately, we have the power to shift our thought patterns and experience more positive outcomes. This process begins during the that drowsy moments immediately after waking, when our minds are highly impressionable. The thoughts we feed ourselves at this time can leave a lasting impact on the day ahead.

Keep our eyes closed and stay in the moment.

Use this time to nurture our alpha state, a brain frequency present during the first ten minutes after waking. In this state we ae awake but deeply relaxed,

transitioning gradually from sleep to alertness.
The alpha state is beneficial for creativity, insight, and **healing** (75).

This is a golden opportunity to practice **compassion** (58), **gratitude** (326) and visualise our goals by setting positive intentions and repeating affirmations.

> I have the power to change.
> I am capable of great things.
> I love money and money loves me.
> I can succeed.
> I am important.
> With positive thoughts and self-confidence, I am unstoppable.
> I am open to opportunities.
> I trust myself and my feelings.
> I feel positive energetic and healthy.
> I stand up to my negative thoughts.
> I am confident in my sexuality.
> I can stay in the present moment.
> I like me, I love me.
> I am lovable.
> Today is going to be a great day.

Hold ourselves in high positive regard. Be kind to ourselves, say loving words about how we wish to experience the day, all before opening our eyes. With consistent practice, we can reduce stress and transform our mindset by working with our subconscious, releasing outdated beliefs and embracing empowering new ones.

Once we are fully awake, take a few deep breaths to oxygenate our brain. Drink water to rehydrate after the overnight fast, and gently rise to begin our day.

If we feel any other emotions resurfacing and have the time and space, take the opportunity to explore them. Seek awareness, engage and release them. **Meditation** (293), or **journaling** (290) helps to bring clarity for the soul. Tune into our breath. Savour the calm, the gentle ease, the safety, the snug warmth, and the quiet restfulness that wraps around us.

Good morning dear soul!

Beautiful Chorus Inner Peace ♪

I hope I don't feel anxious ...

Anxiety

We are More than our Thoughts

Anxiety is a warning light on our dashboard. Indicating: Caution! Slow Down!

Anxiety can disrupt our thinking, emotions, and behaviour, making it difficult to enjoy life or move forward.

When we are anxious, every moment is marred by a constant nagging and unease that we can't quite put our finger on. We begin to feel overwhelmed and unable to cope. We might start to lose sleep or our appetite and feel breathless or panicked. Once anxiety takes root, it doesn't simply disappear, and avoidance becomes our go-to-strategy. Over time, if left untreated, anxiety can be extremely isolating and may lead to panic attacks and severe depressive symptoms.

Unfortunately, anxiety today is often labelled as a problem, like an enemy working against us, something dangerous and destructive, that's simply not the case. When we feel anxious, we fear it and attempt to escape it in many ways, often through distraction to avoid feeling uncomfortable. This behaviour creates more anxiety, which in turn makes us feel even more anxious. So, we continue trying to run from it, rather than learning how to cope and manage it, consequently, it becomes an endless cycle.

Generally, we experience anxiety either from a historical event that has left a fingerprint on our soul, or its projected in the future, focused on events or circumstances that haven't yet occurred. Our thoughts are not reality, we need to work through the illusions pushed upon us by negatively biased thinking. Even if we feel tense, and unsettled, nervous, or even alarmed, anxiety is ultimately on our side. It flags up stuff we might otherwise miss, or that are unfamiliar to us. It gives us the opportunity to gather information and prepare for the unknown.

Anxiety is our friend, simply asking us to sit up and pay attention so we can focus on situations that are new to us. These are usually important moments in our lives that we care about, like, exams, an interview or a date. Foreign situations will come up often in life as a natural part of experiencing the new, so let's face it. Anxiety is simply a fundamental part of the human condition, and we need to slow down and listen.

It's useful to familiarise ourselves with the feeling.

Generally, anxiety is asking for more of us, requesting more information, or greater preparation for that exam or interview. So, help anxiety out, and then let it go!

Anxiety is an emotion that lets us know we can't stay in denial or continue running from our problems. It offers prompts, indications or signals that give us a chance to prepare for the unknown. Once, we recognise that we've done all we can, our anxious friend will stop tapping us on our shoulder. If we haven't been paying attention to our feelings, that started the anxiety, it can subtly set us up for doing unhelpful things or make us feel worse. Understanding the root cause of our anxiety is vital. This often requires seeking professional help to work through the cause of the symptom, enabling us to heal and truly acknowledge anxiety for what it is. Breathing techniques are useful for easing anxiety. Staying in the present means we need to let go of future-orientated thoughts.

If we struggle to stay in the moment, observe our pet dogs, they live only live in the present, they are consciously aware of each moment. Another technique is to hold some ice or rub an ice cube over our palm, or forehead. It demands our attention and the change in temperature quickly draws us back into the here and now.

Anxiety is a part of life. To live a healthy existence, we ned to be open to new experiences throughout our lives. We feel anxious during good times and bad. We're all anxious at various moments, so it's an emotion we must learn to befriend.

You need me, so I'm not going anywhere!

Anxiety is our friend, and it's here to stay.

- Consider changing to a different compound. Wet Tyre.

Sade Keep Looking ♫

I hope I can get past the fear ...

Fear

Low self-Confidence + Poor Self-Esteem + Jumping to Conclusions = Fear

Fear is a warning light on our dashboard indicating: Caution! Slow Down! 💭

Fear is an emotion or a thought that traps us in anticipation of danger or pain ahead. Fear acts as a warning, signalling that the unknown is approaching, something brand-new, unrecognisable and unfamiliar. This uncertainty becomes a perceived threat, giving fear the invitation to trigger a whirlwind of emotions: vulnerability, discomfort, intimidation, horror, fright, alarm, terror, trepidation apprehension, distress, dread, nervousness, doubt, suspicion, stress, anxiety, worry, and many more.

In practice, Sofia, age 26, struggled with her fears of the future. She had a history of making poor decisions, many of which were driven by her anxiety. Each choice felt like a response to the fear of the unknown, fear of failure, rejection and uncertainty. She came to realise that these fears came from her childhood, particularly from the unpredictability of her drunken father returning home from the pub. He would always find something to criticize, to pick apart, making her feel like nothing was ever good enough. This left Sofia with a lingering sense of insecurity and a deep-seated anxiety that affected how she viewed the world.

The fear of suffering is worse than the suffering itself. It restricts us and places limitations on us. Fear can control so many areas of our lives.

What we often overlook, is that fear can be an ally, an emotion that protects us, and prompts us to be on guard, just in case we are in danger. It allows us to be ready to safeguard ourselves from harm. Once we work out that something is no longer a threat we can crack on with our lives. However, if we lack self-confidence and have low self-esteem, we are more susceptible to getting stuck in a fight or flight response, reacting and jumping to conclusions. There's a hitch: we don't know what lies ahead of us because it's in the future. We anticipate what hasn't happened, yet we can only live in the now. The next minute is unknown, we can't predict. The future is unbeknown to us.

A substantial proportion of what we worry about never happens, yet we still spend ninety percent of our time worrying about it. We worry twice; we worry about it happening, and then we worry about it when it happens. Worrying doesn't solve anything; it's simply betting against ourselves. When fear is out of control, it can take a hold of our future. It stagnates the mind, creates an imbalance in the immune system, distorts our perceptions, and narrows our opportunities in life. Consequently, we miss out on meeting many good and brilliant people. It robs us of experiencing freedom and the feeling of being alive.

When we're in our autumn years and we reflect on our lives, we may regret allowing fear to run our lives. The best things in life are on the other side of fear. We can't achieve anything if we are afraid, it's essential that we step out of our **comfort zone** (118).

The best way of conquering our fear is to have power over it. By simply staying in the now, we will notice when we are present, the fear diminishes. To be present we need to ground ourselves by using all our senses in the here and now. Focus on what we see, hear, feel, smell and physically feel to our touch simultaneously, and our awareness will be rooted in the present moment.

We can control our fears by stopping ourselves getting ahead of reality by imagining, overthinking, assuming or speculating. It's important to stop fantasising. It's useful to measure against reality. Without concrete facts and evidence, it hasn't happened and doesn't exist. The less attention we give it, the less power it holds.

Choose love over fear for beyond fear lies freedom. By mastering our fears, we become courageous and trusting. If we don't consistently push ourselves, fear will creep back in.

Reality Check!! Keep our nose out of the future.

- Consider changing to a different compound. Intermediate Tyre.

Doves There Goes the Fear ♫

I hope I don't get annoyed ...

Anger

Our Anger wants to Protect us!

Anger is a warning light on our dashboard indicating: Stop!
It's natural for us to react or respond to a situation, whether it is acceptable or not, anger tells us whether we like or dislike what is being presented to us.

We may find ourselves in situations where someone has taken us for granted, or said something hurtful, insulting or offensive enough to overstep our **boundaries** (215). By nature, we may feel angry, by way of feeling irritated, annoyed or cross. These emotions are often evident to others through our body language, posture, facial expressions, or the tone of our voice. These cues can communicate that we are not in agreement, and we do not endorse or tolerate the other persons behaviour. Often, this alone is enough for them to change their actions. If our body language isn't enough and we need to be vocal; it's healthy to express our disapproval. This supports what our 'angry' feelings are telling us and allows the irritation, annoyance, crossness or displeasure to be addressed, rather than be silently seething.

Healthy anger is often in response to valid concerns we have present dangers. It likes to jump in and take over our minds and hearts sometimes leading us to act on impulse. When something strongly disagrees with us, it triggers angry feelings and emotional discomfort. Through our emotions, we begin to assess, and learn to measure, what is right or wrong, what is welcome or unwanted, and what we are willing to tolerate. This is how we learn about our boundaries and our limitations. Anger is a responsive emotion. If it's left to fester, it can become toxic, consuming our thoughts, feelings, and behaviours, in inappropriate, irrational ways. This distorts our judgement and results in unhealthy, negative anger.

"Anger is an acid that can do more harm to the vessel in which it is stored than to anything on which it is poured." Mark Twain

Do we tend to dismiss anger, fear it, or prioritise pleasing others? There are many who proudly declare...

"I'm not an angry person – I don't get angry."
As a therapist, this informs me that they likely have few boundaries!

It is normal to flow through a range of emotions in a single day. It's healthy to come across situations we're unhappy with, even if we still have to go through them.

Anger is also a cultural tool. Different races and communities are allowed or expected to express anger in various ways, while others are rewarded for suppressing it. What society deems appropriate can depend greatly on gender and cultural norms. There are many cultures including our own 'western' culture struggles with anger, while establishing a clear divide between men and woman.

In general, society allows men to express their anger through hostility and aggression, while it's considered inappropriate for men to cry or be emotionally vulnerable. On the other hand, it is more socially acceptable for woman to cry or express sadness than to be openly angry. If we were raised in a household where anger was unacceptable, we likely learned to discount or suppress this emotion.

As we mature, we continue to feel a full range of emotions. However, we may minimise or mask our true feelings with softer words to conform to societal norms.

For example, we might say,

"I'm upset……but the truth is: I'm actually furious."

What underlying emotion drives the feelings we express?

It's often easier to say we're, *"upset"*, rather than admit we're angry.

A common generalisation is that men express anger when they're actually scared, and woman express sadness when they're feeling angry. These stereotypes reflect broader cultural expectations around emotion and gender.

In relationships, we choose to minimalise or deflect our true feelings creating confusion and miscommunication. Avoiding honest conversations, builds barriers to understanding each other.

> Anger acts as a signal, helping us identify and
> protect our boundaries.

Amerie 1 Thing (instrumental) ♪
McAlmont & Butler Yes ♫

iHope

I hope I can find a way to ground myself ...

Right Here, Right NOW

Past Verses the Future

Dashboard The Green Light indicates: All Clear!

"If you've got one foot in the future and one foot in the past, you're pissing on the present. Be in the moment!" RuPaul

In the present we have our perceptions, mechanisms, thoughts, behaviours, beliefs and feelings that exist in the now. When we find ourselves stuck, swinging between feelings of fear and sadness, it's usually a sign we're no longer in the present.

When we're skipping ahead of ourselves, away from reality into the future that hasn't happened; fantasising, making predictions, assumptions, expectations, second-guessing others, role playing, visualising speaking for others, psyching ourselves up, or feeling insecure, helpless, and anxious, (plus adding a touch of catastrophising to the mix too), this recipe inevitably stirs up feelings of fear.

When we spend too much time thinking about the past, wandering down memory lane, reminiscing, or feeling guilty, ashamed, inadequate, stupid, or depressed, this tends to arouse emotions tied to sadness. Our past serves as a reference point in life. Sometimes life can only be understood by looking backwards, not as a hammock to rest in, to use as a springboard to launch from.

It isn't helpful to keep staring into the rear-view mirror of life, constantly reminding ourselves that we've tripped up. It was a lesson, not a life sentence. Replaying events holds us back. If we stay grounded in the present, the sadness and fear we were feeling will dissolve. They cannot survive in the NOW. Future-based fears and past hurts are deactivated in the present, they lose their power over us.

When we catch ourselves drifting into future or past thoughts, we need to ground ourselves and snap back to the present. We can do this by focussing on our breath, spending time in nature, or a getting quality sleep. There's so much to gain being fully present.

When we are present, we have nothing to judge or compare from the past, we only have now.

If we can recognise that we have the power to control our feelings by being present, we can embrace a state of mind that is open, confident, and non-judgmental. When something captures our attention and keeps us engaged, we're pulled into the present. Certain activities that require focus, like, exercising, following an instructor, driving, writing, studying, dancing, meditating, or teaching, naturally draw us back to the present!

In practice, Miles, 26, struggled to remain present, constantly overwhelmed by anxious and fear about the future. After ending a relationship and losing touch with his friends, he found himself back at home, worried about limited personal space and tensions with his brother.

While working through some of his issues, I introduced him to a grounding exercise that uses all five senses - sight, smell, taste, touch, and hearing, to help him stay present throughout the day.
This technique can be used any place, at any time. anywhere.

Grounding Exercise

- Sit in a comfortable chair, relax and allow ourselves to be fully supported or we can take a walk-in nature.
- Takes a few deep breaths, in through the nose, out through the mouth.
- Roll our shoulders back and forth. Let's begin.
- Look around, what do we see? Keep looking.
- As We observe, listen, what do we hear? Keep listening.
- While looking and listening, notice, what can we smell? Keep breathing it in.
- Whilst we are looking, listening, smelling, what can we taste? Keep tasting.
- Whilst we are looking, listening, smelling and tasting. And finally, what can we feel in our hands? Keep feeling.
- Continue to engage all our senses simultaneously for at least five minutes.

We have reached our destination...Now!!

Each time Miles grounded himself, he noticed that his doubts and fears went away when he was present. Whenever those helpless feelings resurfaced, he realised he had veered off track, into the daydream lane. Grounding brought him back, his anxiety and fear ceased, and he felt more in control and in the here and now. He felt empowered by recognising, that the past had gone, the future had not yet happened, and the present is all we truly have.

The past is a place of reference, not residence. Being present is where life happens. Occasionally, it's helpful to pause and reflect. The following exercise encourages us to stop, think and learn, keeping the past and future in perspective, otherwise the past and future are irrelevant.

Postcard Reflection Exercise

Let's write ourselves two postcards.
1. **Reflection** – If we could go back and speak to our younger self, what advice would we give?
2. **Forward** – Name one thing we would like to achieve in the future?

One postcard may feel more impactful than the other. Keep them until our goal is achieved or discard them when they are no longer useful.

Stay present, it's all we can control.

- Consider changing to a different compound. Wet Tyre.

Alexia Chellun The Power is Here Now ♪

I hope I can understand what I am feeling ...

M.O.T.

Emotional Maintenance

Dashboard The Green Light indicates: All Clear!

If we are struggling to understand how we are feeling, it is likely that we will struggle to meet our needs.
Some of us are not as emotionally intelligent as others, believing we only experience emotions such as hunger, tiredness, happiness and unhappiness, or simply label them as pleasant or unpleasant.
Emotions come in seasons, and we can experience all four seasons in a single day if we're self-aware. It's no surprise we may struggle to recognise what we're feeling or when we're feeling it.

In practice, Ruben, 42, struggled to identify and express his emotions.
"It's such a shame, it limits our experience if we can't pinpoint what we're feeling if it's just generally 'pleasant' and 'unpleasant.'"

We're likely to struggle in relationships and experience a deep sense of unfulfillment, potentially failing to meet the needs required to sustain our emotional, mental, physical and spiritual wellbeing.

Our emotions nudge us towards action to prevent, protect, or to encourage something to happen again so we can repeat positive experiences.
For example, managing stress starts with identifying and expressing our emotions and uncovering their root cause. Only then can we respond and prevent repeat experiences.

As Regina, 32, explains,
"How can I tell people I'm upset, when I can't express or identify the emotion, whether I feel betrayed, disappointed, or humiliated when all I can identify is that it just feels generally unpleasant, or I say to my partner, 'I'm just upset'"
as opposed to;
"'I'm insulted', communication can seem confusing when there's no transparency."

Without recognising the richness of our emotions, we risk becoming invisible and being deprived of many things. When we are unaware or disconnected from our emotions, we lose depth in connection, communication, and personal fulfilment. Our emotions shape our identity. They guide our opinions, preferences, perspectives, decisions morals, values and choices in relationships. They offer a frame of reference that contributes to our uniqueness.

The following method helps us to understand and articulate our emotions by reflecting on the past week to summarise what has impacted our thoughts, behaviours and our outcomes.

Start by focusing on five core emotions: anger, sadness, hurt, fear and joy. Assign each emotion a score that represents a percentage of how strongly we have felt it throughout the week. The scores must collectively add up to 100%. Each emotion we relate to will depend on the events of our week. Our emotions stem from a variety of sources, including past experiences, present circumstances, future thoughts, or self-perception.

This percentage represents the intensity and duration of each emotions impact. If an emotion hasn't been felt, assign it a score of zero. Be 100% honest with ourselves, assessing and acknowledging these emotions.

This tool offers valuable feedback, it can help identify recurring emotional patterns or highlight what's going well in our lives. I like to call this process "Glo", inspired by **The Feelings Wheel** (231), created by Dr. Gloria Wilcox. Over time, various versions of the Feelings Wheel have been developed, tailored to different therapeutic approaches. While there are many adaptations, I find this version to be particularly effective in promoting self-awareness and emotional clarity.

Start by reviewing what has occurred during our week. Use the Feelings Wheel to check in emotionally and identify which emotions we resonate with most. Let this be our guide to reflect on the week emotionally. 'Glo' becomes our emotional reference point, offering a chance to pause, reflect and acknowledge:

"This is how I feel!"

All the categories are useful, they aren't labelled as good or bad, they are all equal.

By Inquiring, we can uncover our true feelings, as Mateo, 27, explains.
"Looking at a constellation of emotions, it's a bit of this and a bit of that why I'm feeling this way."

The five core emotions – anger, sadness, hurt, fear and joy can feel unsettling and impact our lives in different ways.

- **Anger** arises from displeasure or hostility, often feeling tense and overwhelming.
- **Sadness** may feel like giving up, heavy and despondent.
- **Hurt** is emotional pain, like a deep wound.
- **Fear** emerges from perceived threats or danger, causing anxiety or nervousness.
- **Joy** brings cheerfulness and positive energy.

Each of these emotions shapes our experience.

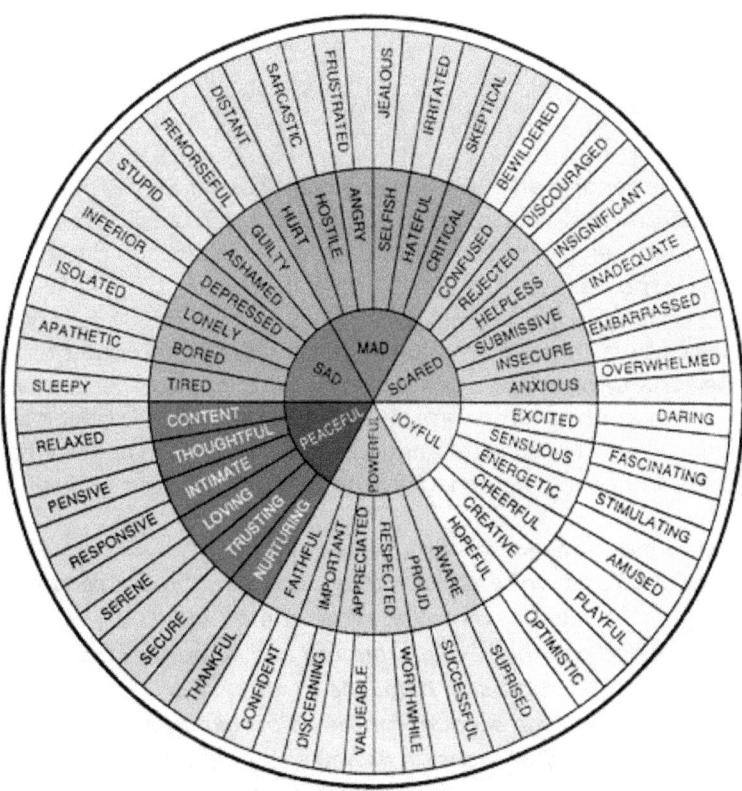

Figure 2. Feelings Wheel, *Dr. Gloria Wilcox.*

Here's an example of how we may score, there are no rules, just ensure the totals equal 100%.

Angry.	Sad.	Hurt.	Fear.	Joy	
20%	20%	20%	20%	20%	= 100%
25%	10%	0	35%	40%	= 100%

**These number are personal and private, and
you owe no one an explanation.**

Now, let's imagine an orchestra of emotions inside us. Our emotions are like a symphony of string instruments; the violin, viola, cello, double bass, and bass and the harp, each representing a core emotion.

- **Bass** = Anger
- **Violin** = Sadness
- **Double Bass** = Hurt
- **Cello** = Fear
- **Harp** = Joy

Our emotions perform an ever-changing composition. Some may linger like a low violin from an old hurt, while other, like a sudden burst of a cello, stretch over days. This metaphor allows us to track the duration and intensity of our emotional responses.

Each week, as we check in emotionally, each feeling contributes differently to our personal symphony. The tune changes with our experiences. Whether challenges, triumphs, moments of joy, reflection, or loss.
This method helps to regulate emotions, and allows us to assess whether a person, event or activity has a negative or positive impact on our wellbeing.

Gertie, 30, found the exercise helpful and insightful:
*"I'm very black and white, all or nothing, and sometimes I can have the worse day ever. When something
has happened and then I've discounted and ignored all the positive things, so it helps me to remember
those as well and I can account for the whole experience, otherwise I could just focus on having a terrible week."*

Here are some real-life examples:

Angry	Sad	Hurt	Fear	Joy
Bass Harp	**Violin**	**Double Bass**	**Cello**	**Harp**
10%	10%	20%	25%	35%

Angry: *"Train was cancelled."* (was an instant response – short).
Sad: *"Missed a long-awaited birthday party."*
Hurt: *"Argument with brother last year."* (still hurts, a small feeling that's constant and lingering).
Fear: *"Worried about exams next week"* (persistent build up all week).
Joy: *"BBQ and night out with friends"* (energising and uplifting for the week).

Angry	Sad	Hurt	Fear	Joy
Bass Harp	**Violin**	**Double Bass**	**Cello**	**Harp**
5%	5%	40%	15%	35%

Angry: *"Ungrateful drivers"* (road rage -fleeting, intense burst of anger).
Sad: *"England lost"* (short- lived, gutted feeling).
Hurt: *"Saw my ex with someone else, ignored me"* (deep burning distraction all week).
Fear: *"Presentation at work"* (small constant lingering feeling).
Joy: *"Parents babysat; slept well"* (Restoration and energy for the week).

Angry	Sad	Hurt	Fear	Joy
Bass Harp	**Violin**	**Double Bass**	**Cello**	**Harp**
30%	30%	30%	0%	10%

Angry: *"The love of my life has left me."*
Sad: *"I miss my love so much."*
Hurt: *"I love them."*
Fear: *"Numb."*
Joy: *"Children and the dog."*

This represents someone navigating grief, with equal measures of sadness, hurt and anger depending on the stage they are in.

This is a good start in identifying emotions and the reasons we feel this way.

Angry	Sad	Hurt	Fear	Joy	OK	
5%	15%	0%	0%	30%	50%	= 100%

Once we've mastered identifying these core feelings, we can expand the chart. Add a new emotion, or instrument, such as, 'OK' (neutral or balanced). Feeling 'OK' implies a sense of balance, we're satisfied, calm and without complaint.

Here's another version:

Angry	Sad	Hurt	Fear	Joy	iHope	
15%	0%	5%	10%	30%	40%	= 100%

iHope helps us to keep focus on long-term goals like a new project, saving for a home, preparing a marathon or working toward personal growth.

Whatever the numbers, they can act as emotional markers. Over several weeks, we may see patterns and cycles emerge, helping us to make better decisions or prevent emotional spirals.

This exercise helps us to recognise the impact situations have on us a, how long those feelings last, and how much emotional energy they consume.
An M.O.T serves as an emotional "oil change," helping to cleanse and maintain our emotional engines for optimal performance and well-being.

Don't wait for the **bricks!** (167)

Time to load up the tyres and hammer the throttle, we can get a fastest lap in.
- Consider changing to a different compound tyre. Red Tyres.

Mr Fingers Can Your Feel It (instrumental) 🎵

End of Racing!

I hope I can hold it in ...

Liquid Truth

Tears Water the Soul!

Dashboard The Purple Light indicates: Action Required! 🟣
Check Rear View Mirror!

When was the last time we cried?

To cry is a strength, not a weakness. it requires openness, vulnerability and courage to engage with the pain in our hearts and to accept and surrender to our hurt and sadness.

It is healthy to release emotions. When our body has been storing pressure and sadness, crying is a release, it is a purge. Crying washes away unwanted toxic chemicals out of our bodies to preventing them from affecting our stress hormones. Shedding tears is healthy for our mind, body and soul. Whether we cried last week, last year or for whatever reason we can't remember, I encourage every human being to shed tears. On average, for women, once every season and men, at least two to three times a year. We keep our physical health in check going to the gym, we maintain our mental health with a therapist, shedding tears is a spiritual workout that allows our souls to breathe.

It's important to clear our windscreens so we don't lose our way or end up in a cul-de-sac. As adults, we learn to park our feelings, waiting for a convenient and appropriate time to express them. If we put our emotions on hold for too long, they can mature and manifest into something much bigger than they originally were.

There's a lot we can learn from toddlers. If we take the time to observe how they emotionally regulate, we'll notice they don't they don't manipulate their emotions or wait for a convenient time to cry, they respond in the moment. For example, an infant experience something that triggers an emotion, their entire body expresses it authentically and completely. When they feel sadness, they screw their face up and physically fall to the side, surrendering their posture to the feelings. They make as much noise as they need to, sobbing, bawling, or wailing and so on.

We are no different. We feel the same emotions that children do, they feel what we feel; we're just older. Their authentic expression is something we can learn to emulate, even if only in the privacy of our own home. We've been conditioned to disregard our emotions, understandably so, in public spaces, yet how long we delay them is what becomes problematic. Often, when we don't cry, it may be because keeping the memory alive feels comforting. Not crying might mean they are still part of our process with no closure.

Whatever stirs our soul, whether it's a memory of a loved one, a photo, a super sad film that makes us weep uncontrollably, or reminiscing over an old text, anything that encourages the tear-triggering stage, please indulge.

The Ugly Cry

To achieve this exercise, create a safe place where we can be vulnerable, with no interference or distractions at hand, and relax.

Slowly, take a few deep breaths to get in touch with those hurts. When the feelings come up and our tears begin to flow, that's the opportune time to give it our best shot. Be as authentic as we can in that moment, let's get our shoulders involved, or even our whole body, and let it out. Let the hurt out. Let it go. Shoo it out the door, and slam the door shut until next time.

The exercise will last as long as we need, perhaps up to five minutes, or more. This allows us to connect with our inner being and surrender to all the pent-up emotion we've been carrying and storing. It helps us to release our hurts, unblock our energies, and allow our spirit space to breathe with ease and re-energise our souls.

It's a guarantee, once those irritations and hurts have been released, we will sleep like a babe tonight. It's natural to release, to let go and to water our soul.

Remember, we're not made of sugar.
We won't dissolve away!

◉ Consider changing to a different compound. Wet Tyre.
Time to get the fastest lap in!

Take That & Sigma Cry ♫

I hope I know when I will start ...

Process

Thoughts and Emotions

Dashboard The Green Light indicates: All Clear!
Every result is shaped by the process!
Each person's process is unique. We may find that the plans in our heads aren't matching our behaviour, or we have a delayed reaction; decision-making is not on cue, we're time wasting, or we leave everything to the last minute.

Everything, our thoughts, feelings, behaviours and actions is all connected to our process. Our process has its own unique and individual pattern; our pattern doesn't change, until we become aware of it. Our process is there for us to learn about how we tick. Knowing and understanding our process will empower and boost our confidence.

Sequence

Everyone has their own unique process.

To process, we all must 'work through' our own individual sequence before we come out the other side. Like washing the laundry, there are no shortcuts. There are several different cycles before the laundry is clean and dry, and ready to go. Our process works on the same principle.

When we are in the midst of processing, we may think more, or think less; be more emotional or less emotional; eat more or eat less, sleep better or experience sleeplessness, be in-active, or over-active. There are certain behaviours we must go through before we reach the destination.

Procrastination (135) may be part of our pattern, finding all those tasks we haven't considered doing for years suddenly attractive, or we reach for our tenth cup of tea in a morning instead of making a start. Avoidance and ignoring may be part of inaction, where we find ourselves doing nothing. It might seem lazy; maybe our spirit needs to be still or perhaps we've frozen, busy doing chores for others. Or, to stay on the run we visit the hairdressers at midnight (that's a new one on me) anything to keep us from making a start.

What is our process?

Whatever the sequence, recognise, there are steps we take, a similar sequence each time. Once we get to know our process, we'll know where we are in our process. Whether we are halfway through, or near the end, either way we must go through our process. This counteracts anxiety and stress once we understand how we tick, we can allow enough time and space accordingly.

Work through our process, be assured we are moving. Even the micro steps count. We are moving, getting closer to reaching the other side.

Ready, steady and Go!

- Consider switching to a different compound. Hard Tyre.

Whitney Houston Step by Step ♪

I hope exercising can become a part of my life ...

Exercise

Not a Punishment but a Privilege!

Dashboard The Yellow Light Indicates: Pick Up Pace!
Exercise is the one thing we immediately regret not doing, and never regret doing. Exercise maintains our health and it is a privilege to be able to move our body and stay comfortably mobile.

Exercise is a sooner or later approach.

We need to include exercise in our lives, to keep our minds and bodies healthy.
There are many different exercises to help achieve different outcomes. One type of exercise that is particularly effective in boosting our serotonin, dopamine and oxytocin levels is cardiovascular exercise. It helps to dispel negative energy, manage our stress, anger and anxieties, and in turn, it improves our sleep.

End of Racing!

Movement is medicine. It makes us feel good, feeds us positivity, helps us stay grounded and keeps us sane. When we're exercising and pushing with effort, we've no time to think about our troubles or negativity, we're only in the moment trying to get through the last five minutes or five seconds still breathing. Unfortunately, we live a very different lifestyle compared to our ancestors.

We live in a culture that endorses an unhealthy lifestyle; most of us sit all day to earn a living, which can cause poor posture and poor breathing, and obesity, unlike our ancestors who were constantly on the move as hunter gatherers.

Let's get out of our heads and into our bodies. Let's leave our worries and woes alone for forty minutes and find an exercise we can fall in love with. Once we've found it, keep it, and maintain it throughout our life. If it's a hobby that incorporates exercise, this can also contribute as long as we remain consistent. It's an incredible feeling to kill our old statistics and create new, better and healthier workout results, especially if we're regularly exercising, committed to a program, and tracking our progression.

Time to shed the old one and embrace the new!

The Fifteen

We can all take 15 minutes out of our day to keep up with our physical health. This is a convenient exercise we can squeeze into our daily schedules without too much disruption to our day.

Marcoco calls, *'The Fifteen'* This requires sprinting for fifteen minutes on a treadmill (only), at zero incline. if pauses are necessary, we can catch breath for 30 second intervals only. This continues until our fifteen minutes are up. Try to beat our longest stretch of non-stop sprinting within the entire 15 minutes. Most people's first score is around 1 minute 10 seconds, and they work up from there to whatever goal they want to aim for.

This activity allows us to track progress and set our personal bests with each session. We can challenge ourselves to beat our last score. Some would call this workout interval training. It's a great way to get fit, build stamina and endurance, and enjoy a quick endorphin release to start the day. *'The Fifteen'* was created for busy people on the move, flying from one continent to another, where exercise often became the first thing to drop off the list.

To consider this activity, we must have reached a certain level of fitness, with no joint injuries, or heart problems. Always consult your doctor before starting.

We all need to exercise, it's like clearing out the exhaust pipes of a car. It's essential that we maintain good health, or else Mother Nature will quickly creep up on us and accelerate the ageing process. If we miss a class, don't worry, one exercise class is better than none. We are all slowly deteriorating, and our genes will also play their part in the aging process. When we reach the ageing bracket, we find we need to spend more time exercising regularly throughout the week to maintain bone density, muscle, and balance, all of which help to sustain a good quality of life.

Keep showing up for ourselves.

Genes load the gun, and the environment pulls the trigger!

🌑 Consider changing to a different compound. Medium Tyre.
Time to load up the tyres and hammer the throttle, we can get a fastest lap in.

Marshall Jefferson & Solardo Move your Body 🎵

I hope this outcome doesn't swallow me up …

Positive Mindset

Seek the Positive

Dashboard The Green Light indicates: All Clear!
When something bad happens and we're left with a negative outcome, it's so easy to fall into negative self-talk, to criticize and tear ourselves down. Instead of focusing on the bad, seek out the positive, rather than letting those negative vibes swallow us up, drain our motivation and soak up all our good energy.

Our thoughts create our world and what we focus on grows. Hence, it's better not to dwell on stuff, it's over, it's done! Go straight to the positive, and get pro-active, if we can't fix or resolve it, check out other options, make different choices and if that's unreachable, don't stress! Let it go and move on.

Protecting our peace is crucial!

Zahra, 36, a mother of two young sons under 4, found herself struggling the night before an event, as she began packing for the weekend.

> " I don't know what to wear anymore because I don't go out in the evening now; I've no idea what a 36-yr old woman wears? I wanted to know what everyone else was wearing because I didn't feel confident, or know the places we were going, are they for casual or glam?" "There was a WhatsApp group to information to interact with everyone; I found it overwhelming and didn't bother. I just threw some things in a case and told myself it was going to be awful, I wasn't going to enjoy it, and I'd feel uncomfortable and out of place. Everybody else will be skinny and excited to be away, I'm going to be the boring one!"

as she was dropped off by her partner.

By the end of the weekend, it was a cruel awakening. Zahra's great at planning for her sons and poor at prioritising herself. She summarised her weekend as awful. Subconsciously, she had set herself up for an awful weekend, and that's exactly what she got! Focusing on all her insecurities, comparing herself, feeling trapped, powerless, and not good enough. Zahra had all the power over her entire being how she thinks, feels and behaves. Instead, she gave it away by not taking care of herself, not planning, comparing herself in ways that fed her insecurities. We have the power to be in charge of ourselves, and that makes a difference to the outcome. That's the power of our minds.

A positive mindset is everything!

Considering Zahra's experience, she learned:

- Avoid assuming the worst. Stay positive.
- Allow ourselves time to prevent panic and anxiety.
- Take time to create a plan.
- Gather the necessary information to make informed decisions.
- Reconnect with social activities and friends to rebuild confidence.
- If we're feeling trapped, take the car have an exit plan.
- Keep the experience positive, and leave when it starts to fade.

Zahra learned so much from her experience; to trust and take care of herself, and to keep a positive mindset.

"I'm going to have a good time!"

Instead of *"I'm going to hell, and I've thrown away the keys.",* (not so helpful.)

From another perspective, it's helpful to find positive meaning in a situation or what's happened to us, to reason with it. Optimism drives resilience, which often leads to more opportunities, allowing us to springboard to bigger and better outcomes that we hadn't considered.

Let go of what we can't control and focus on the present, and what we can control. We can't control the past; its already gone. However, we can take control and pay attention to now, what we can do to move forward and get back on our feet again.

We may encounter defeats; however, they can become detours to life's unexpected opportunities, not dead ends.

A positive and calm mind can handle any situation!

Leave what's passed in the rear-view mirror and stay on track!!
- Consider switching to a different compound. Hard Tyre.

Time to overtake using DRS.

Sounds Of Blackness Optimistic ♬

I hope I can make the most of my time …

Time

To Live our Best Lives is to know Time is Finite!

Time waits for no one.

Time is a precious resource we can't control or buy. Our forever friend when were younger, can become our fiercest enemy in our later years.

We perceive time in different way: if time's flying, we're either too busy or having fun: if we are distraught or in despair, time stands still. When we are grieving, time can play its part in softening the edges of reflection, blurring the intensity of certain hurts, making them seem easier to bear.

As time moves forward, we must acknowledge that we can't afford to take it for granted. For example,

> *"I hate this job, but I've only got another 10 years before
> I retire so I'll hang on..."*

Security aside, tomorrow is not guaranteed, let alone an entire decade.

Is it worth wasting ten years doing something we don't enjoy?
Time also applies to grudges. The longer someone holds onto a grudge, the less justifiable it becomes. it's a waste of time. Our relationships with time will inevitably change over the years. Life is short. When we're young we take time for granted; as it slips away, we learn to respect and value it, especially when we realise how little of it, we may have left.
Time's running out.

We must appreciate the time we're given, enjoy every moment, and do everything we want to do, because we never know what's going to happen. Don't wait!
Creed from Rocky III once said,
"There is no tomorrow!"

Time is precious and can be so easily wasted, especially on social media. Each day spent on social media equates to accumulated time over the course of a year.
We are trading with the most valuable asset we have, and that's the minutes of our lives:

- 1hr a day = 15 days in a year.
- 2hrs = 30 days.
- 3hrs = 45 days.
- 4hrs = 61 days.
- 5hrs = 76 days.
- 6hrs = 91 days.
- 7hrs = 106 days.

For those that aren't punctual, regularly late, or think it's acceptable or even fashionable to be late, time isn't waiting for us. Time is not on our terms. Every person we delay or keep waiting loses time from their lives because of us. Do we know how much time we have?

Time is the only currency we spend without knowing our balance.

Respect the tick tock of time!

AMC Time 🎵

I hope I can survive ...

Rock Bottom

The Awakening

Dashboard The Purple Light indicates: Action Required! 🟣
Check Rear View Mirror!
Rock bottom happens when we crash!

"Sometimes when you're in a dark place you think you've been buried, but you've actually been planted." Christine Caine

From time to time we may experience a meltdown, emotional outbursts that fizzles out. 'Rock Bottoms' are different. There are the 'rock bottoms' when our body shuts down and we stop functioning, or the more common type of 'rock bottom ', which happens when our mood just drops, everything drops and the sound we hear is the bottom of the barrel being scratched.

Alice, 38, expressing her experience of hitting her rock bottom.
*"You don't want to go out to socialise, you stop caring about a lot of things, or having the motivation to reach out and do stuff, you feel you've lost your way and the urge to help yourself is just not there.
That 'push' to be able to give yourself 'a good talking to' isn't there, and you feel you can't pull yourself out of it, knowing you need to talk to someone, need to do something different and find out what's going on in your head to find the source just isn't there."*

These are someone else's words, if we relate to how this person was feeling: We will survive it.
We all have a rock bottom, and it's important we know what that rock bottom tastes, feels, smells, and looks like in case we 'trip up' on life again. We will recognise what's familiar, allowing us to know where we're heading. This gives us the opportunity to act sooner, and prevent it happening the second time, rather than falling down that rabbit hole again. Our personal experience will always be a useful tool allowing us to use that experience as something to measure by, monitor and understand.

Noah, 35, had experienced hitting his rock bottom. After separating from his partner his self-development journey helped him through his adversities. He got to know himself, learning to meet his needs, and felt renewed, strong, and empowered.

> "I've been there, I know what to do to come out of there, and it didn't kill me!"

Rock bottoms can be seen as a spiritual breakthrough. Sometimes we need to go right back to zero to start again, to get off the road that was not serving us well and begin laying solid groundwork. This, in turn brings change, which then leads to growth.

Living a life that supports neglect, abuse, drama, and pleasing others, or living as though we're not even in our own picture frame, are just some examples that are likely to take us to rock bottom. Hitting rock bottom can lead us to discover meaning, purpose, and the opportunity to prioritise ourselves. It's a chance to refill our cup and get our lives back on track.

Our feelings won't kill us. It's the dark, crooked irrational thoughts or voices in our heads we need to keep in check. Our thoughts are not reality, and when we buy into the belief that they are, life can shrink, usually when we're at rock bottom. We may not be feeling much, just a glimmer of hope that shows us the way.

Our feelings are like the dashboard of a car, they provide feedback and notify us, helping us assess, respond, judge, warn, and protects ourselves from life's dramas. This experience can strengthen us with the confidence of knowing.

> *"That's where I was, and that's what happens sometimes in life. I can do this again; I can survive this and recover."*

It can make us feel bulletproof to life.
Life is all about endings and beginnings, over and over again, however big or small. It's like climbing a mountain, coming down, and seeing the next mountain to climb. If we've not learned to take full responsibility for our lives, life will keep sending us the same experiences to get our attention, urging us to learn and get back in the race of life.

Don't stress! In the grand scheme of things, the world will keep spinning. We might have been overtaken, or even lapped, we're all on our own journey. **Life's not for the swift.**

Enjoy getting back on track, knowing ourselves better than we did before. We've acquired new tools to recover and understand how we tick, focusing on our needs instead of our wants. These times can be significant for us.

> All our experiences, no matter how awful they appear
> to be, are temporary.

There is value in suffering!!
No matter how bad things are, or how bad we feel, keep going. We won't feel this way forever. This a chapter in our lives, not a life sentence.

DONT GIVE UP!!!... We're just getting started!

🔘 Consider changing to a different compound. Intermediate Tyre. Time to change to fresher rubber to gain advantage for the undercut. The purple light is flashing on the dashboard.

(If we start thinking dark thoughts, seek medical help)

Lewis Capaldi Survive ♪

I hope I can calm myself down anytime, anywhere in real time …

Breathing

Inhale Hope and Exhale Doubt

Dashboard The Blue Light indicates: Leisurely Slow the Pace Down!

The power of breathing to improve our wellbeing is a remarkably effective tool to use.
Breathing can help to relieve stress and anxiety and make us feel calmer and more composed, when done correctly. Most of us breathe shallowly into our chests, which in turn stresses us out creating more anxiety and even panic attacks. We can change our health simply by changing how we breathe.

Most of us are breathing in a dysfunctional way, we are breathing through our mouths, which bypasses our natural filter system that helps prevent dust and other particles from entering the body. When we inhale, we suck in our stomachs, which is unhealthy for our lungs and lower organs. If we are stressed, or anxious we tend to hold our breath, and this can lead to various chronic conditions later in life.
To prevent further problems or health conditions, here's a better way of

taking in oxygen to keep our cells alive, and breathing out carbon dioxide efficiently: Place a hand on our abdomen feel the expansion of our stomach and breathe in. Then exhale, allowing our stomach to return inward. Next, place a hand on our chest, inhale to feel the expansion begin in the stomach and rise into our chest, then slowly exhale as the chest lowers again.

It's important to pay attention to how we breathe life into our body. Once we've mastered how to breathe normally, we can try some breathing techniques that can reduce our stress, panic, and anxiety, helping us to cope, ground and centre ourselves in real time.

3-4-5

An easy exercise to do anytime, anyplace, anywhere, with or without others around us, in public or private, that is suitable for any environment and uses three easy numbers to remember if we're ever in a panicky situation,

- Breathe in for **three** seconds.
- Hold our breath for **four** seconds.
- Breathe out for **five** seconds...and repeat.

Box breathing

This technique can help to clear the mind, calm the body, and refocus. It's based on the count of four each time. Some people find it helpful to imagine drawing a square box in the air, in front of them, using forefinger. We can choose to keep our eyes open or closed, whatever feels most comfortable. Each count of four represents one line of the box, continue until our box is complete. Repeat until we reach a calm state.

- Breathe **in** and draw our line for **four** seconds.
- **Hold** our breath for **four** seconds.
- Breath **out** for **four** seconds.
- **Pause** for **four** seconds...and repeat.

On the Double

This breathing technique uses a double deep breath to help de-stress and calm the body down in real time.
1. Inhale a big, deep breath through the nose until our lungs are full.

2. Sneak a little more air for our second inhale before exhaling.
3. Slowly exhale through our mouth until our lungs are empty.

Take a breath, look what we can do for ourselves!
- Consider changing to a different compound. Wet Tyre. Time to get a fastest lap in.

Ariana Grande Breathin' ♫

I hope I have a healthy relationship with my money ...

Financially Faithful or Unfaithful

Money Talks!

Money exists to save, spend or invest; money is powerless without us. It's our choices that give money its purpose and direction. We are the ones who control how it's used, whether to create security or opportunities for our enjoyment. Only we control what we do with our money.
We control our money!

I have observed many who shy away from discussing money, because of its connection to power, control and identity. Our friends, colleagues, partners, even parents often avoid the topic altogether. Yet, money remains deeply intertwined with our lives and relationships.
It's time to talk money!

When we think about relationships, we often think of people, not our relationship with money. Yet we all have one. Whether we are friends with our money, estranged from it, constantly chasing it, or stuck in a dysfunctional cycle, money influences our lives deeply.

What our parent's teach us about spending and saving shapes our relationship with money as adults, leaving a lasting impact on how we navigate financial decisions. Where there is money, there is always a relationship, or a situationship at play.
Now we've established the relationship, let's explore the power money holds in our lives. Money represents far more than currency, it symbolizes security,

freedom, and opportunity. It threads through every aspect of our lives, providing for our basic needs, and enabling choices, and opening doors or creating obstacles. This makes it a powerful force in our lives. Nowadays, a new dimension has. emerged: invisible money. Invisible money has changed how we spend. In the past, physical cash made it easy to track our spending and stop when it was gone. Today, a simple **'ping'** detaches us from our finances, making overspending effortless.

How do we keep track of our invisible money and understand the value of money when our pockets are empty, and we're spent?

Money carries emotional weight. It influences our sense of self-worth, status, and belonging. It touches nearly every decision we make.
Debt creates obstacles that drain us and redefine us as a statistic. It acts like a sponge, soaking up our power and leaving us feeling helpless and insecure. It brings toxic emotions that make facing our truth difficult. It breeds fear, and fear breeds anxiety, shame and anger. These emotions chip away at our self-esteem, confidence and pride, keeping us trapped in a cycle where debt becomes a shameful secret.

Temptations to spend are everywhere, especially on our public image. Image brings kudos, credit, and power, as well as lead to overspending to fit in, belong, or gain approval. Peer pressure and feelings of inadequacy often drive these choices, pushing us to use money to compensate or validate ourselves.

"Why do I want the latest trainers or a trip to Ibiza with my mates?"

Power dressing shows how much our outward appearance matters. It can distract from how we truly feel inside, both to others and ourselves. Money temps us to define our worth through external symbols – houses, cars, clothes, shoes, watches or holidays.
We can be lured into a false sense of security, believing our external world can fill the void within us. Yet our souls don't thrive on material things. Our souls seek simplicity connection and meaning. While buying something new may offer a quick fix or instant gratification, the high fades, the sensation dissipates, and the cycle repeats – KERCHING!

These things can make us feel valued and validated. The more attractive we seem, the more attention we attract, and the more we crave it. There is often a deeper reason behind our financial struggles, emotions and patterns we may have overlooked. Understanding these feelings is key to breaking free from the cycle and rebuilding our relationship with money. If we are someone who gets into debt because we overspend, there will be reasons behind our behaviour.

We may be big spenders, with deep pockets overly generous, with big personalities and tendency to be impulsive. We may act before we think and do the same with money. We may overspend because we feel lonely or bored and the initial temporary pick-me-up, or retail therapy, keeps us distracted from sadness, grief or depression. If we've experienced abandonment in the past, we might seek security in expensive items rather than in people, who may feel less reliable or more likely to leave us in this way.

Money becomes a mirror, reflecting our values, priorities and insecurities, if we believe,

I'm not good enough.
I'm not important.
I'm unlovable.

Does money make us feel important, loved, or enough?

Our insecurities often dictate how frequently we flex that credit card, yet this behaviour won't create lasting change in how we feel. Materialism can't heal, repair or validate our emotions indefinitely. Money alone won't make us feel whole or fulfilled. To break the cycle, it's important to educate ourselves, understand our needs versus wants, and make informed decisions about money.

What if we paused before reaching for the latest trainers?

Take a moment to check in with ourselves and ask:

Which emotions are driving us to spend?

The relationship we have with money is deeply emotional. Money speaks to us through our feelings, and our emotional wellbeing often dictates how we spend. To stop debt, we must break free from seeking external validation and neglecting our inner needs. We must first connect with our emotions.

Overcoming emotional and financial debt is empowering. By understanding the emotions driving our relationship with money, we can take control and manage it more wisely.

Money talks but our emotions speak louder!

- 🟢 Consider changing to a different compound. Soft Tyre.

Koelle The Void 🎵

End of Racing!

I hope I can let go and enjoy light-hearted fun ...

Playful Story wheel

Opening up to Possibilities

Dashboard The Yellow Light Indicates: Pick Up Pace!
Story wheels invite us to be playful, to leave the stresses of our lives behind and simply escape into a story.

Using creative theatrical techniques can help liberate our playfulness. We create a story together, typically in a group of ten people, where one person says two or three lines, then the next person picks it up and develops the story further as it goes around the group.

Here's an exercise that's frequently used in drama and storytelling for acting and improvisation. If we didn't have a script, we would work with someone and create something out of nothing. Someone would say something and that would be called 'an offer'. We would have to accept the offer and believe the truth of what's being said to develop it further.

The goal is to consistently nurture the creation of the lie, the fantasy, to embrace the playfulness.

"What if...?"
"Anything is possible...?"

The intention is liberation.
The story wheel helps to liberate our thinking and encourage playfulness. It is a fun way of learning how to play, embracing new possibilities and experiencing a sense of freedom.
To start, create a story together with a friend or partner. Using ourselves as the character, whatever age or stage in life, there are no rules.
We can have as many superpowers as we like and be as disposable as we wish. Fabricate a story that is not serious, a-non-productive story where everything in it has to be a lie. Be as outrageous as we like, the more ridiculous, the better. The story can last for up to 15-30 minutes each time.

Both players will engage in the process and soon find themselves properly laughing out loud together, in fits of laughter.

Go for it, release the playful energy and have fun!!

The Allman Brothers Band Jessica ♪

I hope I can show I care ...

Our Condolences

Reaching out to the Bereaved

Death comes to us all, the uninvited guest when we least expect it.

If we know of someone close to us who is bereaved and we're not comfortable with emotions, or we've never experienced a loss of a loved one. Here's an idea of how they may feel a peep into their world that's come crashing down.

As Gracie explains,
"It's like looking out the window and always seeing a building that's there and then all of a sudden it's gone, as though part of the landscape has been removed..."

According to Emerson, 41,
*"Grief is love with nowhere to go! It can't be put anywhere so it pulls in the corners of your eyes and the
lump in your throat..."*

Or, Jerome, 39, shares,
"Grief on the inside can feel like a burden, relentless, tiresome and it hits you like truck. It's difficult adjusting from your normal everyday routine to find your world had just been flipped upside down and you feel lost, like paralysis where nothing's moving and everything is still, this is part of the process of grief ..."

Grief feels unspeakable and beyond reckoning, it can feel like the deceased has taken the future away from us, we must learn how to live
a different existence without them.

I've experienced those who struggle to empathise or comprehend the situation, and they don't reach out. They want to help or support, but don't know how to. Under no circumstances dither, procrastinate or avoid, deny, or ignore reaching out. If we are scared of saying the wrong thing, or we don't know what to say,

it's okay. Reach out.

This is a shocking time for everyone, especially the bereaved. There is no excuse. It is better to communicate in words or gestures than to communicate with inaction or deafening silence.

In the initial stages of their grief, they won't be judging us, they are devastated, shocked, numb, heartbroken. They will be so grateful and appreciative of some effort rather than no effort at all.

In practice, I have seen many, who have shared their lived experience of grief. On reflection, their brethren, or members of their tribe holding their silence exacerbates the initial feelings of abandonment and loss. They feel outcast or alone in their grief.

The Key Practices

- Pay a short visit to see them.
- Spend some time with them.
- Take them out of the house, even if they don't speak.
- Stop by to give them a hug and leave.
- Phone them.
- Send a text.
- Send a voicemail.
- Send an email.
- Write a note.
- Post a card.
- Send flowers or a gift.
- Leave a plant on their doorstep.
- Bring food, drink, chocolates, or whatever else they like.
- If we draw, knit, crochet, paint, leave a small gesture to say, "I'm thinking of you," *"I'm here," "if you need anything..."*, or even *"I don't know what to say!"*

Even if we don't know how they're feeling and struggle to understand, we are reaching out to show we care, in our way.

Say something, anything is better than nothing!

I hope I can take care of my health ...

Medicine v Medication

Use food as Medicine before Medicine becomes our Food

Dashboard The Green Light indicates: All Clear!

Health is the foundation of everything.
When it comes to nutrition, our health is our wealth. We have to consider a 360-degree approach regarding all aspects of our health.

Movement, nutrition, thoughts, beliefs, wellness, what we choose to watch, and our environment all have an influence and a role to play when it comes to our health, good or bad. If we make unhealthy choices, we are likely to become unhealthy. That then leads to a myriad of conditions. For example, depression isn't always caused by trauma. Depression can be related to nutritional deficiencies in vitamin B, or vitamin D, or to mercury that's found in our environment which encourages inflammation of the brain.

In certain cultures, when we become unwell, it is expected that we go to a doctor, where we are likely to be administered drugs that we call medication, either for treatment, cure, or to prevent of the illness from spreading. By this point, we may not be able to consider an alternative approach. Understandably, not all of us have the choice. Some medication has its place, preferably for temporary use rather than long term. If we are taking medication for a lengthy period, it can lead to further complications.

Naturally, over time, our bodies become used to the dosage, which means the medication loses its potency, encouraging us to increase the dosage each time to achieve the same outcome. Repeating this cycle of medication makes our bodies dependent on it. The longer we are on the course of medication, the more likely it is that side effects will occur. Generally, all drugs bring a cocktail of side effects that can compound the original problem. This unhealthy cycle isn't working for many of us.

If we can catch it early enough, the alternative to medication could be food, herbs, and well-balanced meals, eating food that looks like food, meat, fish, vegetables, potatoes, rice, pulses, nuts and seeds. Avoid sugar, processed and ultra process foods, fast food, convenience foods, or any carbohydrates that come with barcodes. For many of us, this means going back to the source, making the time to cook our own food from scratch. Only then will we know what we are eating. If we consciously use food as our medicine, some conditions can become stagnant, cured, or reversed simply by eating the right nutrition. We can adapt what we eat to prevent certain deteriorations or conditions from occurring.

In practice, I would focus on my clients' problems as well as looking at their wellbeing, identifying nutritional deficiencies to change their diet based on the basic principles of food. For example, a client was feeling fatigued and run down. Their nutrition consisted solely of ready meals, which they would cook in the microwave, no fruit, or vegetables. They started cooking fresh food and well-balanced meals and turned their health around.

In practice, Harry, 21, who was struggling with a history of daily migraines throughout his teenage years. He was experiencing poor focus and concentration, stress and anxiety. When we explored his daily eating and drinking habits, he was only consuming two or three cups of tea a day. He had a history of bed wetting as a child, because of nocturnal enuresis his parents had conditioned him to drink very little. He quickly developed daily migraines, taking a substantial amount of medication to control the episodes. The truth was, he had outgrown nocturnal enuresis, yet his behavioural habits had not caught up with him. The dehydration had caused stress and anxiety that contributed to a barrier to studying. We increased his intake of fluid from one to two litres of water daily. He started recognising when he was thirsty, drinking one to two litres of water daily, and the migraines stopped within one week. He came off the medication. There are many other reasons and different remedies for migraines. People suffer with migraines for various reasons, it's not always so straight forward, however this made the difference for him.

We live in a world where convenience is key. We are seduced and enticed by brightly coloured packaging and trends like highly processed foods that drive our biology in many ways that aren't serving us well.

There is a myriad of herbal remedies from plant medicines that we can use to prevent and heal many symptoms and conditions.

What we put in our mouths is either fighting disease or feeding it. Eating nutritious foods makes a difference and will help the fight against diseases. If we understand the nutritional value in food, for instance, eating more calcium-dense foods protects our bones. It is important to increase the variety of different plants on our plate. Consider eating 30 different diverse plants a week in our diet, different colours, every nut and seed, with a little spice all help to improve our gut microbiome.

Microbiome is known as our gut brain, which is responsible for many aspects of our health, particularly our immune system. If we eat a high protein diet (unlimited amounts of meat, fish, cheese, eggs, and limited amounts of carbohydrates – pasta, potatoes, bread etc), the quicker our cell renewal, and the more muscle growth, which protects our joints. Complex carbohydrates, such as lentils, oats, brown rice, quinoa, vegetables, whole grains, nuts and beans, etc to help stabilise our blood sugars. Foods rich in fibre help protect our bowels. Plant foods that are rich in phytonutrients help to build up the diversity of our microbiome. Foods rich in omega-3 protects our brain function. If we eat more anti-inflammatory based foods, we are likely to suffer less with inflammatory conditions like arthritis and so on. We can find what we need in food. A good start to getting off the hamster wheel is to simply eat food that looks like food, and if we can't pronounce the ingredients in our food, don't. eat it.

Once we understand food and our bodies, we stand a chance of becoming the CEO of our own biology. We have access to our own medical history to research, educate ourselves, and work out some of our own internal biology.

Doctors have their place, yet we can help ourselves with good nutrition, which nourishes our body, mind and soul and helps to protect and heal our bodies. Let's put an end to taking medication for something our lifestyle, or the right food can fix. If we do our research, we will discover that there are foods that make a difference instead of popping a pill.

We want to be in rude health, so let's look after ourselves.

Eat to live!

🏁   Consider changing to a different compound tyre. Red Tyre. Time to hammer the throttle, we can get a fastest lap in.

UB40 Food for Thought ♬

I hope I can remember to keep myself safe ...

The Fruit Bowl

Prepare to Taste the different Fruits of Life

Dashboard The Yellow Light Indicates: Pick Up Pace!

When we reach the legal age to have 'consenting' sex, it is a time to explore our bodies and our sexualities. Unfortunately, we still live in a time where double standards persist, particularly around gender and sexuality. A man's value is often perceived to increase with sexual experiences, celebrated as a sign of prowess or status, while a woman's value is unfairly judged to diminish, subjected to criticism and shame.

These outdated and unjust perceptions reflect deeper societal inequalities, underscoring the need to challenge and dismantle such biases to promote true gender equality and mutual respect. The respect does not end there.

It's equally important that we embrace sexual liberation and enjoy our bodies safely, with awareness and care. Honouring our boundaries and prioritizing our well-being are essential aspects of this journey. This involves encouraging a culture of respect not only for us, for others.

I recall, a long time ago, when I was single, a student and broke, I had to make the most of decorating on the cheap. One day, I thought I'd get creative with my fruit bowl and create an arrangement on the coffee table.

The fruit was looking a bit dull, and in need of a lift, I used tinsel, glitter, and creatively arranged bright-coloured square aluminium foil condom sachets (sealed), placed amongst the fruit. It started out as a joke, a little pinch of seasonal humour. Nevertheless, it ended up being quite an expensive arrangement. Friends who would visit helped themselves and pinched one because they had run out or didn't find the time to pick one up. As well as being very thankful, the arrangement became a great talking piece. Many 'hit and run' hookups were revealed.

Today, things have advanced. Before we go any further than kissing, we can also have STI (sexually transmitted infections) testing. Some sexually transmitted infections, especially the more extreme or long-term ones, can't be cured, they last forever. This is the best way to ensure we are clean and safe.

If we're going to do it, do it safely. Always be prepared.

Enjoy safe sex by protecting ourselves and our partners!

🌑 Consider changing to a different compound. Hard Tyre.

Jorja Smith Little Things x Gypsy Woman (L Beats Mashup) 🎵

I hope I make it through to the other side ...

Break-ups not for Make-ups!

A step closer to 'The One', or ten steps back, our Choice!

Dashboard The Purple Light indicates: Action Required! 🌑
Check Rear View Mirror!

We all a have a story about a break-up, whether we fell for the words instead of the persons actions, turned a blind eye to deception, or simply outgrew the other. When we break up with someone we are madly in love with and still choose to walk away for ourselves, on the grounds of loving ourselves more, that is when we know our self-worth. Not all of us can say we've had the self-esteem to make autonomous decisions, so here's a start.

**Relationships do end, they are a part of life.
Don't give up, this time will pass.**

When someone walks out on us, the end of a relationship can hurt like hell and leave us in deep sadness in the aftermath. Our hearts don't always break evenly, it's a loss we need to grieve, we may need more time than the other party, whether it's grieving for the past, for ourselves, or for our future hopes and dreams we will no longer share together. When we break up, our brains process the heartbreak as physical pain; it's not uncommon to feel heartache, headaches, or feel sick. Just hold on.
We've got this!

**It's time to turn this around and have this time in
our lives work for us.**

The story we tell ourselves about that person will determine how long it takes to recover. If we believe we've lost our soulmate, it's time to change the narrative, they clearly weren't our soulmate. They bailed out. They didn't choose us.

I have seen a variety of souls, to know relationship break-up give us the opportunity to actively rebuild and create the life we want, with us at the top of the list. We need space to grieve, to grieve for ourselves not for them, so give a good amount of distance and cut contact from our ex. Only then can we find ways to overcome heartbreak.

It is important to emotionally disconnect.

Avoid persecuting ourselves with substances like drugs or alcohol, skipping meals, or boozy late nights, trying to drown our sorrows, or pushing away those unwanted feelings. It won't work, we'll still wake up the next day feeling the same. This slows the process of getting back on our feet. It only creates more pain for us: more stress, anxiety, confusion and helplessness. It's destructive. Getting ourselves in a state is the ideal invitation to show our ex they have won!

Once we've had a few days or weeks (no more) apart to lick our wounds, it's time to gain a new perspective and understanding from our experience. This is where healing begins. When we let go of the emotional attachment, we realise how ordinary they really were. The love will start to fade. This allows us to take a step back and see that it was our love that made the connection special, not theirs. If we have been hurt from our previous relationship, we may have developed an anxious, or avoidant emotional attachment. Never let what happened turn us bitter, pain doesn't define us. We are bigger than that!

Before stepping into another relationship consider taking a year or two to focus entirely on ourselves. Removing the distraction of dating allows space for self-discovery, healing, and personal growth. Use the time to reinvest and pour into ourselves through **therapy** (284), self-reflection and intentional solitude. Speaking to a neutral party can help to process past experiences and gain clarity. Many of us pour so much into our relationships that we lose sight of ourselves. We may not know who we are outside of a partnership or what we truly want from life.

It may be worth reflecting on:

The Key Questions
- What are my values?
- What are my non-negotiables?
- What kind of life do I want?
- Who do I want to become?

The journey requires self-care, **spiritual hygiene** (260) and **high wellbeing** (272), **self-compassion** (58) and **self-love** (191).

Sometimes, heartbreak clears the way for something better. They weren't the one, and that's okay. We can step into our next chapter with a renewed sense of self, and a clear vision of what, and who, truly aligns with us. We are responsible for our own healing. No one else can rescue us. It's up to us to rise and move forward.
We will be okay because we are here for ourselves!

🛞 Consider changing to a different compound. Intermediate Tyre.

Adele Rolling in the Deep ♫
Oasis Stop Crying your Heart Out ♫

I hope I can cleanse my spiritual energy to make space for...

Spiritual Hygiene

Preparation to embrace our Highest Potential

Dashboard The Green Light indicates: All Clear! 🟢
Spiritual cleansing is an essential step in this process, enabling progression and positive momentum.

Before achieving **high wellbeing** (272), it can be beneficial to take a few preparatory steps to clear the cobwebs and lay some groundwork for renewal. Spiritual hygiene is an intentional practice of maintaining and cleansing our energetic and spiritual bodies. It clears negativity, aligns our energy and creates space for new opportunities.

End of Racing!

Imagine ourselves as a vehicle in need of a valet, the interior is unkempt, cluttered with remnants from the past: crumbs, empty bottles and muddy paw prints. The exterior is dirty and covered in bugs or tree sap.

Until everything gets cleared, cleaned, buffed and polished, it remains chaotic. Just as a 'deep clean' transforms a car, spiritual cleansing revitalizes our energy, brings clarity, and makes space for peace and growth. Together high wellbeing and spiritual cleansing create the foundation to feel unclogged, clear, and balanced.

Life can fill us to capacity with unresolved past experiences and overwhelming present demands, leaving no room to meet our personal needs. This leads to poor concentration, chronic stress, and feelings of disconnection, anger, hopelessness, or stagnation which lead to negative thought patterns, making us believe we are undeserving or incapable. This can block the flow of blessings and opportunities, preventing us from embracing our highest potential. If we are unavailable, we are less likely to meet 'our person' or attain our *iHope*.

When practicing spiritual hygiene, we can maintain a high-frequency state for growth and connection. It helps us to focus on self-love and diminish fear, to opening ourselves to new possibilities.

The Key Practices

- **Meditation** – Calming our minds and connecting with the present moment.
- **Detox Baths** – Using water as a tool for energetic cleansing.
- **Nature Connection** – Grounding ad recharging through natural elements.
- **Smudging** – Clearing stagnant energies with smoke or other rituals.
- **Prayer and Visualisation** – Setting intentions and visualising goals with clarity.
- **Movement** – Release blocked energy through physical activity.
- **Healing Sounds** – Using frequencies to elevate and balance energy.
- **Journaling and Solitude** – Reflecting and reconnecting with inner truths.
- **Crying** – Let go and wash away built-up tension and emotions.
- **Tidy Space** – Maintain a clean and organized environment to reflect inner clarity.

This is especially useful to practice before manifesting, as it requires space and alignment.

Spiritual cleansing ensures we are energetically aligned and ready to receive. If we are unprepared or 'cluttered', blessings remain on hold until we create the capacity to embrace them fully.
Spiritual hygiene allows us to hold space for our dreams to be felt and visualised with clarity, enabling us to step into a reality where they are possible. Consistent spiritual hygiene allows us to have agency, to create a life filled with clarity, purpose, and openness to embrace our fullest potential.

Be ready for what we wish for!

- Consider changing to a different compound. Wet Tyre.

Cymande Dove ♪

I hope to find a time each day when I'm at my best ...

The Owl and the Lark

What type of Creature are We?

A vast majority of us are either an owl or a lark. and we don't have any choice in the matter. Neither is right or wrong, it just is!

It seems that this is how we're wired, we are born this way. Right from childhood, the kid that hated waking up for school, miserable, untalkative in the morning, won't go to bed, difficult to fall asleep -" hello ***owls***!" The child that leaps out of bed at 5 or 6am, wants to play, hungry for breakfast, and easy to settle at night -" hello ***larks!***"

Throughout my years as a therapist, I discovered that each client had a certain, rhythm. They would struggle at certain times of the day that would impact their mood, so I identified whether they were a lark or the owl, and each had different needs.
Larks are 'morning people' 6am rises, 9-10pm sleepers. Up at the crack of dawn, bright-eyed, bushy tailed, ready to start the day, they generally love breakfast first thing in the morning. Whereas owls are 'night people' 10am -

12pm risers, 2 - 3am sleepers. They struggle to start the day and are generally not fans of breakfast instantly when they wake, they can easily wait for two or three hours.

Unfortunately, we live in a world where the lark is at an advantage, the nine to five conventionalist culture the mainstream is programmed into, or the school run which dictates the proper time to start our day. Anything beyond these times is often considered, late, inconvenient or difficult. The owl's body clock is generally viewed negatively. Larks may struggle to understand an owl's body clock, or bed routines positively: *"You should be up by now..."*
This can make life difficult for the owl. Larks and Owls have different chronotypes; they sing different tunes depending on the time of day.
What's important is knowing when to take the opportunity to sing our tune according to the 24-hour clock.

Larks and owls have the same amount of energy yet perform better at different times during the day. Larks naturally have the most amount of energy is the morning until mid-afternoon, whereas owls naturally start waking up much later, typically reaching their peak energy between 8-9pm and 2 or 3am. This means any tasks are more beneficial to undertake during the peak performance hours of our day -and that's okay. It's not the owl's fault if they prefer to wash up or study at midnight.

Both creatures naturally change with age. As we grow older, we require less sleep, more afternoon naps creep in, or hormone changes manipulate our creatures' tunes. Also, if we've had a job most of our lives that's been against our natural clock, we may get used to not feeling fully rested, yet feel tired or sluggish most of the time. With solo ventures, work around our body clock, the most productive time of day. Larks harvest energy in the morning, and owls harvest energy in the evening. When deadlines, or exams loom, use our time according to the tune we sing!

I've travelled extensively, and one thing we all have in common is rush hour traffic, as the working world generally favours the larks. The system rewards and affirms the larks, who click neatly into the 'nine-to-five' culture. Meanwhile owls spend half their day with one-eye open, struggling to catch up. So, give props to the owls; they've had to live against their natural clocks, endure harassment and criticism, and are labelled 'lazy' or 'time wasters. They simply tick differently from the way the world chimes.

Are we birds of a feather?

In relationships, it helps to acknowledge our differences, especially if we are different birds, who sing at opposite ends of the day. One partner has full experience of nightlife and clubbing, the other significantly less. One socialises over breakfast, the other over dinner. One prefers sex in the morning the other at night, and if we're both lucky, anytime. When living together sleep can become an issue. Things can get personal, not going to bed together at the same time, or the owl staying in bed until late morning on weekends:

"You've wasted the whole morning in bed!"

The truth is, morning time is wasted on an owl; however, the night is not. They still have their time of day to sing. If the owl has gone to bed at the same time as the lark, guaranteed they won't fall asleep at the same time, they're only midway through their evenings at 9pm, not winding down like the Lark who started their day at 6am.

When it comes to chores, we all have a time of day when we have most energy and drive. Larks tend to be better in the morning, whereas owls are firing on all cylinders in the evening. Instead of ruffling each other's feathers, consider the differences, we simply operate at opposite ends of the day. This isn't personal.

Strike a balance by making allowances for our responsibilities. By adjusting our schedules to suit our energy banks, we avoid burnout.
We are of no use if we're bankrupt.
Perform to our own tune!

- Consider changing to a different compound. Medium Tyre.

Air All I Need ♫

I hope I can recover from my loss …

To Grieve Loved Ones

To Love comes with a Cost

Dashboard The Purple Light indicates: Action Required!
Check Rear View Mirror!

"The day after, I woke up and they're not with us anymore, I have to do everything for the first time. my first coffee, getting dressed the first time I have a bath since, the first thing I'll wear, my first dinner, my first walk, my first day sober, my first day food shopping, my first day back to work…." Margot

Bereavement lets us know we have loved. Grief has a way of showing us we are not in control of our lives. Grief is physical, our hearts break or feel a tightness from our loss. Grief comes in waves and can surprise us when we least expect it, sometimes for a long period of time.

Grief is on its own terms, yet we must grieve our loss to heal ourselves to be able to move on with our lives. There is a process of grief we must go through and it's crucial not to minimise our grief, to feel the full reality of it.
At the beginning, grief is like carrying a heavy backpack, it doesn't get lighter, we get better at carrying it!

There are five different stages to grief we may experience.

- **Denial** – Feeling numb is very common in the early days of grief.
- **Anger** – Death can seem cruel and unfair, it's very natural to feel angry.
- **Bargaining** – It's common to go over things, "what if." Questions, wanting to go back in time.
- **Depression** – Waves of Intense painful feelings – Life feels like it no longer holds any meaning.
- **Acceptance** – We may never get over a death, it's possible to accept what has happened and learn to live again.

This process may take months or years to feel we have reached a place of acceptance. Most of us get stuck in anger, especially if we're uncomfortable with the emotion or don't know how to express it. It is helpful to embrace all emotions, they are key to carrying us through to the other side, to acceptance. We need to grieve, to feel our loss in order to move on.

We all have our moments, we are all entitled to feel all our emotions at once, when all our feelings are blended together to feel sad, angry, fearful, guilty, or even relieved, and to own them. To help us to move forward, we sometimes need to force ourselves out of the house. Having pets, especially dogs can help by getting us out in the fresh air and keeping us to some kind of routine. Joining groups and surrounding ourselves with others who are experiencing similar pain can help us become more comfortable talking about our loved ones. Sharing stories about them, helps to validate our emotions.

In time, we will find comfort in watching their videos, treasuring the memories, and celebrating their life. Creating a memory book filled with memorabilia; like photos, mementos, ticket stubs can recount the narrative of the love that was shared and help us document memories of them.

It is better to remember the wonderful person that we've lost than to remember that we have lost a wonderful person.

Over the years, we may still find ourselves trapped in the memories. The pain can remain overwhelming, and we feel stuck in a loop of repeated feelings, like a scratched record we can't get past without help and support. Seeking therapy could be the next step to consider.

At times, men may feel an obligation or a responsibility to be strong and supportive for their families, in turn neglecting their own grief. We all need to talk and feel our loss. We are entitled to be vulnerable to let go of our grief.

There is no right or wrong way to grieve.

There isn't a prescribed amount of time to grieve. There is no timeframe, and there are no rules. Eventually, we will come out the other side. As human beings, we are far more resilient than we think. We have the capacity to survive loss if we surrender to our grief.

We all grieve differently, in different ways. Let it be!

- ◉ Consider switching to a different compound. Wet Tyre.

Tom Rosenenthal It's Ok ♪

I hope who I am reflects how others see me …

Who are you? Vs. Who am I?

Identify our Identity

Dashboard The Green Light indicates: All Clear!

Who am I?

There comes a time when we ask, *"Who am I now?"*
Becoming parents, losing a job, moving to another country. Life shifts, and we question where we sit in the world, where we belong.
We discover who we are by acting naturally, free from conditions, expectations, or judgement. Life presents situations and opportunities that challenge us, and help to redefine who we are.

The Key Questions

- Can I….?
- Am I…?
- Am I into…?
- Is this within my power…?
- Am I equal…?
- Am I capable…?

Let's bring some clarity, how would we, or others, describe us?
Check out who we are, to see if we relate to or connect with any of these qualities.

I am……

Loyal. Passionate. Intelligent, Kind, Respectful. Enthusiastic. Supportive. Considerate, Emotional. Funny. Trustworthy. Responsible. Reliable. Efficient. Loving. Lenient. Caring. Resourceful. Creative, Honest. Powerful. Fun. Generous. Understanding. Authentic. Accountable. Spontaneous. Compassionate. Empathic. Unique. Bold. Assertive. Reassuring. Serious. Bold. Grounded. Warm. Mischievous. Patient. Approachable. Courageous. Courteous. Tolerant. Assertive. Diligent. Conscientious. Playful. Dedicated. Sensitive. Diplomatic. Brave. Optimistic. Interesting.

These qualities are what make us human.

They are valuable and transferable qualities that can be used across different areas of our lives, for ourselves, relationships and employment.

We can find solutions for some of our personality traits which may steer us into different professions.

Personality Traits
- **Bossy** – Natural leader, manager.
- **Dramatical** – Passionate and expressive.
- **Hyperactive** – Enthusiastic and energetic.
- **Talkative** – Enjoys interacting and communicating.
- **Impulsive** – Instinctive and passionate.
- **Defiant** – Bold and determined.
- **Stubborn** – Tenacious and persistent.
- **Fussy** – Eye for detail. Knows what we want.

We're all a work in progress. If some of the above aren't ticked, there's room to grow, choose a **'nudge word'** (328) to set as a goal to focus on, practise and make our own.
"I can…!"

We have so much to offer!

Florian Christl Natural 🎵

I hope I can share my problems with ...

The GQ Collective

Brotherhood

Dashboard The Green Light indicates: All Clear!

Friendships are about time. Nowadays we have less time to prioritise friendships and end up spending our free time on social media or working longer hours. Since becoming fathers, we may have had less time to rebuild friendships. There seems to be a struggle for some men to have deeper and more meaningful friendships, to be able to share and talk about their problems. By the time many men are 50, they have no personal friends.

The situation that seems to arise for us, is most male friends are acquaintances and they let friendships slide. They are left with no real friends they can talk to. Instead, we have gym mates; pub mates, football mates, golf mates or gaming mates, yet no friends per se, or a best friend.
Men's language is often centred around banter, or the casual brutality of mocking each other, rarely about the 'real' stuff, the intimate stuff. They don't convey affection to one another. Their form of intimacy is to be outrageously rude to each other, as a way of showing closeness, as though there is an unspoken rule not to talk about their feelings or show vulnerability. Additionally, in times of grief or trouble, they tend to talk 'idle chit-chat' instead, not as receptive to the deeper story.

Men need to get over that hump in friendships to be able to openly talk about their feelings, instead of holding their emotions back by holding themselves through such rigid restraint and barriers, alongside being regularly on probation as to whether their friends rate them.
So much pressure.
Let's take the pressure off and focus on making our own community where we can talk. It can build a bond, create new friendships, and become a brotherhood. It has to be intentional. Mark a day of the week in our diary, put that day in our schedule so it becomes routine. Let's say, we meet for padel on Tuesday, meet at the gym on Fridays, keep these semi-regular meetups in the diary.

To start a level of cohesion within a group, it often takes one person to get the ball rolling, to lead the process. When we're casually talking in the group, expand on the content, not just about padel, or football or any other sport.

Be mindful to add some intimate, or vulnerable chat, or even light-hearted gossip, to engage in deeper conversation and show a little more of ourselves. It always starts with being the first to crack the shell, thereby giving permission to the other men to open up. We may have to take on the role as the leader of discussion for a while. Lead, and in time, when these types of discussions become normalised, others will feel comfortable enough to naturally take the lead in the discussions.

Once the group is established, whoever we choose to lead, ensure that everyone shares the same goals, to grow and be the best they can be, for themselves and their families. That's a popular aspiration for most to get on board with. Choose a subject that we all have in common to support each other. Consistency is key to opening up, seeing the same faces supports safety and helps maintain the dynamic of the group.

There's so much to gain from exploring the question, **who am I?** (267), and from openly talking and sharing our thoughts and concerns. It will encourage us to grow, learn and motivate and support each other on a different level, in times of crisis or mental health issues, being a part of the group can increase our confidence and extend our emotional wellbeing. When we feel our emotions, we can feel vulnerable. Vulnerability is the backbone of confidence. Vulnerability makes us strong, brave and courageous.

If we benefit from our group and are curious about therapy, therapy can be another way to help to get 'private matters' off our chest. Imagine therapy like a toolshed. It tidies up the tools by getting rid of the negative psychological habits that were holding us back and leaves us with the tools that work for us so we can get on with our life.

Men can be super supportive, yet firm with each other. Each time, we will take away different things from a group. To share our story can keep us surviving and keep us walking through life.

Redefine masculinity and create space to talk!

Consider changing to a different compound. Intermediate Tyre. Time to load up the tyres and hammer the throttle, use DRS.

Wookie (feat Lain) Battle ♫

I hope I can show my love, that they're seen and celebrated ...

Royalty

Kings and Queens

Dashboard The Green Light indicates: All Clear!

If we're fortunate enough to find royalty, it is essential to learn how to keep them and let them know they are royalty and how much we love and appreciate them!

If he treats us like a queen, treat him like a king!

A **King** deserves to be treated well, championed, cherished, supported, encouraged, reassured and cared for, to support the risks, and encourage the 'firsts' and to reassure him that his efforts are appreciated. He should feel secure, celebrated, praised, and complimented – of his handsome qualities, and occasionally have his crown loving adjusted.

There is no competition; her successes are his successes.
The best way to hold our king is in our arms.

If she treats us like a king, treat her like a queen!

A **Queen** deserves to be treated well, cherished, supported, encouraged, reassured and cared for. Support her risks, encourage her 'firsts', and reassure her that her efforts are appreciated. She should feel secure, celebrated, praised, to be complimented – for her beautiful qualities and occasionally have her crown lovingly adjusted.

There is no competition; his successes are her successes.
The best way to hold our queen is in our arms.

Love royalty wholeheartedly, without fear.

Now rise together! 👑

D'Angelo Cruisin' ♪

I hope I can attract the right partner for me ...

High Wellbeing

Alright! Alright! Alright!

Dashboard The Green Light indicates: All Clear!

The most important decision we will make in life is the partner we choose. The key is to focus on our own wellbeing and invest in ourselves before entering a relationship.

Many clients in my practice have asked,
What do I need to do to find my person?

Often, we think we are upgrading ourselves because we have changed our standards. Have we raised our qualifications to match our standards? The package may shine and sparkle on the outside, does the interior match the exterior?

To get the person of our dreams, we must be the person of their dreams!

To fully experience high wellbeing, embracing our **spiritual hygiene** (260) is essential.
There are several aspects to support high wellbeing:

The Key Practices

1. Participate in activities that we love, activities that are light-hearted and fun.
2. Be open to meeting new people. Keep expanding our world, the more people we meet, the more likely we are to meet a potential partner.
3. Build a fun social life: go dancing, join groups, get out and have fun at least once a week. Have something exciting to look forward to each week and keep our energy and vibrations high.
4. Do whatever makes us curious, explore different interests we've never experienced before. Let's step out of our comfort zone.
5. Surround ourselves with loving family and friends who love and respect us. A solid support network is vital; they help set the bar on a loving relationship.

6. Be more appreciative and respectful of ourselves. Learn to treat and pamper ourselves more often or enjoy an occasional spa day with friends. Rewarding ourselves helps boost our self-esteem.
7. Sleep well. Get in some early nights; sleep is the only time our bodies repair themselves from our daily grind. It prevents burnout. Learn to nurture ourselves and feel refreshed for the day.
8. Practise good nutrition. Consider 2-3 well-balanced meals each day, breakfast being the most important for keeping our hormones, energy and emotions in check.
9. Learn to ground ourselves and relax. Practice being present by attending exercise classes, e.g. yoga, or pilates.
10. Meditate to take some quality time to hear ourselves, slow down and develop a relationship with ourselves. Give time and space for those questions to emerge, for the hope of something more meaningful to be acknowledged. It's important to go a step deeper, because someone else will.

Practising good health, self-discipline, independence, rest and having a varied lifestyle helps us to develop and meet our own needs. Learning how to nurture and love ourselves provides us with confidence and so much more to offer another. Once we know how to give to ourselves, we are ready to receive love.

We require, rest, recuperate, repair, relieve, recover, relax, refresh, revive, reset, reboot, reconstruct reclaim, redefine, renew, refine, and reward, and most of all. Be ready to re-invest!

Recognise that love, care and attention to ourselves is what gets us over the finishing line. When we pull over into the pits and take time to refuel, we can get back on track,

Get high on our own supply!

🛞 Consider changing to a different compound. Hard Tyre.
Time to load up the tyres and hammer the throttle, we can get a fastest lap in.

Thee Sacred Souls Live For You ♫

I hope I can optimize my alertness in the day and sleepiness at night...

Circadian Clock

The Bookends of our Day

Dashboard The Green Light indicates: All Clear!

We all have an internal master clock.
Our circadian system helps us to adapt to our environment, preparing our bodies for expected changes throughout our day. It tells us about the best time for activity, the best times to eat, and the time to sleep.

This 24-hour biological clock controls our brains and has two important purposes: to regulate our alertness and sleepiness by responding to light changes in our environment. Not artificial light, DAYLIGHT. The sunlight sends a direct signal to the brain to wake us up and put us in a better mood, helping us maintain daytime focus and alertness throughout the day. When we step outside in the morning, the process of looking at the sun at the beginning of our day sets a timer for when our bodies are ready to eat and when they are ready to sleep, allowing us to experience better and deeper sleep. If we don't maintain regular rhythm patterns of sleep, we will lose rhythm and alignment to our internal clocks. To know when our rhythm is off, we generally experience extreme daytime sleepiness, decreased alertness, and problems with our memory and decision-making.

We may experience problems, such as:
- Falling asleep.
- Waking up too early and being unable to get back to sleep.
- Staying asleep.
- Feeling alert during the day.
- Getting sleep and not feeling refreshed.

Our circadian clock also affects our processes like our hormones, digestion and body temperature. For those who are 50 and above, or experiencing menopause, we may naturally have decreasing levels of melatonin. Speak to a specialist for guidance.

Let's prepare our body for the days natural changes.

End of Racing!

The Key Practices

- Morning daylight. Our 15 – 30minute daily dose.
- A regular bedtime routine.
- Keep regular meal schedules.
- Avoid daytime naps in the afternoon.
- Exercise. Regular physical activity, preferably daily.
- Limit screen time at night.
- Avoid alcohol and caffeine.
- Keep to a routine.

These practises help us find our rhythm, to reset and strengthen our biological clocks.
The tick to our waking, and the tock to our sleeping!

🌀 Consider changing to a different compound. Medium Tyre. Time to gain traction and get a fastest lap in.

Milk & Sugar Feat Lizzy Pattinson
Let the Sun Shine (Terrace Club Mix) ♬

I hope I have the energy to keep this up ...

Recharge Our Battery

We can't Pour from an Empty Cup!

Dashboard The Green Light indicates: All Clear!
To keep the engine purring, practice kindness!
Being social butterflies is fun and exciting, mixing and interacting socially with others.
As fabulous as some of these social events may be, whether it's birthdays, family gatherings, networking events, work activities, weddings, dinner parties, or chilling out with family, they all require energy.

Every one of us has a social battery. This doesn't mean we have a real battery inside of our bodies, it's simply terminology that refers to the level of energy we have stored, which depends on our lifestyle and capacity to socially interact with others; the energy we require to socialise. Socialising takes a lot of energy. Simply put, a continuous stream of verbal and non-verbal communication, meeting new people, managing expectations, and engaging in conversations can deplete our batteries. We may experience socialising as tiring, stressful or over stimulating. Some batteries drain and deplete quicker than others, and we need to recharge our batteries more frequently.

Social batteries are all rechargeable.

If we imagine a battery, a battery cell can have an extremely long lifespan if we take care of it, battery management is key to giving us the longest service. To illustrate, we all have different sizes, whether we're an AAA, AA, C, D, or 9V, depending on how frequently we need to recharge, or regroup.
I have observed many, to understand different personality types have different ways to jump-start their batteries. From the great 'social climbers', the extroverts, whose batteries have the highest current, highest performance, and longest lifespan, and who require the shortest charge time. To the introverts, who may last half as long, putting out the same amount of power, but need frequent rand longer recharging periods. There are all the personality types in between. Some may specialise in reliability; a long shelf life, longer-lasting power; others may have lower energy counts that need to top up and recharge accordingly.

Introverts are a little more special than the rest. Their capacity for socialising is lower and will deplete quicker than others, as they are susceptible to becoming overwhelmed, stressed or anxious. To recharge their batteries to the same level as everyone else, they generally require alone time, 'me' time. Their batteries operate differently, running on a deep current that rewards them with creativity. Generally, introverts are the creators and inventors of life. They are wired differently and require solitude to regroup. Creativity is energy. To be creative, we require the energy to drive it. No energy, no creativity. This can be vital if we have occupations that require a creative output.

We all have a social battery that corresponds to our attachment types. If we have experienced trauma, or mental health conditions, or personality disorders, e.g. ADHD, borderline personality disorder (BPD), or bipolar, our batteries require even more careful management.

Some personality types can zap our energies quickly. Their energies and vibrations, good or bad, can leave us feeling more emotionally drained than others, especially those known as the 'energy vampires. We all have our own individual triggers and warning signals that tell. Us when we are becoming draining. Signs such as feeling tired, anxious, overwhelmed, stressed, irritable, or fatigued, leave us feeling wiped out.
This may affect our behaviour, we may withdraw, engage less in conversation, lose our sense of humour, seem more vacant, or simply prefer to go home. These are warning signs that our batteries are low and need recharging.

If we choose to ignore the warning signs, we get stressed, burned out or feel frazzled. It is valuable to know who we are, to acknowledge and understand our weaknesses, so we can manage ourselves appropriately. Consider setting some **boundaries** (215) to ensure that we are servicing our battery life efficiently. Scheduling time after social activities or events to recharge, rest, and regroup ourselves is vital. If we've run out of steam, sometimes dropping everything for a few hours of one-to-one time, meeting our best mate, or having a laugh to lift our spirits can re-energise us. Alternatively, resting; relaxing, mindfulness, drawing, journaling, reading, or meditating are all forms of quality time well spent to recharge our batteries.

Recharging is essential for our wellbeing and our quality of life!

If there's fuel in the car to carry us onto the next lap, we're fine. If we don't recharge appropriately, it will cost us our pace.

- ◉ Consider switching to a different compound. Wet Tyre.

I hope my menstruation doesn't stop me ...

Hormonal Cycles

Adapting to Golden Opportunities

Foe many women, periods, can be a challenging time. They often bring discomfort, disrupt daily routines, and affect how we feel physically and emotionally. Every woman's experience is unique.

For women who have menstrual cycles, there are opportunities to adapt our lives according to our hormones. It is beneficial to recognise that certain phases of a menstrual cycle change how we feel about ourselves due to hormonal fluctuations. These are moments we can take advantage of, which are beneficial if we tune in, get to know ourselves, and understand how our hormones affect us.

There is scientific evidence to suggest that with the fluctuations of our hormones, we can benefit by adapting our lifestyles to flow in tandem with them. Once we understand how we tick, we can navigate through our monthly cycles and make the most of what mother nature has given us.

There are four different phases to our menstrual cycle: the menstrual, follicular, luteal, and pre-menstrual phases. Different hormones make us feel different things:

Oestrogen makes us feel like superwoman. Progesterone is the anti-anxiety hormone, that makes us feel calm and relaxed. Testosterone gives us extra energy and makes us feel strong.

The Key Practices

Phase 1 – Reflective and Creative
Oestrogen and progesterone decrease.
Our energies are low, yet we tend to be creative and reflective, so take the opportunity to explore new ideas for assignments or schemes.

Phase 2 – Superwoman
Oestrogen and testosterone peak.
We feel more confident, our energy levels are higher, and our libido increases. It's the best time building muscle, so it's the prime time to work

out. Take the opportunity to deliver presentations, go on a first date, or even run a marathon.

Phase 3 – Clearer heads and Sharper brains
Progesterone dominates.
We feel calm and collected. Take the opportunity to discuss, debate, negotiate, or set goals.

Phase 4 – Reflective and Creative
Hormones drop to levels similar to the menstrual phase. We tend to feel flat or low. Focus on creative energy and developing new ideas.

Take the opportunity to adapt our lives to make the most out of our hormones!

I hope I'm ready to fall in love ...

Dating

We Attract who we Are!

Dashboard The Green Light indicates: All Clear!

Most of us are searching for love, and the beautiful truth is, there's no expiration date on that.
Meaningful relationships can blossom at any age, at any stage of our lives. Let's be honest: the journey to finding love can sometimes lose its sparkle and become a chore, after endless searching, swiping, the ghosting, love-bombing, bread crumbing, or getting catfished, it can all feel exhausting. Sometimes, what people are looking for isn't love at all, it's help, support, or even escape. When these patterns repeat, it's easy to feel disheartened or worn out.

These days, it's tough for everyone. We're all juggling busy lives, endless distractions, and the pull of social media, on top of trying to connect meaningfully. If we're feeling weary, know that we're not alone. Be kind to ourselves, stay open-hearted, maintain high wellbeing, and true to our values. Love has its own timing and often shows up when we least expect it.

Dating can be a brutal business, if we're not mentally and emotionally resilient, it can feel especially brutal. After **break-ups** (258), it's easy to feel worn down. Rejection is part of the journey, it's not a reflection of our worth, it's just part of the process.

Before jumping back into dating, it's important to ask ourselves:

"Am I ready to face not just the highs, but also the setbacks?"

To open ourselves to love again, we also have to be strong enough to face heartbreak, and still stay open.

There are three ways to meet our significant other in today's dating scene.

- Friends and family can help to set us up with someone they know.
- Search outside our social circle to increase our gene pool, by visiting different cities nearby and connecting with people who share the same values and interests, through hobbies, such as dancing or a sport.
- Online dating – different strokes for different folks. With internet dating, we can plug into what we want, with no restrictions.

It can feel a lonely pursuit, so if we're not feeling confident going solo, why not choose a dating buddy? We can debrief together and have a laugh. Whether we're looking for meaningful pursuits, or disposable pleasures, we might just bump into 'the one" along the way.

To know when we're ready to start dating, be sure we have learnt from our previous relationship and know what values are important to us. Be sure we're not choosing the same person with a different name. It also helps to have a clear vision of our goals for the next year or so.

Who we choose as a partner is the most important decision of our lives!

In dating, we often find ourselves drawn to the outside package – their style, charisma, cheekiness, career, finances, or even what car they drive. Instead, let's focus on what's inside the package. The engine might have exceeded its mileage. It's what beneath the surface that counts.

The Key Practices

1. Are they **proactive**, reliable, kind and trustworthy? Do they share our values and ideas of fun?
2. Do they **show interest**, ask questions, and stay in touch? Do we feel seen and heard?
3. **Trust our instincts.** How do we feel in their company - scared, anxious, or at ease?

Occasionally, we can confuse lust with love and want everything in one person. That supports the culture of instant gratification we live in today. It is to our advantage to hold back and delay sex when forming a new relationship. Our 'love bubbles' are all about physical touch - bonding, stroking, cuddling, holding hands, and sex. These are associated with the hormone called oxytocin, the 'love hormone'. We release oxytocin when we connect with physical touch.

Bonding is essential to a long-lasting relationship. Try to build a connection and strengthen the bond first, until there is sufficient trust. Focus on being consistent, having regular contact, and getting to know them slowly, slowly. Commitment is a far more attractive quality for a keeper.

When things are going well, let's not create red flags or even pink ones. Sometimes we search for the negative that isn't there. For instance, if we find it hard to trust, we may prefer others to earn our trust rather than giving it freely until they prove otherwise. Stay present, and positive; this is not a time to sabotage ourselves from receiving the love we deserve.

Celibacy

The word 'celibate' is often whispered, out of ear shot for others to hear. It always feels like an awkward and uncomfortable conversation to have when we start dating, yet it's an important one. If we've been out of the scene for a while, and have been celibate for some time, it helps to let people we are dating know:

*"I'm really enjoying getting to know you, but
I need to take my time."*

Lay it all out on the table so the other person knows where we stand. It helps to take the pressure off both parties and sets the pace of the relationship. On the apps, we think we have endless perceived choice, there are endless variations of relationships and goals today, which makes it more difficult to match well.

I have seen many to understand that being in love and being ready for a relationship are not the same. Love is a commitment of emotional intimacy and friendship. Love takes effort, and relationships need preparation. We must fall in love with ourselves to believe we're worthy of loving another. The strongest unions are those with longevity. They share values and, most importantly, like themselves. Only with high personal satisfaction, they put in 100% effort into the relationship.

Key Characteristics

For a healthy relationship includes being emotionally available, open minded, honest, trustworthy, willing to compromise, tolerate, fun and staying curious about life. These qualities start with us, if we don't embody them ourselves, the relationship will be out of balance.

Prioritise our wellbeing by focusing on self-worth, **self-love** (191) and **high wellbeing** (272). Surrounding ourselves with loving family and friends is key to making the right decisions for ourselves first. That way. we attract the right person into our lives.

When we step into the game of love, we must accept that mistakes, disappointment, hurt, and heartbreak is part of the journey. The one's who aren't right for us aren't necessarily wrong. It's just part of love's price. Our hearts are precious, and they may offer only a handful of chances before resilience fades.

Keep it positive and keep it real, and only when we are truly ready, say after me,

" I am ready for my next great relationship!"

Padam. Padam, I hear it and I know... Padam, Padam....
        Safeguarding: Check out 'The Angela Scheme'. And 'Claire's list'.

🌀 Consider changing to a different compound. Hard Tyre.

                                      Olivia Dean It isn't Perfect but it Might Be 🎵
                                  Justin Timberlake Suit and Tie (radio edit) 🎵

I hope I can do this without asking for help ...

Help

One hand can't Clap!

Dashboard The Green Light indicates: All Clear!

We all have pride that gets in the way of what we need from time to time. However, when our pride, or the risk of feeling vulnerable or awkward starts to deprive us to the point that we're not progressing in life, we need to make a decision:

Which matters most in life, our needs or our pride?

Support lightens the load. If we keep doing what we always do, we'll get what we always got! There's no harm in asking. We've nothing to lose and possibly everything to gain, we're never too big for help!

We all need help, or the world will come to a halt.

We are all a part of a bigger, wider community, a global community that is trained, qualified and skilled to help each other along the journey of life. The global community offers services, and in exchange, we pay for those services, which are professionally prescribed to help us. We do it all the time without thinking. If our car breaks down, we need help from a mechanic who has the skills to fix it. if we are buying a house, we need help from a qualified solicitor to legitimise the contract. If we break our leg, we all need a trained, skilled and qualified surgeon to repair the injury. We cannot do everything on our own. It doesn't define us or make us any less of a person to ask for assistance. Lending a hand, doing someone a favour, or giving someone a leg up in life is a rewarding experience. We all know how it feels to be stuck or hampered by a task. We all require help to keep us moving and progressing in life. Civilization cannot function if everyone acts alone. We're all links in a chain, each with the power to help.

**By picking up our teaspoons, we can support one another.
Together we rise.**

Help is what makes the world go round!

🟢 Consider changing to a different compound. Intermediate Tyre. Time to load up the tyres, use DRS.

Germaine Rose Rouge 🎵

I hope I can find someone who's neutral to guide and support me ...

Therapy

A time for Healing, growth, and Support

Dashboard The Green Light indicates: All Clear!
"Until you heal the wounds of your past, you will continue to bleed into the future." Iyanla Vanzant

For some of us, it can feel easier to talk to strangers about what we're going through because our struggles are too personal to share with friends. Therapy might be the answer.

I have worked with many different types of people in support and healing, and it all began with reaching out for help, through a phone call or an email. I often view each soul like a tree. When someone contacts me, it's usually because one of their branches is loose. We would focus on the roots, the root causes and eventually, the branches take care of themselves. Everything begins at the roots, breaking down faulty foundations to rebuild a solid structure. In other words, we create a new life that serves us well, centred on our true needs. Along the way, we can reinvest in ourselves, and pour into our own growth.

There are so many different types of therapy to experience. They all have their place, especially talking therapies. Having been a therapist for over twenty years, I cannot overlook the countless benefits therapy offers. Therapy can save lives and positively transform them indefinitely. For many, therapy is what turns on the lights. It can be the greatest investment we ever make in ourselves. A wide variety of treatments exist to help to clear our windscreens, identify our troubles, and heal our wounds so that we can fall in love with who we truly are.

Every one of us has at least two things in common: we all have a story to tell, and we all want change. It's important to recognise we cannot change the outside without first changing ourselves internally. We all have blind spots, and self-awareness is the gift that therapy provides. Therapy helps us understand ourselves, identify how we got to where we are, and gives us the tools to resolve, heal and dissolve our troubles. As we transform from within, our outer lives begin to reflect that change.
Many of us are simply curious, asking:

"How did I become me?"

We explore the beliefs and perceptions we hold about ourselves. Often, discover that we've been defined by limiting beliefs such as.

Unworthiness.
Stupid.
Not good enough.
Unlovable.
Hurt.

We swallow these untruths and distract ourselves through blaming, rescuing, complaining, soothing, avoiding, judging, criticising and picking at ourselves or others. We may unknowingly carry around unseen emotional debris that keeps us stuck. Recognising these shackles and breaking free to rediscover our authentic selves, whether again or for the first time, is incredibly empowering.

Through our rear-view mirror, we can map out the path that led us to where we are. The journey often requires revisiting our childhood, to revisit the scene of the crime, and clear out the emotional debris This may involve revisiting old mental tapes we repeatedly play and choosing to discard them so we can live our own stories as their truest version of ourselves.

Once we have that map, we can understand how to translate our experiences and navigate our way out of what we once felt stuck in. By connecting with our inner child and learning to reparent ourselves, we can finally live our stories authentically. Without this work, we risk reverting back to old habits and patterns of blaming, complaining, judging, criticising, soothing, and distracting because we are still responding from our unloved selves. Therapy is not a resource to indulge in victimhood. We must focus on solutions, not just the problems.

Therapy offers a dedicated space to commit to ourselves, to be honest and explore our unmet needs so we can move forward. Everything starts with us; it is our responsibility to keep ourselves happy and content. One of life's medicine's is laughter. Enjoy being the author of our own life and start making some fabulous memories. We can travel light, with less 'junk in our emotional trunks'.

Most souls that I've had the privilege of working with have said,
"I wish I'd done this sooner!"

There comes a time when we all need to invest in our emotional, mental, and spiritual wellbeing, because we're worth it!

"I am not who I was a year ago."

And that's something worth celebrating!!

🎯 Consider switching to a different compound. Intermediate Tyre.
Load up the tyres and hammer the throttle, we can get a fastest lap.
Time to change to fresher rubber to gain advantage for the undercut.

Tracy Chapman Change 🎵

I hope we can work things out …

Chemical Romance

Diesel Vs. Petroleum

Dashboard The Green Light indicates: All Clear!

In every relationship, there will be ups and downs, inflated ego, laughter, fun, words said in anger, smiles, hurt, arguments and misunderstandings.

A couple, Colman, 39 and Joanie 37, were struggling with communication and vulnerability in their relationship. Colman explains,

"When I don't know how I'm feeling I can't communicate with someone. I'm getting angry and frustrated, feeling guilty of upsetting her any further. The slightest thing I say would tip her over the edge, she would shut down and that would create more distance between the two of us by her not reciprocating back."
"I felt like an idiot!"

"Trying to express my emotions and being open with her made me feel uncomfortable, not knowing if my thoughts and feelings were going to be rejected. Opening myself up to possible rejection felt like giving my power away, it felt too risky in knowing my confidence would take a battering."

End of Racing!

Petrol vs. Diesel

We often experience what I call a "chemical romance" in relationships, when each partner responds differently to conflict. I categorise these responses as 'petrol' and 'diesel'. This is much like how different cars are designed for different types of journeys.

Petrol engines are built for quick, agile, short-distance travel, while diesel engines are more suited for slow-paced, long-distance endurance. Similarly, in conflict, one partner (petrol) may become hot-headed and reactive, while the other (diesel) may withdraw and turn cold. These clashing styles can lead to a stalemate, fuelling the ongoing 'power-struggle'. We try to navigate our world through expectations, judging others the by what we would do ourselves, and end up feeling let down.

Generally, our partners don't share the same moral coding or values as us, which means they have different perspectives or genuinely make mistakes. Nonetheless, one of the main reasons couples separate is their inability to resolve conflict, which becomes a roadblock. Roadblocks often involve the 'silent treatment'. We need to hear their voice, not their silence, if they don't express how they feel, we tend to fill that space with our own insecurities. Communication is key.

Couples usually struggle in one of three areas. If we want to establish and maintain loving relationships, we must surrender the need to control.

- **Power and control** – ignoring a partner's needs, vulnerability, crossing boundaries, and competing for influence and money.
- **Care and closeness** – Lacking emotional connection, and intimacy, leading to a dull sex life.
- **Respect and recognition** – habitual bickering, one partner consistently blaming the other, with no accountability.

When seeking resolution, consider putting some ground rules in place.
- No violence.
- No throwing or smashing objects.
- No name calling.
- No disrespectful behaviour.

It's better not to get too caught up in the details, as this can avoid addressing the core issues. Forget about the details: take a step back, narrow the issue down to one of the three areas above, and start talking.

Listen. Allow each other to be vulnerable. Share openly and communicate respectfully with one another.

**A Duel can become a Duet,
if we work together as a team.**

For a relationship to thrive, we need balance. The most important elements are honesty and acceptance. We must reveal 'the good and the bad', the qualities we love and those we love less about each other. It's essential to accept our partners fully for the relationship to grow and keep progressing. This sets a strong foundation built on truth and acceptance.

If our objective is to be with who we think they night become, we are wasting our time.

The worst thing we can do is fall in love with potential!

Louie Vega Can We Keep This Going ♪

I hope I can accept challenges …

The Climb

We are all Students of Life's Challenges

Dashboard The Green Light indicates: All Clear!

We are all students of life. We're not supposed to stop learning.

Challenges never cease. Life will always bring moments of hardship, they're a natural part of growth and self-development. We all encounter situations that make us feel unequipped or pushed to our limits, where unwelcome emotions like anxiety and stress arise. To be challenged is simply to be alive.

Often, life's challenges hit us head-on. If we haven't been taught how to live positively and flourish, we may adopt dysfunctional coping mechanisms and unhealthy habits based on what we've seen and experienced. Don't give up. We must keep looking, find what works for us. Painful experiences offer a unique opportunity to heal parts of our consciousness. Growth requires us to reflect on our experiences; by recognising our role we have played in them, and understand how we may have contributed to or co-created the narrative.

Overthinking is the art of creating problems that don't exist. Avoidance is the engine that keeps those problems running. Lessons often repeat until we acknowledge, understand, and learn from them. Only then can we adapt and make different choices. Learning never stops.

Get comfortable with learning. Each of us has the power and the resources within to overcome life's challenges.
Embrace the challenges and move at a pace we can manage. There is so much to gain: challenge expands with boundaries, matures us, strengthens our character, and instils lasting confidence.

Without challenge, no change, without change, no progression!

Time to hammer the throttle, and use DRS

○ Consider changing to a different compound tyre. Red Tyre.

Oliver $ & Jimi Jules Pushing On ♩

I hope I can connect with my inner truth ...

Journaling

Our Internal World in Words

Dashboard The Green Light indicates: All Clear!

Dear me.
A journal becomes an extension of ourselves. A personal record of our life experiences, thoughts and feelings. Our souls laid bare on paper, handwritten rather than typed, allow us to connect more deeply with our emotions. When we write, we engage with our inner world in a way that devices simply can't replicate.

Journals encourage our internal world to speak, to reflect, ruminate, assess, question, **enquire** (267). They help us focus, confirm our opinions, and measure our thoughts, **emotions** (204), and past actions. Through journaling, we hold ourselves accountable and gain clarity on our feelings and perspectives.

Set a dedicated, specific time each day to write, making it a regular part of our routine. This consistent practice will help to ground us, offering space to reflect and process our thoughts and emotions.

Morning writing is helpful for being with our purest selves, without the distractions or influence of devices and the outside world. Bedtime can be useful when our minds are busy or we're struggling to sleep. It's an opportunity to de-stress, unpack the day to make space in our heads to unwind and rest.
Journaling is a lifetime tool for clearing out the traffic and debris of our day, helping us to connect with what really matters, to validate our authentic selves in writing.

Welcome to our private world!

◎   Consider changing to a different compound. Wet Tyre.
Time to load up the tyres, we can overtake.

Travis Writing To Reach You ♫

End of Racing!

I hope I can mark this occasion ...

Celebration

Praise our Progress to Process Progress!!

Dashboard The Yellow Light Indicates: Pick Up Pace! 🔔

Celebrating is about taking a moment to acknowledge and appreciate what we've achieved.

Whether it's dancing the night away, having a feast and a jolly, or simply sharing joy with others. Celebration lets us honour our journey and the milestones we've reached.

Celebration replenishes our souls with serotonin, endorphins, oxytocin, and dopamine, sparking happy emotions, such as joy, pride and validation fuelling us to springboard into the next chapter, mission, or race, allowing us to truly recognise.

"I did it!"

When we take a moment to acknowledge our achievements, big or small, when we look back, we reinforce what's possible. This boosts our self-belief, strengthens self-esteem, and fuels our resilience; determination and confidence, allowing us to claim our own validation.

Celebrating accounts for acknowledging our blood, sweat, and tears, the hard slog of the road we have travelled; to know we have reached the end. It's time to be rewarded for reaching the finishing line, for achieving our desired results, and to take pleasure and rejoice in our glory.

Recognising completion is essential for closure and growth.

Acknowledging when something has finished marks the end of a journey, an episode, or a season and allows us to fully embrace the present and move forward with clarity. Closure allows us to give ourselves permission to stop, to acknowledge what we've achieved without overextending. Rewarding ourselves reinforces,

"We did it. It happened. It's over!"

It helps us to celebrate progress, release any lingering attachments and make space for new opportunities.

We're free to feel good!

Played-A-Live The Bongo Song 🎵

I hope we can make a fresh start ...

Marriage Sabbatical

A chance to Reignite Love

Many of us tend to measure the success of a relationship by its duration rather than their quality. Yet sometimes a partnership can feel like being stuck in repetitive mundane routines. Like a computer needing a reboot, a relationship may need a fresh spark to bring it back to life, rekindling the connection and making our hearts grow fonder.

If the trust is strong and they're our still deep feelings and no deep wounds, having a break or space from our spouse, to live apart (staying with family or friends) can be as good as a rest. Set a deadline, no meetings, only the occasional messages/phone calls to each other, for a period of 2-4 weeks. It might be helpful. It's healthy to recognise what we have worn out, taken for granted, or missed, rather than focusing on constant bickering or the annoying peccadilloes of our spouses. We can't keep having gridlocks anymore.

To undertake this new arrangement the relationship requires being in a strong enough position to endure emotionally. No sabbatical should involve children; both parents must always remain available to their children. The children choose which parent to stay with, communication remains the same and consistent.

The break requires both of us to reset **boundaries** (215), that meet our own needs and values to trust, with no involvement with any other parties, etc. If we're in a perilous place or there are some major cracks in our marriage or partnership, we may need a third party that can remain neutral to both of us to decide if the relationship is retrievable; seek professional help.

Sometimes, we have to lose each to find each other.

When we have survived the sabbatical, and it's ended, it can feel like a fresh start. In many ways, this can be a starting point for some realness. Now we have a blueprint, it's time to do our work, talk to one another, communicate again, communicate about our communication:

"How do you feel about what I've said?"
"How are you feeling about what we've agreed upon?"

Actively listen; as a tip, watch our tone. A large proportion of friction in relationships can be caused simply by the wrong tone of voice. With healthy communication and equal effort, we can rekindle the feelings of the early days that we lost or got buried beneath the distractions of life. Leave the past behind and start with good intentions. Work towards dating again, or, if we're back to living together arrange regular quality time together and take it from there.

Romance can be revived in a relationship. Keep it alive with paying attention to detail, understanding our partners, their needs, and being there for them. Just remember what brought us together in the beginning.

Communicate. Communicate, Overcommunicate!!
Good luck!!

- Consider changing to a different compound. Intermediate Tyre.

James Bay Let it Go ♫

I hope I can get my mind in gear. Neutral …

Meditation

Inner Peace Translates to outer Peace!

Dashboard The Green Light indicates: All Clear!

"Silence is essential. We need silence just as much as we need air, just as much as plants need light. If our minds are crowded with words and thoughts, there is no space for us." Thich Nhat Hanh

I recall staying at my grandparents, making a mess, endless playing and fooling around, making memories, and Mama would say,
"Hush now, let my ears eat grass."

Other than calm down and be quiet, I never quite understood what my Mama meant at the time, now I know. She wanted stillness, quiet, to quiet, to quiet her mind enough to listen to our surroundings, our natural environment, and ground herself. We can take the time to sit with ourselves and quiet our minds in various ways and thrive in silence.

Our brains are the most important resource, we must turn the noise down. Meditation helps to grow our intuitive muscle and can be seen as a daily exercise we take to maintain our brain health. Meditation isn't just about breathing; there are emotional and physical benefits from meditating. It can be used to go within to listen. We can boost focus through creativity, manage stress, tap into deep meditation, and manifest the future we desire.

Firstly, mediation helps to silence the noise and the chitter chatter of self-doubt. Meditation improves our sleep and immune system; it reduces our blood pressure, helps us to cope with pain, melts away our loneliness and has a positive impact on our mental health. Meditation helps to develop peace of mind, calm, to have calm in our hearts and minds. If we were able to maintain peace, by accessing calm as part of our daily routines with meditation, we would manage our stress and anxiety better, and have a positive impact on our mental health.

Finding 10 minutes each day to step out of chaos to still our minds is of great worth. With daily practice of meditation we can put the brakes on irritability and be less reactive, de-stressing ourselves and reducing negative thoughts. We become more self-aware, giving us a new perspective on matters, connecting with our creativity, focusing on the present and practicing patience. Meditation clears our crowded minds leaving behind complicated notions to gain presence in the world. We can shift from feeling like we're constantly in mini emergencies, sweating the small stuff, to taking control by choosing to respond differently. Instead of letting challenges flood us with stress, we can stay calm and let them roll off.

For some, mediation is not so easy; it requires discipline and practice to experience absolute relaxation, which can be just moments away. All **emotions** (204) are to be felt in stillness. Spend a few moments listening to our thoughts, repeating self-affirming notions, shutting down the negative committee, and weeding out the negative chatter.

So, breathe in love, breathe out everything else.

Quieten the mind, silence is full of answers!

◉ Consider changing to a different compound. Wet Tyre.
Time to hit the throttle, we can get a fastest lap in.

Asake Peace Be unto You (PBUY) ♫

I hope I can find my own routine of loving myself ...

Self-Love Language

Maintenance

Dashboard The Green Light indicates: All Clear!

We all have expectations of the 'love language' in romantic relationships.
What's our love language?

A guideline is to learn how to love thyself to help promote **self-fullness** (210).
We may have a primary language that we prefer.
Here are the five love languages to keep a check on our wellbeing. To tweak or make improvements, or to inspire us to choose our own checklist.

What are our top three preferred love languages for ourselves?

Here are some examples to choose from:

Acts of Service

>   **Cleanse** - Home (260)
>   **Cook** - Nutritional Food – New recipe (254)
>   **Exercise** - New Workout Class (238)
>   **Organise** - The Closet
>   **Therapy** - Self-Development (284)

Words of Affirmation

>   **Gratitude list** - Count our blessings (326)
>   **Meditation** - De-Stress (293)
>   **Journaling** - Clarify Thoughts (290)
>   **Manifesting** - Focus Energy, Attract Possibilities (320)
>   **Praise** - Acknowledge Achievements

Physical Touch

>   **Facial** - Pampering
>   **Shaving Rituals** - Cleanliness
>   **Mud Ritual** - Relax and Release Toxins
>   **Massages** - Reduce Tension / Relaxation
>   **Body Drumming** - Invigorates Energy and Circulation

Receiving Gifts

    Spa weekend - Sleep and Stress Management
    Holiday - Relaxation and Fun
    Clothes - Confidence Booster (304)
    Tickets - Sports Events – Pursue a Hobby
    Time - Space to Be (242)

Quality Time

    Meditation - Stress Buster (293)
    Lie-in - Reduce Sleep Debt (212)
    Me-Time - Space and Self-Reflection (323)
    Wellbeing - Balance, Health and Fulfilment (272)
    Drawing - Creativity and Stress Relief (301)
    Walking - Maintain Mental and Physical Health (313)

Enjoy practising!

🎯 Consider switching to a different compound. Wet Tyre.

Kendrick Lamar | 🎵

I hope I am aware my body will change, naturally …

Menopause

We Pay for our Curves

"Menopause was an age thing, and now I realise it's a woman thing." Davina McCall

We all have a mother, maybe a girlfriend, sister, niece, cousin, friend, colleague or neighbour, who will experience menopause.
Half the global population will go through menopause, which means the other half of the globe will be impacted.

End of Racing!

Women can do other women a disservice, especially their daughters; young women are not prepared for menopause because it's not talked about enough or at all. Understandably, it's been shrouded in fear or shame because there's been little knowledge and support from our health services. We deserve better. No woman is pleased or joyful with being menopausal. Unfortunately, mother nature is in charge. We may look years younger on the outside, unfortunately our hormones keep score, so this is a wake-up call to woman of all ages.

Women are transitional beings, from puberty to fertility to perimenopause to post menopause. Our bodies are incredible; they do phenomenal things. Our shapes and curves are mind-blowing to admire. Our hormones do a magnificent job that most care not to recognise until they start to deplete. The menopausal journey can be a high price to pay for our curves.

The journey of menopause isn't the same for every woman.

Menopause can start early for some. It's important for a woman to know, from as young as being in her twentie's, to prepare herself mentally and physically so she can realistically plan ahead. Menopause is a gradual process; we find that we can't pin symptoms to a specific date. it's a drip-by-drip effect that creeps up on us, sometimes it takes a while for the penny to drop.

Menopause can be debilitating for some women, not all.

Generally, women aged 25 years have on average, 15 years left of being in the same body before change starts to occur and creep in. Everybody is different, and every woman can have a different experience. Generally, menopause interferes with every part of our being, from head to toe, inside and out; our brain, teeth, eyes, hair, bones, joints, skin, weight, sex, and all that's in between, everything.

Our thoughts, feelings, and behaviours change, as well as our judgments, confidence and concentration. It impacts our sleep, which in turn encourages weight gain. Menopause challenges our bodies, including our identity. After menopause, we can no longer rely on hormones; in the same way, our bodies require more maintenance.

It's favourable not to leave things to the last minute to prepare and take care of ourselves. There are different avenues to consider, such as, lifestyle, food and exercise. A few suggestions may help, breakfast is key. What we eat will carry us through our day and either lessen or increase our symptoms.

Sunlight is vital to balance our hormones and help with sleep; smoking, alcohol and sugar dramatically exacerbate symptoms; take supplements, especially vitamin D. A high-protein Mediterranean diet ticks many boxes; strength training is vital. Keep moving, as long as we're exercising, they all help to make the journey more manageable and we're able to cope better.

How confident do we feel about ourselves?

Ladies, enjoy our bodies whilst we can before things get a little complicated, and have as much meaningful, creative, knee-trembling pleasure as we can. Sex isn't over, it simply changes. Some of us have the best sex of our lives through menopause, and other libido's flatline. A lot is based on our genetics or how desirable we feel about ourselves; low testosterone levels can play their part too. Let's be honest, while this may be justified in a few cases, it's common for some of us to fall into the habit of withholding sex as a form of control in relationships. Using intimacy as leverage, without open communication or mutual understanding, isn't a healthy way to express dissatisfaction, especially if we're also neglecting our own emotional and physical needs.
Once we stop having sex and being intimate together, then what?

Do reconsider our bodies and find a healthier way to communicate and make our point heard.

There are alternatives and medicines that can help lessen the symptoms of menopause, such as supplements, natural relief and (HRT) hormonal replacement therapy, available for most to consider.

More knowledge about menopause enables us to make informed decisions. Knowledge helps us to prepare for the physical and emotional changes, as well as providing a choice of better treatments to relieve our symptoms. Understanding menopause and talking about our experiences, and our differences, is also beneficial. Discussing different types of HRT with other woman helps to empower us, reduce isolation, and minimalise the sense of feeling so alone.
Support is essential during this significant life transition. It is possible to find our sweet spot with HRT, we can get back to feeling ourselves again, it just takes some time. When we reach the other side, we feel a greater sense of contentment than most post-menopausal woman experience.

Men

What also helps women is to let men in. Inform the men in our lives. Men need to understand what's going on with our bodies to fully support us. For instance,

- Accompanying us to the doctor or clinic.
- Joining us for daily walks.
- Helping to cook the right foods for us.
- Helping us to get a peaceful and unbroken night's sleep.

Let's not forget, they have their own too. It's just not as intense as ours. A hormonal imbalance or decline will affect their energy, personality and mood too. They might experience low mood, anxiety, and weight gain around the middle.

They won't have fluctuating hormones that cause the symptoms women experience. However, men at this age are also going through their own transition called Andropause. Their testicles shrink, libido decreases due to the decline of the hormone called testosterone. It is important to know that if we have partners of a similar age to ourselves, that we can be there for each other.

Conversational cards about menopause can be useful to help to prompt a couple to have those uncomfortable conversations. They can be informative and help to encourage us to share our stories and reflections.

It's important that we separate fact from fiction and understand how our bodies work, to give us a sense of reassurance that everything will be alright in the end.

These are times of great vulnerability for us, this is also a time in our lives we can take the opportunity to reinvent ourselves.

Mother nature encourages us to become top priority, to give ourselves the attention menopause requires, and a new focus rather than putting everyone else first.
As Marriella Frostrup and Alice Smellie wisely said,

> *"Watch out for the menopausal woman, for she is driven and passionate, and she seeks pastures new."*

The more we know about the magic of menopause, the better our outcomes can be.

- ◎ Consider changing to a different compound. Wet Tyre.

Sterling Void It's Alright (House Mix) ♫

I hope I can get in touch with my frustrations and angst...

Screaming

Scream our Hearts out, and Breathe

Dashboard The Green Light indicates: All Clear!

Sometimes words aren't enough, that's where screaming comes in.
It's a primal instinctive release that can help us let go of intense emotions we might not know how to express. Screaming is a very primal method of turning up the volume; getting in touch with and releasing emotions that we may struggle to express or vocalise. It can be a quick method of releasing many uncomfortable emotions – frustration, tension, anxiety, irritation, **anger** (224), and annoyance.

Screaming can appeal to a soul that is not comfortable expressing anger, as it may feel unfamiliar, or because angry emotions are perceived as negative. This primal therapy often appeals more to woman than to men. If we listen to children in the playground, we'll hear that it's generally easier for girls to scream than boys.

Screaming therapy can open the door to getting in touch with old baggage and release stuck or suppressed emotions, such as old hurts, anger, or rage. Screaming can help us access deep grief or trauma allowing us to scream them out safely and process them too emotionally.

After screaming, we may experience a rush of endorphins that can help to calm the nervous system. Screaming is a powerful tool for releasing resistant, stubborn, suppressed emotions. However, this approach is not a permanent solution to mental health issues.

Join a screaming group and scream all the way to the moon!

I hope I can retreat to my calm place ...

Zen

Anything that Costs us our Peace is too Expensive!

Dashboard The Blue light Indicates: Leisurely Slow the Pace Down 🔵

It is vital in this chaotic, demanding, fast-paced world that we recharge, re-energise, and reset our spirit, retreating into our souls at least once a week, to have the best chance of getting through the week to come.

Zen promotes calm, relaxation and peace of mind.

Zen requires total relaxation, chill, calm, and letting go of everything else. A worry-free zone purely focussed on ourselves. In Zen, work is unwelcome.

It helps if our zen is flexible, portable, easy to step into. The easier it is to access, the more likely it is that our zen can become a regular part of our routine. Perhaps zen can be found, in a shed, bedroom, dining room, garage, wherever we are least distracted.

Let's find our own zen, a space that's always available to us, where we can escape, switch off from the world and fully engage in our own passions. Find something we love doing, something that makes us feel alive, makes our hearts sing, and helps us escape the grind of daily life. It may even be an activity linked to our childhood that once allowed us to disappear into joy and imagination.

What's our Zen?

Jigsaw. Reading. Train sets. Weight training. Meditation., Knitting. Yoga. Painting. Walking. Writing. Sewing. Scrap booking. Solo sport. Fishing. Lego. Gardening. Swimming. Model building. Puzzles. Star gazing. Cooking. Sewing. Cycling. Drawing. Jewellery. Flying drones

Do more of the things that make us forget to check our phones and allow our spirit to breathe. Escape and take ourselves off into our own Zen. The responsibility-free and worry-free fun zone offers us time to slow down and enjoy ourselves.

It's one of the best ways to maintain wellbeing and find balanced in life.

Follow our bliss and immerse ourselves in our pastimes!

Time to get a fastest lap in.
- Consider changing to a different compound. Wet Tyre.

October London Mulholland Drive ♫

I hope I can make a connection …

Talk-in-Trifle

Social Interactions and Connections

At times we feel intimidated or pressured with expectations that we place on ourselves when we meet others. Generally, we like to take our time before revealing our true selves, so we stick to small talk. The weather, light conversation or everyday topics that don't require much emotional effort or attachment.

Connecting with others requires having the confidence to talk and open up, or choosing a person we feel comfortable with to say,
"Actually, I'm not fine."

When we do start opening up, we realise everyone has a little bit of the same thing going on, we share more in common than we think.

If we have an exam, a driving test, or a big speech to give at a wedding. It can leave the best of us feeling anxious. By sharing with someone, we realise that other may feel the same, or that someone else has been through a similar experience. Connection makes a positive difference, try not to bottle it up.

Everyone has their own thoughts and feelings, and it's okay to talk about them. Hearing other opinions or experiences can offer new perspectives. By sharing, we can feel so much better. A problem shared can be a problem halved.

Being more open with others and sharing emotional experiences helps us bond by revealing a part of ourselves. It encourages others to open up about their emotional encounters too, and we can walk away feeling okay.

These connections are more fulfilling and engaging because we've shared a piece of ourselves, we've *"put ourselves in the picture,"* so to speak. By giving and sharing, we create impact and influence. When we reflect, it's often the exchange of genuine connection that stays with us, helping us to get to know others through shared experiences and commonalities. We feel seen and heard, so much so that we remember the occasion. This gives us the opportunity to pick up where we left off next time, rather than returning to polite, surface-level chats where we remain invisible. Next time, take the risk and have the courage to show up in conversation.

We bond through shared experiences, building memories, and spending time together. Experiencing loss or life-threatening events can sometimes forge stronger bonds, although bonding doesn't always have to happen quickly, it takes time.

Bonding begins with asking questions and receiving answers, when both people can be seen and hear. The emotions that arise from talking validate our presence and help us to get to know each other. This is where connection starts to emerge, and with time and consistency, we can build a friendship, possibly even find a compadre for life.

I use the good old-fashioned trifle as an analogy to represent the different generalised levels of interaction we participate in.

All conversations have different levels and purposes.
There are five distinct layers to consider.
Where do we feel most at ease?

From top to bottom, we have 'hundreds and thousands'; cream, custard, jelly, and the 'fruit and sponge' at the bottom.

- **Hundreds and Thousands** – Represents the sugar-coated presentations of many different masks we wear for the world. Conversation consists of exchanging pleasantries, e.g. weather.
- **Cream** – Small talk. Low levels of trust; formal conversations. We may feel 'talked at'. This level is whatever we feel most comfortable discussing. We are generally closed –e.g. current affairs, or gossip.
- **Custard** – Generally where men feel most comfortable, the speaker plays no role in the story. Avoid asking too many questions. This is where, banter, and light-hearted camaraderie occur.

- **Jelly** – Friendships, transformational conversations. A shared experience of disclosure with trusted friends. We feel safe and secure. Conversations sharing information, offering insights and perspectives, asking questions, listening deeply, and discovering. It's an influencing relationship.
- **Fruit n Sponge** - Partnership and Intimacy. Get down to the real substance. No holds barred - open, honest and heartfelt exchanges. At this level, we are on a level playing field, exchanging and bonding through **emotion** (204) and engagement. We talk openly with vulnerability and honesty, and we listen deeply, creating a sense of trust and safety, matched by physical intimacy.

Each stage of connection has its place.

Small talk may seem insignificant, but its impact is real. 'Hundreds and thousands' are the first steps to connecting and getting to know someone. It can feel awkward or unpredictable even, we can't always guess how someone will respond. Yet these 'hundreds and thousands' of everyday exchanges are healthy and make a difference in someone's day.

From an effortless, *"Hello"* to chit chatting at a bus stop, or a casual *"How are you?"* with a colleague, carry more weight than we realise.

Even a simple, *"Are you OK?"* to a stranger can be life-changing.

Sometimes, it's not the words, it's the connections words ignite that matters.

Keep Connecting.

I hope I can find the confidence to …

Confidence is Power!

Copy and Paste

Dashboard The Green Light indicates: All Clear! 🟢

Confidence is contagious; its powerful and attractive.

It embodies trust, reliance, self-assurance, and belief, all key traits of effective leadership. To others, confidence is universally appealing, and to ourselves, it boosts our self-esteem and influences our thoughts, emotions and behaviour.

Confidence looks good on everyone.

Confidence is not, *"I'll be fine if they like me."*
Confidence is.
"I'll be fine if they don't like me."

Confidence is choosing to say "No" to the things we want when we know it's not the right time for us, because we can accept, trust and believe in ourselves, knowing our strengths and weaknesses, as well as having a sense of control in our lives.

Confidence is the key ingredient in business. It's beneficial for communicating assertively, making decisions, or handling criticism. Insecurity creates doubt, vulnerability and unreliability and promotes a lack of leadership, control, and authority. Confidence is quiet; insecurity is loud. Most successful people are confident or know how to act with confidence. We can all smile.
Confident people behave differently. It's a language we can recognise across a room: their posture, strong eye contact, natural assertiveness, tone of voice, speaking slowly, calmly, without seeking approval or caring for others' opinions of them. Confident people hold a presence. They are in the here and now, confidence naturally commands attention. All these qualities are positive.

Confidence makes everything easier. When we're feeling good, we trust ourselves and gain the courage to take charge of our lives, to open doors that can take us far beyond our dreams. When we work on these qualities, no one can take them away from us. We become unstoppable. That's the true power of confidence.
If we're struggling with confidence, it helps to remember that it's not just something we're simply born with. It's a skill that can be learned and strengthened over time. However, when life feels challenging or threatens to shake our confidence, remind ourselves the price to pay is too expensive. It's too valuable to lose. Choose our battle wisely, let go of unnecessary fights, and protect our confidence at all costs.

Find someone we admire, a role model whose traits inspire us. And mirror those qualities. It's absolutely okay to imitate and practise, practise, practise. Repeat, refine and rehearse, as long as we stay connected to who we are and like the person we're becoming. We've got this!!

Power Dressing

Power dressing has become a forgotten tool that can instantly inject confidence into our day. The right outfit has the power to shift our mindset, elevate our mood and influence how we carry ourselves.

When we feel stuck in a routine with our outfits, we might experience wardrobe fatigue, which can dampen our spirits. Our wardrobe can become a secret weapon. A way to step into a more empowered, self-assured version of ourselves. Dressing with intention isn't just about fashion; it's about harnessing the psychological power of clothing to feel positive, bold and ready to take on the world.

Power dressing isn't just about looking good. It's a tool that helps us become more empowered. Studies show that what we wear can trigger positive emotions and even boost dopamine, the feel-good hormone.

- **Dressing for Confidence** – When feeling low, putting on something bold or expressive can instantly lift our mood.
- **Playful and Creative** – Experimenting with colours, textures, and mixing masculine and feminine styles sparks creativity and adds excitement.
- **Making an Impression** – Bright colours and statement pieces helps us stand out and leave a memorable impact.

For big moments like interviews, first days at work, or important meetings, to seek the appropriate attention. Power dressing can enhance confidence and help command attention.
When we look good, we feel good.
We can slay the day.

Give it some attitude and confidence will take us places.
Wear it well.

Time to load up the tyres and hit the throttle, use DRS.

James Brown The Boss ♬

End of Racing!

I hope I can find my happy ever after ...

Happy Ever After...

Wedded bliss isn't the same as Marital Bliss

We can be perfectly focussed on planning our wedding and trying to please everyone that we lose sight of the reason why we are getting married. Having a long-lasting, loving relationship can be a tremendous support and joy in our lives, yet the process of creating and maintaining an intimate bond with another person can be one of the most challenging.

Some of us want to get married, but we don't want a husband or wife, getting married might have sounded like a good idea, only to discover down the line that getting married was seen as the desired destination.

Nonetheless, getting married is the start, not the end of the chapter.

> *"Now we've married them, we need to learn how to keep them."*

We invest in our relationships because we believe they will work. We wouldn't invest our money into business if we knew it was doomed to fail. Marriage requires both parties to dive fully into the pool of love and give 100% to see if it's going to work, not just dip our toe in, or hold back 25 % for self-preservation purposes. Love is a risk we have to take; we can't expect to get in the pool of love and not get wet.

Some of our perceptions of love are what society would have us believe, love shaped by fairy tales. Disney left us at the "*happy ever after....*", but how do we accomplish *happy ever after?*

Romantic love is temporary. We base our love on the Disney version rather than reality. "Happy ever after" takes work. Nobody mentioned, it's an inside job.

True love starts with us first.

I have encountered a variety of souls in practice; each revealing the love that they didn't receive in childhood is the love they seek in adulthood. Naturally, we will seek that similar kind of love that we didn't get, because our nervous system is set to that same familiar energy, one that will attract and match our wounds.

We are drawn to a match from deep within that reflects. What we lacked. This happens on a subconscious level. We aren't aware of what we are attracting. The person we're drawn to will mirror back to us the emptiness, the wounds, the lack, or the hurt. Showing us what we didn't receive by nature, we may act out; resist moan, complain, criticise, withdraw, or blame to distract and create further hurt and division until we do our own work to heal.

Our partners are not responsible for healing our wounds. It's not for them to fix or rescue us.

It's not their fault!

They have given us a gift, a prompt to heal our own wounds, to become secure in our own right. The power of love from a healthy and secure relationship can allow us to become our best self.

We all deserve to be loved, to feel safe in a way that we don't need to question anything. The way a secure partner loves us can have an impact on our attachment style, which can help to undo some of our wounds.

Loving deeply requires courage in holding space for one another, in doing our own work to secure ourselves and build trust with each other. They can love us more fully when we know exactly who we are. Then, and only then, will *happy ever after* have a chance of lasting forever.

Ram Pass wisely explains,

"I can do nothing for you but work on myself. You can do nothing for me but work on yourself!" happy ever after."

To love is an honour, to help them feel loved!

🏁 Consider changing to a different compound. Intermediate Tyre. Time to load up the tyres and hit the throttle, we can get a fastest lap.

Elmeine Light Work ♫

I hope I can have the last say and put these feelings to bed, safely ...

Dear 'Unfinished Business...'

Role Play

Dashboard The Green Light indicates: All Clear!

When we end a meaningful relationship, or a loved one has passed away, grief is a natural process we all experience. When a relationship expires and we're struggling with some unfinished business with a family member, friend or an ex from a situation that is still taking up too much rented space in our head. It can leave us hanging, feeling suspended or in limbo with the process, we are unable to let go and move on. We must honour an ending for each situation to free ourselves of our sorrows and **grief** (265).

A healthy approach to finding our own closure is to create our own ending, to have the last word, get our point across, or let them know just how much we miss and love them. This entails having the courage to be painfully honest with ourselves, and get in touch with those unresolved feelings; to let go, sob, **scream** (300) or shout, call them all the names we can muster, by way of speaking our truth to them through writing, in the form of a letter.

This can be quite an emotional exercise, so it's important to prepare ourselves.

Find a safe space with no distractions, turn our phone off, and choose the best climate for this. Get really snug in a blanket on the sofa, or if we choose, sit at a table, wherever's comfortable for us. Have a big notepad and several pens at hand just in case the pens run out when we're in mid flow. Have tissues at hand, in case we're emotional, a glass of water, and get comfortable.

This exercise can be applied to situations regarding frustration and injustice or heartache and anguish. There are two very distinct letters I shall briefly demonstrate. Each letter is addressed to one person at a time.

Each letter will be titled; the first exercise is called '**Let them have it...**' The second exercise is called '**I miss you so.**' There are no rules for what we write, other than the letter must be handwritten, not typed or written on a device. Start by saying all we need to say in writing. If we choose to repeat a sentence over and over in writing, that's entirely our choice. A way to express whatever we needed to say when the opportunity was no longer available us.

Imagine that very person sitting opposite us. Imagine what they look like; from their facial features, to what they're wearing, shoes, hair, a hat, the position they would sit, cross their legs, lean etc. Once we can visualise them, imagine they're sitting in front of us, looking directly at us, with whatever expression they might have, waiting to hear what we have to say.

It's our turn now, it's over to you.

A letter can start however we like, Dear xxx, or '*look at me you xxxx...*', '*It's me you son of a bitch!...*' whatever our truth is, begin.

Letter One – *Let them have it!!!*

Let out all our painful, cringe-worthy memories, thoughts, hurts and frustrations, do all our screaming, shouting and cussing on paper. You have my permission to swear like a trooper.

Letter Two – *I miss you so!!*

Get in touch with the pain and the sorrow of missing them, the shock of them not being here. Acknowledge what isn't the same anymore, feel the sorrow and the loss of how much we're missing them.

Imagine the person is responding to our words in our head whilst we write, what gestures would they be making in response? We may notice our body language as a way of expression. Just keep writing, let our emotions write for us and don't stop until our hand naturally slows down to a halt; that is the sign to know there is nothing more to say, we've finished. Sign it off as you will:

"Goodbye", "good riddance" or 'xxxxxx'

MUST NOT re-read the letter or keep it, once it's written and we've wiped away our tears, tear it up or burn it. TRASH IT!

For completion, imagine all that we've visualised and fantasied in our head as though the letter has covered our body from head to toe in cobwebs. Use our creative power to physically brush all the cobwebs off our body until all the cobwebs have gone and we're cobweb-free.

We now have closure!

This exercise can be used to help us clear away the cobwebs.

If we find it's becoming a regular exercise, and a pattern emerges, seek professional help.

Mike Drop!

🌐 Consider changing to a different compound. Intermediate Tyre. We can get a fastest lap in.

Letter I. Alanis Morissette You Oughta Know 🎵
Letter II. Olivia Rodrigo Driver's License 🎵

I hope I can be open to receive comfort …

Hugs

Are for Free!

Dashboard The Green Light indicates: All Clear!

Did we know there's an 'International Hug Day'?

If everyone learned to hug one another, what a difference it could make to the world if we embraced the invitation to extend our arms and offer affection to each other. International hug day is the perfect excuse to start.

The power of a hug helps to boost our mood by releasing hormones such as serotonin, dopamine and oxytocin to calm us down for free. Oxytocin is the antidote to all the cortisol that we are pumping out with life's daily stresses: school runs, difficult relationships, kids, or the demanding job. We all have the hormone called oxytocin. It's the bonding hormone associated with love and trust. It is how we bond with our children, significant others, friends, and family. We release oxytocin through physical touch, when we are cuddling, stroking, hugging and being held.

Hugs are universal. There are different types of hugs for different occasions, each with its own etiquette. Whether they are cultured hugs, business hugs, bro hugs, bear hugs, flirty hugs, group hugs, one arm hugs, wrestle hugs, and many more.

Hugs are a powerful form of expression, a way to connect closely with someone, offer comfort, and convey warmth. Whether we gently fall into a hug or approach playfully like a wrestle, it's a shared moment of personal space used to greet or say goodbye.

Never underestimate the power of a hug. It speaks when words fall short or when we don't have the courage to say what's in our hearts.

Thank you.
I'm so grateful.
You're not alone.
I care about you.
I'm so proud of you.
I'm sorry.
I've missed you.
You mean so much to me.
I love you.

A single hug can express countless emotions and unspoken words, letting someone know how much they mean to us without saying a thing. The longer the hug, the more intimate and meaningful it can become. It makes a real difference when we hold someone until they're ready to let go, letting them be the first to withdraw ensures the message has been fully received.

To offer a truly affectionate hug, embrace with both arms, and hold for at least 10 seconds, allowing our intention and warmth to be fully felt.

When we're alone, and in need of comfort, we may only have our own arms to rely on. In these moments, the 'butterfly hug' can be a powerful and soothing alternative.

The Butterfly Hug

When we've no other arms except our own, gently cross both arms across our chest in the shape of a butterfly, with one hand on our heart and the other hand to mirror the other side gently and securely hold the hug.

Pay attention to our heartbeat and the rhythm of our breathing. Take a deep breath in, then slowly exhale. Connect with any feelings of sadness as we gently form our arms into the shape of butterfly wings. Softly tap our shoulders in time with our heartbeat, like the gentle flutter of wings.

Focus on our heartbeat and pat in harmony with its rhythm. Then hold and hug ourselves firmly for a minute or so.
Affirm ourselves simultaneously:

"I love you", "I'm here..."

Then release. If we become emotional, allow our tears to water our soul.

This exercise helps to soothe, comfort and calm our anxiety.
We all need to be held!

The Blessed Madonna Shades of Love (feat The Joy) 🎵

I hope I can feel better, one step at a time ...

Nature Walking

Walk it off to Work it out!

Dashboard The Green Light indicates: All Clear!

"I go to nature to be soothed and healed, and to have my senses put back in order." John Burroughs

My beloved dog gave me so much and introduced me to so many things in life.
I learned many things: play, daily exercise, and I fell in love with nature. Each day while walking, I immersed myself in nature through a gentle practice known as forest bathing. I tuned into the sights, sounds, and rhythms of the natural world, using all my senses to mindfully connect as it quietly transformed from season to season. Nature would inspire me in many ways, keeping me grounded and in touch with time. Walking is the best exercise, if we just take a thirty-minute walk every day, our physical and mental health would improve immeasurably.

To observe nature is a privilege.

Take the opportunity to be fully present, in the here and now, and use all our senses to experience nature at its best. For example, being mindful of feeling the breeze on our skin, the light in our eyes, hearing the rustle of leaves and smell the aroma of freshly cut grass in the peak of summer. By using all our senses, we can learn to ground ourselves and be fully present.

Practicing 'colour walking' encourages mindfulness by focusing on a specific colour. Choose a colour, e.g. yellow, notice yellow objects around us in our surroundings. This practice grounds us, boosts our mood through the release of endorphins, and supports **circadian rhythms** (274) with natural light.

To experience nature at its best is to observe nature transforming from season to season, which can mirror to reflect the seasons of our lives. There is a time to sow and a time to reap, a season for questions, a season of answers, a season to weep, laugh, mourn and dance in our lives.

This is a time when we can be with our thoughts, undisturbed, out in the elements. Walking is the best way to process things, to process our thoughts and feelings. If we are searching for the answers and feel stuck in our heads or stuck in an emotion, take a walk and clear our minds. The best time to go walking is when we don't feel like it. Trust in our process; the steps we take bring us closer to what really matters. Let's take each season as it comes, step by step.

Nature keeps rolling on, and so can we!

Alysa Marie The Woodland Realm ♫

I hope I have what it takes to get on with life ...

The Survivors of Bullying

Don't allow ourselves to Internalise someone else's Bullshit.

Dashboard The Green Light indicates: All Clear!

"I will NO longer shrink myself to be more digestible for you, I'm going to be myself and let you choke!!!!"

If we have been bullied, know this: our time is coming, because all that resilience, strength and courage have built up a defence, an armour, and a belief within the essence of who we are, along with the promises we made to ourselves to get through each day.

We have unknowingly been in training, earning 'Survival Honours', a step ahead of everyone else.

We won't break like the average person; we've been tried and tested; and we've earned our stripes. Nobody leaves this world unscathed, we all face personal battles, whether they are self-inflicted or inflicted by others. We are part of the human race, facing the obstacles together.

Bullying forces us to recognise our weaknesses. Most bullies have been bullied themselves, and all their insecurities are projected onto us. Their bullshit isn't ours to inherit. It's not our truth; it's theirs. Don't buy into it!

We learn to turn our weaknesses into strength; giving ourselves a voice takes guts. The painful existence of being the victim of a bully requires endurance and a will to survive. Out of adversity comes our own strength, providing an opportunity to grow and survive.

Now, we are the ones to be reckoned with!

Never be bullied into silence; speaking our truth is the most powerful tool we have!
   Speaking out truth is the most powerful tool we have! Congratulations!

   ⚪ Consider changing to a different compound. Hard Tyre.
Put our foot on the throttle and let that positively drive us forward in life!

Anastacia Welcome to My Truth ♫

iHope

I hope I can make the most of this opportunity ...

Life Changing Goals

What does it take?

Dashboard The Green Light indicates: All Clear!

Discipline is the only practice to avoid chaos, and confusion.

To truly discover what we're capable of, we must stay disciplined and let go of others' opinions. Whether it's starting a new job, preparing for exams, or re-sitting a year.

When we have the opportunity to pursue a goal that could potentially be life-changing, the strategy and plan to achieve it requires our full commitment. This means giving 100% focus, dedication and dedication, and effort.
No distractions or excuses.
We place ourselves at the top of our priority list; everything and everyone else must wait. This is our opportunity to improve, honour our potential, validate ourselves, and shine. This opportunity is not up for negotiation. Take advantage of the opportunity to go all in and seize what's rightfully ours.

**Meet that moment. It's our moment. Don't be intimidated by it.
It could be our only shot.**

Let's adopt the approach of champions and winners. They, too, have had to follow the same strategy to succeed. Athletes can undergo continuous training: physically, mentally and nutritionally. For example, boxers in boot camps. To become champions in their respective leagues they must make sacrifices: they switch off from the world, leave their families and homes for months at a time to advance. This commitment fuels consistency, focus and helps eliminate distractions.
We may not have the privilege to do what champions do. However, it's useful to understand that something has to give to achieve. If we can afford to take some time off work to dedicate time to giving ourselves the best shot, we're lucky. Know that discipline and dedication require sacrifices, these are only for a temporary period in our lives.

Opportunity is not up for negotiation!

🞄 Consider switching to a different compound. Soft Tyre.

The Chemical Brothers Galvanize ♫

End of Racing!

I hope we can work it out ...

Relationship Ding-Dongs

Quarrel V Squabble

Dashboard The Green Light indicates: All Clear! 🟢
If there's a phrase that makes us stop in our tracks, it's
"We need to talk!"

The power of those words creates a sinking feeling in the pit of our stomach, warning us that this is the time for an important conversation. A conversation which may lead to honesty, vulnerability leading to less, or more **connection** (302) with our partners.

In intimate relationships, mistakes are inevitable, none of us are perfect. At times, our partners may disappoint, or hurt us. Occasional arguments are part of human experience. In fact, healthy conflict can signal a real, evolving partnership, that's moving beyond the honeymoon phase, into what's often called, "reality". Understanding is the cornerstone of any lasting relationship and open communication is essential. When couples quarrel, or bicker, trying to prove their value to each other, it can often show how much we care, however, true growth comes from accountability. Saying **"sorry"** (70) is a powerful act of love, it takes vulnerability, and courage, yet builds deeper connection. Arguments aren't about winning and losing at the other's expense, there moments to understand each other.

It's not uncommon for people to avoid long-term relationships due to fear of commitment. Imogen, 33, and Tyrone, 36, came to me at a breaking point. Their relationship had stalled. Tyrone had become argumentative, blaming her minor issues that escalated into hurtful fights. Imogen felt confused, guilty, angry and resentful. Imogen wanted to move the relationship beyond the casual stage, while Tyrone remained emotionally distant and hesitant to commit.

Eventually, Tyrone opens up for the first time about his past:
*"I got stung badly. I went through a tough break up a few years ago and it messed up a lot of things for me.
I care about you, and I like where this is going, but you keep pushing me.
I need time. I need to get used to the idea because
I'd given up on relationships, full stop."*

Despite they're compatibility, Tyrone's fear of being hurt again was sabotaging the relationship.
Two key issues were conflict and commitment. Tyrone to communicate healthily, owning his emotions instead of projecting them onto Imogen. Understanding Tyrone's struggles, Imogen was patient and supportive. Together they set boundaries and learned to navigate conflict with more understanding and respect.

The primary reason couples separate is unresolved conflict. It can make or break a relationship, especially if issues repeat and apologies are withheld. When we find the relationship in retrograde, connection stalls and becomes stagnant.

Are we led by our feelings, thoughts or behaviour?

When we are under stress, our mental capacity is reduced, making it harder to operate at our best, which inevitably impacts our relationships. We often default to a specific mode of communication.

We approach conflict through one of three lenses: feeling, thinking or doing, each shaping how we communicate and resolve issues. Such as,

Feelings
"I feel so upset the way that…"
They are seeking a response to how they are feeling.
Thoughts
May approach using facts or make the decisions.
They are seeking a logical response to work things out.
Doer
Get stuck into doing something to remedy the situation.
They are seeking action to remedy.

When we start 'butting heads', it's often because we're approaching the issue in different ways, which can lead to feeling misunderstood or overlooked. This disconnect may trigger frustration and stall resolution. The first step to managing conflict is acknowledging each other's feelings. Understanding where the other person is coming from helps us find compromise. By identifying and respecting each other's perspectives, we create space for mutual understanding and healthier responses. Active listening and open dialogue can bring new energy to a relationship. Every healthy relationship requires some compromise or thoughtful gestures, whether through words, time, touch, gifts, or acts of service. These expressions often reflect our own love language (Love Languages by Gary Chapman) and the hope that these gestures will be reciprocated.

How do we treat our partner?

The next time a quarrel, arises, a helpful way to manage conflict is by using "I" statements. Instead of saying,

"You don't do this anymore..."

Try expressing how their actions make us feel. Focus on defining our own experience, not the other person.

Try not to define the other person; define ourselves:

"When you do X, I feel Y..."

For instance, consider Imogen and Tyrone 's situation: Tyrone could communicate from a feelings position, defining himself by only speaking about himself.

"When you leave and we're talking, I feel sad"
"I miss you when you're not here"
"I feel neglected when you leave..."

Instead of blaming or defining them.
This is a healthy way of getting our point of view across, when we focus on our own feelings. This approach encourages understanding and reduces defensiveness, allowing for more constructive conversation, rather than pointing blame. For a relationship to thrive, a partner's willingness to work together makes all the difference by working as a team, not opponents. Combative behaviour encourages toxicity and sustains division, while collaborations build connection. Relationships are meant to be tender, intimate, like a duet, not a duel.
Consider a monthly ritual of sharing three reasons why we love our partner. This simple practice encourages appreciation, offers gentle guidance, and strengthens our bond through praise, not criticism. Small gestures like these keep the relationship warm and connected.

In every relationship there will be ups and downs, there will be ego, fun, laughter, things said out of anger, smiles, hurt, arguments, misunderstandings, and don't forget to cuddle more!

None of us are perfect, we all have our flaws.
It's up to us to find the one that is worth suffering for!

The Jimi Hendrix Experience Crosstown Traffic ♫

I hope I can put my aspirational thoughts into practice ...

Manifesting

Joy in our Hearts and Minds, Brings Joy to our Lives

Dashboard The Yellow Light Indicates: Pick Up Pace!

Manifesting is aligning thoughts with the law of attraction.

Manifesting is a great approach to becoming aware of actions and intentions, focus, and preparation. Using the power of our mind to change and create the reality we want to experience. Manifesting is a lifestyle that can empower our souls from within.

Before our manifestations begin, it is essential to consider our **spiritual hygiene** (260), let's not block our blessings. It is becoming what we want to be before it happens, believing it before we see it. Expectations shape our reality, for our incredible brains will seek out confirmation of what we believe. If we believe something doesn't exist, then that is what we will encounter. Manifesting is re-scripting our self-talk and taking positive action to align with the intention.

The secret to manifesting is to believe that we are worthy of receiving, to know we are worthy of receiving joy, and stepping out of our comfort zones to achieve desired results. Manifesting requires self-love that is deep rooted in practice. If we don't believe we are worthy of love and success, it will be difficult to attract and experience love and success in our lives.

The Key Manifestation Techniques

Manifesting the life we want starts with intention and action. Here's how to align our energy with our vision:

- **Set clear Intentions** – Define what we want and why, directing our focus and energy.
- **Affirmations** – Use positive, present-tense statements to reinforce belief and shift our mindset.
- **Gratitude Practice** – Appreciate what we already have to attract more abundance.
- **Meditation** – Clear the mind, breathe, and connect with our inner desires.

End of Racing!

- **Scripting** – Describe our ideal reality as if it's unfolding now.
- **Energy Work** – Practices like Reiki, or EFT help remove blocks and align our goals.
- **Vision Boards** – Create a collage of images and words representing our dreams.

With every intention there is an outcome.

Be clear about our intentions and the outcomes we desire, and stay ready, even if it hasn't arrived yet. Stay ready, or we might miss the opportunity. When we combine intention with action, we can create the life we truly desire. Stay positive, trust and believe.

We can rise to anything when we claim our own personal power!

🌑 Consider changing to a different compound. Intermediate Tyre.

Cleo Sol Life will Be 🎵

I hope I can find someone to aspire to …

Role Models

To Inspire, Guide and Show us what is Possible!

Dashboard The Green Light indicates: All Clear!

Having a source of inspiration or motivation can be incredibly beneficial for our personal growth. If we didn't have a positive parental figure or caregiver to guide us or help us recognise our potential, that's okay. Let us find our own role model.
Role models can be found in many forms, through books, social media, the news, politics, magazines, tabloids, podcasts, or TV.

Positive role models offer a blueprint for the kind of person we aspire to become. It's natural to seek guidance or inspiration, even from someone we've never met. Sometimes, a single idea or example from a stranger is enough to ignite a spark within us to plant the seed that fuels our motivation, rev's our engines and drives us forward.

Think of ourselves in five years' time and choose someone or a character, who is healthy and positive, who demonstrates a few steps ahead of where we're aiming to be. It is okay to copy the individual's behaviour, appearance, style, attitude, manner, approach, technique, etiquette, decorum, voice, make-up, walk, fitness and so on. We can put our own spin on it, add our own flavour for the character to become our own. Enjoy and have fun experimenting until we discover enough options and choices that represent and express who we are. Have the courage to create a new version of ourselves, and then allow ourselves to grow in confidence. The journey continues.

If they can do it...Yes, I can!

⚙ Consider switching to a different compound. Soft Tyre.

I hope I have the courage to go solo ...

Me Dates

"Would I like to join Me, Myself, and I on a Me-Date?"

Dashboard The Green Light indicates: All Clear!

We all need time alone, especially if we live a busy lifestyle and everybody wants a piece of us. This is the time to take flight and indulge in time with oneself. To reinvigorate our spirit and lift our confidence. A time to be with ourselves, no need to worry about feeling obliged to fill the silence with another. This is a time to do as we please, without excuses or approvals.

Whether it's hitting the gym, enjoying a good book in our favourite café, soaking up live music at a bar, dining out or escaping on a city break or holiday. Our me-dates are designed to fit whatever we need. It might be a short getaway over a long weekend, or an extended break of a week or two. If it's our first solo holiday, it's best to start small and gradually build up. The goal is to feel comfortable, not too comfortable, after all, growth rarely happens in our comfort zone. This is our chance to prioritise ourselves fully, to nourish whatever our soul is craving, without the pressure to accommodate anyone else's needs.

The experience invites us to connect with who we are, away from familiar surroundings. There's only one guiding principle: we can't drive or hire a private vehicle. We must use public transport, allowing us to be present, open to chance encounters, and naturally exposed to meeting new people.

The kind of me-date we need depends on our lifestyle, and it may vary each time. Sometimes we might crave rest and relaxation, other times, unfiltered fun, light entertainment. Or the joy of being a sightseer. We might need silence and space to think, to work through things on our own, to connect with like-minded souls, to experiment with new experiences, seek inspiration, let go of emotional weight, make important decisions, or take part in tours and activities.

Perhaps we want to dress up, feel glamorous, wine and dine ourselves, or simply be at peace. Whatever it is, this time is about tuning into what we need most. Along the way, our values, principles, and boundaries may be challenged, and tested. This is a great opportunity to discover more about who we are, by pushing the limits, rising to meet challenges, and doing things we've never done before. Let's face our fears and do it anyway. This time is just for us.

Choose a destination and choose a word. Perhaps a '**nudge word'** (328) a single word that acts as a compass for our journey. Make a promise to ourselves to explore that word during our trip. It could be adventure, confidence, fun, glamor, control, peace, play, or relax, say "yes", interact, extravagance, decisiveness, tolerance, no goals, creative, excitement, nurture, flirtatious, or presence. Whatever we're struggling to prioritise at home. Whatever personal growth has taken a backseat, this is the time to focus on it fully, without distractions, guilt, or compromise. This is the moment to show up as our truest self unapologetically.

Travelling solo like this can be a transformative experience. We'll naturally find ourselves talking to strangers, building connections and opening the door to new friendships. It's a valuable chance to observe who we are when we're outside our comfort zone.

This kind or experience is a powerful boost to our **self-esteem** (144) and self-confidence. Many return from their me-date feeling uplifted, empowered, and proud, having embodied the word we set out to explore.

The benefits are so enriching, it's worth making this an annual ritual.
Once we get started there's no looking back!

Butcher Brown Ibiza ♪

I hope it's okay just to be …

"I'm Home!"

We are human Be-ings, not human Do-ings

Dashboard The Blue Light indicates: Leisurely Slow the Pace Down!

If we were the kind of child who, upon hearing our parents pulling up on the driveway or putting the key through the door, leapt into action through fear. Fumbling around swiftly trying to find a house chore to pretend we were busy, busy doing something, then we learned early on that stillness wasn't acceptable.

We couldn't be caught relaxing, busy doing nothing. I was raised to be productive, always doing something, always in motion with a chore, activity, and sometimes even busy with someone else's task. In turn, I learned that my body and wellbeing had little worth. Believing I had to earn it by helping, working, tidying, cleaning, sorting, cooking etc... It wasn't seen as favourable for me to relax, nap in the afternoon or go to bed when I was tired, not under this roof. Things needed to be done.

Most parents are doing their very best for a better life and future for their families. Both my parents were never out of work! Building careers that helped them progress from working-class roots to a middle-class life, driven by a strong sense of responsibility. All duties, business and chores came first, before anything else; the 'fun' only began once the work was done.

I was young and busy with school homework, however, to my parents, that didn't warrant being tired. I quickly learned that being busy did not rock the boat or stir things up in the house. It was a way to survive without contention, and this was how the house was run. I found the same to be true for single-parent families, especially communities of first and second-generation immigrants. Life wasn't about fun and relaxation. They came to another country to create a better life, and that required hard work. Our parents were on a mission for our better good. They were absolute grafters, not afraid of hard work to establish a place in society. Parents busy working all hours expected a hand at home with the chores to keep things running like clockwork. This usually meant that the household was run by a strong work ethic, based on the principle of hard work to make ends meet. Growing up, we quickly learned that it takes something to keep the lights on! We were expected to use our initiative and become 'mummy's little helpers'. We subscribed to become a part of a team within the family framework; parents didn't stop, we didn't stop, until the work was done. We were all in it together.

We learned to keep the 'productive' tap running, and often found ourselves doing something, believing we had to earn rest, to have permission to stop. Consequently, in our adult years, we continued. We never learned how to stop, to relax, to rest or to appropriately take care of our bodies.

We deserve to understand and embrace our **love languages** (295), to have rest and relaxation, to conserve our energy for ourselves, to regain, sustain, and maintain a healthy life. Rest is our right. It's not a reward. It's not a privilege. Rest is about realigning, reconnecting and rebuilding our bodies. It is important that we normalise pausing throughout the day to rest. Allow ourselves simply to BE. Our bodies depend on us treating ourselves right.

Enjoy being busy doing nothing!

I hope I can live life with gratitude …

Celebrate Life

Congratulations, Life is Good!

Dashboard The Yellow Light Indicates: Pick Up Pace!

We are alive!!
It is okay to celebrate simply because we are alive, to enjoy being alive, and to appreciate when life is treating us well.

Generally, when life is good, the essentials are covered and our needs are being met, we feel loved, or have love in our lives. So, celebrate what we have now. If we are fortunate enough to live the life we want and have the opportunity to strive and create the life we desire, then, celebrate. Celebrate the stability, security, and good health in our lives.

We are free to alternate between many different spaces. Spaces that offer different forms of nourishment or 'currencies' to support balance in our lives: such as pastimes, good times with friends, visiting loved ones, to learning, having an occupation, enjoy a hobby, intimacy, adventure, exercise, for comfort, or peace. We have built and created this life, so let's celebrate it. Let's celebrate whilst we can. Life has a way of changing suddenly, often when we least expect it, and with it, our reasons to celebrate can disappear. Whether its loss, conflict, hardship, or illness, we never know what tomorrow may bring. So, let's celebrate our fortune, no matter how big or small, while it's here.

Let's count our blessings and toot our horns!

Celine Dion I'm Alive ♫

I hope I can recognise my blessings ...

Gratitude

Acknowledging Enough is Recognizing Abundance!

Dashboard The Green Light indicates: All Clear!

When we start to doubt ourselves, remember how far we've come, everything we have faced and overcome.

Gratitude is the practice of recognising and appreciating the positive aspects of our lives, both big and small. It shifts our focus from what we lack to what we already have, encouraging a positive mindset and attracting more abundance.

Take a moment to write down five meaningful things we value and appreciate in our life. This simple act of recognition is the essence of gratitude.

Gratitude is the mindset of recognising and appreciating what we have. A genuine thankfulness for our blessings, big or small. While it might seem difficult to list ten things we're grateful for, start with just three small ones. Like a muscle, gratitude strengthens with practice, the more we use it, the more natural it becomes.

Practising gratitude brings positivity into our lives and changes our outlook and optimism. It helps us to identify and acknowledge our blessings, to recognise that we are fortunate, to keep us grounded and humble, and to avoid taking things for granted.

Focus on the positives of how fruitful we are, rather than the negatives in life. Gratitude is like a magnet; the more thankful we are, the more we will receive.

The Key Practices

- **Gratitude Journal** – Write down 3-5 things we're grateful for each day. They can be as simple as a good cuppa or a supportive friend.
- **Express Appreciation** – Tell people we're grateful for them. A simple, "thank you" can strengthen relationships.
- **Mindful Gratitude** – Pause during the day to appreciate little moments – a sunrise, a gesture, a deep breath.
- **Gratitude Letters** – Write a heartfelt letter to someone who has positively impacted our life. We can send it or keep it as a reflection.
- **Evening Reflection** – Before bed, reflect on one moment that made us smile that day.

Practising gratitude regularly helps rewires the brain for positivity, leading to greater happiness fulfilment. As we develop the habit, we begin to realise just how much there is to be thankful for every day. The more we open our eyes to the present moment, the more deeply we connect with the richness of our lives.

A glass half empty can be a glass half full!

Count rather than discount our blessings!

◉ Consider changing to a different compound. Wet Tyre. Gaining traction!

Theresa Phondo Blessings ♪

I hope I can do what I want to do for the new year ...

At the Strike of 12

Start as we Mean to go On!

Dashboard The Purple Light indicates: Action Required! 🟣
Check Rear View Mirror!

5... 4... 3... 2... 1... Nudge!

Everyone is given a 'new year'. An invitation to begin again.
On the count of five, do we feel our anxiety start to rise?
Many of us struggle with the commercialised expectations of the new year. The pressure to feel joyful, dressed in glitter, and celebrating as the clock strikes twelve. For some, the chime of midnight and the melancholic tune of *Auld Lang Syne* brings more dread than delight.
It's okay to step away from the noise. Allow ourselves to let go, skip the festivities, or even have an early night.

There's no obligation to feel celebratory if we're not in the spirit. Honor our feelings and embrace what's right for us.
Our new year can begin on our own terms.

This perspective invites a refreshing approach to personal growth and self-reflection. 1st January is just another day; our true new year can begin whenever we choose. Alternatively, it can begin the day after our birthday, by aligning this with the anniversary of our birth, it becomes a personal milestone, a time to reset and realign our intentions.

Nudge Words

After reflecting on the past year, **Yearly Reflections** (330), we can identify areas for growth and choose one guiding word that gives us a little nudge in the right direction. This word can encapsulate, encourage, and support the person we want to become. The word acts as a compass, influencing our actions and helping us to stay focused on achieving our goals. The word we choose can shape our behaviour across all areas of our life, helping us to clarify our goals and guiding us towards the person we aspire to become.

These guiding words are called 'Nudge Words' – (Professor Cass Sunstein and Richard Thaler), the objective is to support and encourage our decision-

making process, helping us to clarify our goals.
- How do we want to change?
- What do we want to become?
- What are the new values and behaviours that our 'nudge word' requires?
- What limiting beliefs we need to release to become a new version of ourselves?

Focus on one word for the next 365 days. A word that holds meaning and inspires growth. Let it guide us towards progress, create meaningful change, and positively impact how we feel each day. Let this word be the anchor of our year. If we're struggling to pick one, here's a few words to help us set our intention and inspire the year ahead:

Quality. Execution. Peace. Discipline. Yes. No. Boundaries. Kindness. Abundance. Care. Patience Ease. Release. Positivity. Cherish. Expansion Shine. Strength. Moderation. Playful. Forgiveness. Acceptance. Trust. Connection. Focus. Fun. Firsts. Compassion. De-stress. Joy. Reset Respect. Commitment. Confidence. Balance. Pause. Fitness. Engage. Growth. Intimacy. Loving. Empower. Grounded. Present. Fulfilled. Courage. iHope.

The Key Practices

Once we choose a guiding word to represent our aspirations, put it into action.
1. Frame it. Display it on all devices, make it part of our environment.
2. Incorporate it into our routine, so it becomes a daily practice.
3. Manifest our word.
4. Research a deeper meaning, explore books or resources that support us in developing it into a lasting **habit** (83).

Everyone's journey is different. Our word may reflect our unique path, even if it differs from others.
Spend the year fully understanding and living this word, feeling it, learning from it, and noticing how it evolves as we integrate it into our life.
Our word carries energy and presence. Step into the frequency it creates and let it guide us through the year ahead.

When the clock strikes twelve, here's to taking ownership!

⚙ Consider changing to a different compound. Intermediate Tyre.

Riccardo Muti & Vienna Philharmonic
Freiheits-Marsch, O. 226 (Live) ♫

I hope I can learn from last year....

Yearly Reflections

Give and Take

Dashboard The Green Light indicates: All Clear!

The new year is a time to look forward, however, it is equally important to reflect on the year we've just experienced. 'Give and Take' offers us the chance to look back before moving forward.

The year we've left behind has gifted us a wealth of experiences and emotions. It has also taken from us, bringing emotions tied to both new encounters and the loss of things that have ended. Reflecting on these moments helps us to recognise their impact, allowing us to appreciate each experience individually.

As we reflect on the past year, let's take it month by month, beginning with January. We'll mark the significant moments, compliments, announcements, confessions, occasions, anniversaries, holidays, celebrations, heartaches, losses, achievements, hurts, wounds, joys, and loves that shaped our year. This exercise holds deep significance for many, offering insight in unique and personal ways.

Have we noticed,

> When one aspect of our life is going remarkably well, another may seem to unravel.

To help us along, here's a few queries to prompt our thoughts:
How much do we remember from the last twelve months?

The Key Practices

1. Identify each significant episode or experience that has changed who we are?
2. Have there been significant experiences that have altered how we see things?
3. What have we learned?
4. What more do we want to take with us in the new year?

End of Racing!

5. Have we noticed any repeated patterns. What lessons have we not learned?
6. What challenges have we overcome?
7. What do we want to leave behind in that year?
8. What did our year give us, and what did our year take away from us?
9. What have we learned about life itself?

Each of these experiences leaves a mark on our spirit in its own way.

Through observation, we learn that life has a way of balancing itself, of exchanging, and levelling out the highs and the lows, the good and the bad. It often surprising us, usually when we least expect it, by presenting moments that shift our priorities and demand our attention. Some moments stand out more than others, reshaping our path and challenging us to adapt.

Experiences bring with them emotions, and they often take away certain feelings while replacing them with new **emotions** (204). These emotions either support or challenge how we navigate the experience. Just like the tides that rise, and fall, challenges and victories come and go. Every setback carries the potential for a comeback, and every struggle offers a lesson that strengthens us for the journey ahead. It's life's ebb and flow that gives our journey depth more meaning.
Throughout the year, we ride a wave of emotions, feeling empowered one moment and overwhelmed the next. We may experience joy, relief, pride, or contentment, yet also encounter, guilt, anger, sadness, fear or regret. Each emotion marks a distinct chapter in our journey, contributing to the person we are becoming.

Take a moment to reflect. List every achievement, no matter how big or small. Acknowledge the highs and the lows as well as everything in between. Celebrate our victories, learn from the struggles, and recognise how far we've come. Honour the strength it took to keep moving forward. Everything life has given us, has left an imprint on our spirit. Write It all down because every step, no matter how small, counts.

We are far more resilient than we think.

Deadmau5 & Kaskade I Remember (Extended Version) ♫

I hope I can set out a clear vision of what I want to achieve ...

New Year, New Vision

We can't Be what we can't See!

Dashboard The Yellow Light Indicates: Pick Up Pace!

As the new year approaches, it's common to feel weary, uninspired, or even disheartened by the events of the past year. If we're longing for a fresh start, a sense of direction, and renewed motivation, now is the time to begin planning. By setting our intentions in November, we can ensure everything is in place, ready for us to dream big and step confidently into the new year come January 1st.

New Years are about new beginnings and an improved version of ourselves. The only things we can control are the thoughts we think, and the images we visualise. What we think translates into what we do.

A vision board provides guidance and focus to stay on track throughout the year, (or whatever period we've for ourselves to feel we're working towards something meaningful, giving us a sense of purpose and motivation). Human beings need goals, this primes our subconscious to help us reach the intended goal and achieve what we want.

The Key Practices

1. Firstly, let's separate our professional life from our personal life. We can't be successful in professional life if we are struggling with our personal life. Success requires balance. Start with our personal life first.
2. To start our visionary board, reflect on the past year and ask:
   What did I take from this year?
   What didn't I achieve last year... Why?
   What would be our answer if we thought,

   "I wish I had more time to do ...?"
   "What can I do to make these goals a reality?"

3. Decide what we would like to prioritise this year and list our top 5 reasons that will help motivate us.

4. Start with brainstorming, then research and explore images from different social media platforms, e.g. Pinterest, Instagram, Facebook etc. Stay focused on how we want to be or want to be, live, or achieve.

5. This is the time for authenticity, transparency, vulnerability and honesty. Be specific, be exact, be ambitious, and optimistic about love, state of mind, discipline, positive emotions, house, job, exams, new activities, interests, hobbies, or motivations. Include as much detail as possible. Consider goals outside of our comfort zone. Ask ourselves:

    "What fears are. Holding me back?"
    "What's something I never imagined myself doing?"

6. Set our goals into different specific categories, e.g. love, work, health, fitness, hobbies, family, social, and wellbeing, to ensure that our goals are clear and achievable. Then break them down into realistic manageable chunks, focussing on monthly or weekly habits. Keep refining and breaking down our goals until they feel attainable and worthy of taking into the year ahead. Ask ourselves:

    What needs to happen to transform these goals into reality?

7. Commitment is key to achieving our goals. This may involve developing new habits, to encourage consistency and support change.

8. Download a planner for guidance, to encourage and keep us on track with our new daily habits.

9. Gather the information and images that we've collected to create a collage displaying our intentions.

Where there is no vision, there is no hope!

🔘 Consider switching to a different compound. Soft Tyre.

Jasmine Sullivan Dream Big ♪

I hope I can count my blessings ...

Memory Jar

Memories are Moments that cannot be bought, only experienced!

Dashboard The Green Light indicates: All Clear!

The start of a new year is a time for new beginnings. Another opportunity to scrap the old and start again, to get things right for us. The very moment the clock strikes twelve, our new year begins.

Any significant event, compliment, achievement, lesson learnt, acknowledgement, or favourite time, start collecting all our most meaningful, purposeful and fabulous moments and pop them into a jar.

The jar is a container for us to collect a year's worth of memories.

Simply write down the experience in note form on a small piece of paper, fold the paper and pop it in the jar. Keep building and storing our memories in note form throughout the year and when the end of the year is upon us, open the jar and reminisce on the good times we've been blessed with.

Enjoy reflecting on the positive aspects that we've experienced throughout the year and count our blessings. This tells us how blessed we've been. As a result, we feel a sense of pride, fun, unity from the times that we've shared with our tribe, together with a sense of excitement to springboard into the new year.

Life is a collection of memories; they become mementos.

Enjoy every moment of living!

End of Racing!

I hope I can experience a pure calm state ...

Gong Baths

Sink into an Immersion of Sound

Dashboard The Blue Light indicates: Leisurely Slow the Pace Down!

A gong bath is a sound healing meditation where we are immersed and bathed in various vibrations and frequencies and healing sound waves emanating from instruments such as gongs, drums, crystal bowls, bells and chimes.

Gong baths are not an activity for doing. They are a practice in being. They can help rebalance the mind and body allowing us to reconnect with ourselves. Gongs can heal our soul by allowing us to rest and listen to sound. Their power is multi layered, capable of changing our chemical imbalance, influencing neural pathways, and altering how our neurons fire.

Unfortunately, most of us live in a constant state of stress, predominantly filled with cortisol, and remain in our heads much of the time. For some, this state can resemble being in a 'fear state'. Cortisol, (a hormone naturally released by our adrenal glands) floods our bloodstream, when we're feeling stressed, burnt out, or overwhelmed with pressures, demands and worries occupying our minds. This becomes our default: living in fight or flight mode, moving from one crisis to another. Whether work related, within our community or involving family.

In contrast, a 'meditative state can feel similar to being in a 'love state': calm and peaceful, and restorative. As a result, our cortisol levels drop. The release of cortisol affects our nervous system, immune system, emotions, weight, sleep patterns, behaviours, and even our eating habits.
When we relax and switch off our minds, our bodies begin to take over, and cortisol levels decrease significantly, replaced by dopamine, serotonin, and oxytocin. Gong baths can help change the relationship we have with our minds. Our minds often believe they know what's best for us and default to memory, replaying our past experiences. While each of us carries different experiences, our bodies and souls all crave the same things: peace; calm, love, and flow. We all share these essential needs. We simply need to step out of our own way, quiet the mind, and let our body lead.

**This process shifts us from cortisol-fuelled stress
to a calm, restorative state.**

To experience a gong bath, no actual baths required. Simply lie flat on the floor, fully clothed. Floors are very unforgiving; so, use a yoga mat or even a bed for comfort. Most people lie on their backs, we can turn onto our sides if needed to relieve pressure. Wrap ourselves in a blanket as our body temperature may drop when we enter deep relaxation. Close our eyes, allow our body to sink into position and relax. Focus on our breath, the mind will eventually follow the body. Let our mind switch off and allow our body to take over. Relax, relax, relax.

The more comfortable we are, the better the experience. The instruments are played by an instructor for one or two hours. More experienced practitioners may engage in longer sessions.

A gong baths is a blissful experience. We emerge deeply relaxed, with no energy or interest in conflict. We are brimming with peace.

Happy days!!

Pick up a slipstream to gain speed.

Hans Zimmer Now we are Free ♫

I hope I can believe and trust …

Faith

Finding our Spirituality?

Dashboard The Green Light indicates: All Clear!

What is faith?
Some of us are devoutly religious, while others are quietly spiritual. Keeping faith is a personal journey rooted in our beliefs, values, and connection to something greater, offering inner peace and fulfilment.

Each day, I would walk my beloved dog in the woods and forests, surrounded by a cathedral of trees. Observing the naked branches, begin to bud as leaves appeared. I'd witness the changing of the seasons. Being present in the splendour of nature clears my vision, grounds me. We all find something in nature that speaks to us; for me, it resonates deeply with the spirit.

Nature is everyone's experience, and nature connects with my faith. When I see a view, of rolling hills, blue sky, and the many shades of green, blue and yellow, I feel a profound sense of connection and freedom.

We are all part of this landscape.
We are all deeply connected.

For many, finding meaning and purpose in life through faith can bring comfort and reduce stress. We may turn to prayer in challenging times, often finding solace in familiar words. Prayers can be a source of strength and comfort in times of adversity and deep sorrow.
Even for those who don't pray may have heard of this well-known Catholic prayer by Reinhold Niebuhr (1932) and felt inspired:

The Serenity Prayer

God, grant me the serenity to accept the things
I cannot change,
the courage to change the things I can,
and the wisdom to know the difference.

The stories of lived experiences I have been privileged to hear have been unforgettable, astonishing at times, even beyond ordinary comprehension. The different souls I've encountered seem to have crossed my path for a reason. Their presence mirrored certain moments in my life, taught me lessons I needed, or drew my focus to areas I'd previously overlooked. These encounters, often arrive just at the right time, sometimes even enabling me to save someone from ending their life, makes me believe there's something greater than us at work. Or is it simply uncanny?

My faith began as a child, attending church and Sunday school with my grandparents. As I grew older, hormones kicked in and life led me away, yet at pivotal moments, I found myself drawn back. Certain experiences have made me realise that I'm here for a purpose: to help, inspire and change people's lives, and sometimes to save them from harm.

We all have a choice: to embrace the signs of something bigger; guiding, protecting, giving us a leg up or nudging us forward in the right direction. Or to dismiss them.
For me, I call it ...

Stormzy Blinded by Your Grace Pt23. (Feat. MNEK) ♪

iHope

I hope I can keep a healthy daily routine …

Ode To Joy!

Daily Thrive for Wellbeing

Dashboard The Green Light indicates: All Clear!

The choices we make consistently shape the outcomes in our lives. Consistency is the key to seeing progress and achieving our goals.

I've noticed that the most beneficial routines are those that nurture the body, mind and soul. Our bodies thrive on structure and consistency. When we incorporate healthy habits into our daily routines, we create a foundation for overall well-being. This doesn't mean that pushing our limits with challenges such as, cold water exposure or interval training isn't valuable. It's about finding balance. The key is to blend both consistency and healthy challenges for growth.

The Key Practices

- Exercise.
- Daylight. A 30-minute morning walk.
- Start the day with a nutritious, wholesome breakfast.
- Drink 1-2 litres of water.
- Meditation.
- Relaxation.
- Communicate or socialise with loved ones.
- Sleep, sleep sleep. Aim for 6-8 hours.

Routine gives us structure. Our brains love routine.
These luxuries of life are priceless, things money can't buy and that we can't purchase from a shop.

Consider ourselves truly blessed with:

Time
Health
Love
Dreams
A Quiet Mind
Home full of Love

End of Racing!

Friends
Hope

Spend more time outdoors rather than under artificial light. Nature wants to heal us. Walking is exercise, fresh air and sunlight all in one. Don't forget our past and learn from it. Our strongest weapon is patience, and laughter is the best tonic. Acknowledge and care for our emotions, a calm mind can handle any situation. Ensure that we strive to thrive in excellence supporting our wellbeing. If something happens to us, the world will move on, and we will be left behind.
Time waits for no one, no matter how special we are!

Raise our standards, to live life as stress-free as possible!

- Consider changing to a different compound. Wet Tyre.

Time to change to fresher rubber to gain advantage for the undercut.

Jill Scott Golden ♫

End of Racing!

Chapter 12

Student

The Student Study Chapter guides ...

Student

Study Smart.
Support mental health and wellbeing.
Hitting our goals.

We'll cover ways to study effectively and maintain a positive and healthy mindset toward reaching our goals.

We all experience times in our lives when we are tested through the pressure of exams and adapting to student life.

We have the potential to graduate with a 1st grade, if we focus and put in the effort.
Let's go!

343 **Student Life**
345 **The Hustle**
346 **Time Management**
347 **Turning Thoughts into Reality**
348 **The Wake-Up Call**
349 **H_2O**
350 **Nutrition**
351 **Sunshine Vitamin**
352 **Unwind**
353 **Downtime**
354 **Master Momentum**

I hope I can get through this course ...

Student Life

Aim low, there's nowhere else to Go!

Dashboard The Green Light indicates: All Clear!

The first time I was a student at university, there was a group of us from every corner of the UK. Six housemates, with six different accents; Welsh, Irish, Mancunian, Liverpudlian, Cockney, and me from the Midlands. One of the housemate's dads would visit and mutter with a smile.

> *"The road to hell is paved with good intentions."*
> St Bernard of Clairvaux

His son Keanu was always on top form, full of character and charisma. He could talk the talk. However, when the morning alarms rang around the house and everyone was flying out the door, he would laugh and stay in bed for the day after partying hard the night before. Ironically, Keanu was the one whose intentions led him to fail his course, He was devastated once he recognised the opportunity he had wasted, that everyone was moving on and leaving him behind.

Being a student can be the best time of our lives, to learn, meet our new tribe, explore ourselves, experiment and attempt new stuff, to have fun times. Let's not get too wrapped up in having a good time and forget why we are here. We're here to learn, gain skills and qualifications, and build a better life.

Many students I have encountered struggle with the pressures that university life often brings. Especially the freshers, everything is different.
Being away from home for the first time, managing finances, food, living accommodation, and missing family and friends are not readily available for support. All of this can be overwhelming. Along with pressures of social media, trying to fit in, or feeling burdened by expectations and the pressure to get it right; to perform, the tests, the exams. This is an academically, socially, physically and mentally challenging time, and these factors can create or fuel stress.

Some students are juggling external responsibilities, being a parent, working, or caring for family. Combining these roles with the pressures of university life can be challenging, exhausting, and overwhelming.

Getting the right help and support
we need at these times can be crucial.

We need **help** (283) and support to get us through our course; to meet deadlines, pass exams, achieve desirable grades, rand navigate romantic relationships, or build healthy friendships. Realistically, this is an experimental time for most students, so drugs and alcohol are a recipe for disaster. These ingredients are off the table, or, if necessary, for special occasions only.

Join as many societies, as possible, especially the ones
we know nothing about.

Try them first before rejecting them, get an opinion. It's a great way to find our tribe, build friendships, and explore new hobbies which supports a full student experience.

If we've lost direction and struggle to prioritise, or time manage time, it's beneficial to communicate with our tutors. We're paying for their knowledge, a service. Our tutors are on our side, there to help us, so use them. Let them know where we are. We won't be the first or the last to find ourselves in a sticky situation. When we have to put ourselves through the mental gymnastics called studying. The following sections outline a **winning formula** (199).

It's beneficial to know what we're putting our bodies through, especially our brains. Revision is an intense crash course, that needs a helping hand.

Exam time requires a different routine and demands more of our brain. This winning formula maintains our mental health, gets us on track and stops us from crawling to the finishing line. Remember, facts don't care about feelings when it comes to our grades. To ensure our feelings don't get in the way, we must keep to a balanced schedule. Decide the desired grade we're aiming for. It's time to invest. The best project we will ever work on is ourselves.

Remember, we're good enough to be here. We're in.

As cliched as it gets, this will be one of the best times of our lives.
So, enjoy it!

Time to buckle up and turn the key in the ignition!
                               Green Day Good Riddance (Time of your Life) ♫

I hope I know what I need to study ...

The Hustle

It is worth the Slog

Dashboard The Green Light indicates: All Clear!
For our brains, studying is intensive.
Start by consuming a high protein diet, this will help support our brain function. Graze on as many nuts, seeds, and chicken (if preferred) while studying rather than reaching for high sugar or caffeine-based energy drinks that cause blood sugar fluctuations and result in energy crashes. Protein nourishes the brain and also helps to keep us alert.

Sleep (212) is paramount when it comes to supporting our mental performance. When we're deep in study, we're putting our brains through a marathon, a crash course of memory processing, as well as relying on its moment-to-moment function to keep us healthy. Our brain's need extra sleep to recover and maintain the resources required to perform efficiently. Consider getting an extra hour of sleep when studying intensely; aim for no less than seven hours, if possible.

Time (242) becomes the sacrifice we make for study. If we lead a busy lifestyle, carving out time each day for study can be a tight squeeze. Food preparation, including shopping for food, putting it away, preparing and cooking our meals can soak up valuable time. This is when our partner or parent can help support us. If they're able to take on those tasks, we're fortunate. if not, online shopping and batch cooking or freezing for the weekend. There are also healthy takeaway options that can nourish our brains.

If we're a student, treat our study like a full-time job, follow standard hours, studying nine to five around our classes. Depending on whether we're an **owl or a lark** (262), adjust our schedule accordingly.

　　◎　Consider switching to a different compound. Soft Tyre.

Time to hit the throttle!

Self Esteem Focus is Power ♩

I hope I have time to catch up and manage my time effectively ...

Time Management

Reduce Stress to Boost Productivity

Dashboard The Green Light indicates: All Clear!

A timetable helps us to manage our time efficiently. Be brutally honest about how we spend our days. Take note of our daily commitments identify the gaps in **time** (242) that could be used for revision. To be time efficient requires being savvy with time. If we can shave off one hour from our social diary, that gives us 7 hours a week, it's the equivalent of a working day that we can devote to studying. Two hours a day adds up to fourteen hours a week that we can use for study, and so on. Weekends provide a valuable opportunity to claw back some time in order to catch up. If we are busy in the week, make use of evenings and/or mornings. Then take full advantage of the weekend by following a structured schedule. Treat the two days like a nine to five working week.

Timetable

A time table helps us stay organised and prevents us from wasting time.
It's great to have direction and focus by creating a timetable that, we can refer to easily at any point during the day. An A2 size whiteboard is useful for creating a timetable that displays relevant information across a timescale of one week and up to a full term, accessible at a glance on our wall as our 'study' calendar. Across the top, write a countdown showing the number of weeks until the deadline or exam. It's satisfying to achieve a goal and tick off ✔ each week as it passes, by counting down each week, so we always know how much time we have left to work with. Use symbols and colour coding to represent the different areas of commitment e.g. classes, free time, revision time, time to unwind, and time to play. We can then easily tally up the number of hours we're committing to study each week, ensuring we're on track to meet our goals. This is also a great way to build a rhythm and make the most of any free time available to studying. Once we've drawn up our timetable, we'll have a clear view of when to work rest and play. This method helps us stay on top of things and maintain a sense of organisation by managing our time effectively.
Time to pick up pace!
  🟢 Consider changing to a different compound. Soft Tyre.

Olivia Dean Time 🎵

I hope I know the difference between positive and accurate mindsets ...

Turning Thoughts into Reality

Reality Check - Is this Accurate?

Dashboard The Green Light indicates: All Clear!

Is this Accurate?
We all have intrusive negative thoughts that can impact our relationships, work, finances, and our mental health. Here's the good news, thinking positively or negatively is a habit we can change. To thrive we need to shift our mindset not just toward positivity, but toward seeing things accurately.

It's important to understand the impact that our negative thoughts and beliefs create. Our beliefs shape everything. When a situation unfolds, our thoughts about it sparks feelings, leading to behaviours, and actions, in turn seek validation.
When we believe toxic thoughts, we risk spiralling into unproductive habits and tunnel vision, a narrow focus that makes us miss the bigger picture. This is why accuracy matters more than positivity, we need our thoughts rooted in reality, thoughts that are balanced and grounded, rather than wishful thinking. That means giving truthful, balanced attention to both negative and positive thoughts. It's not the negative thoughts themselves that hurt us, it's what we do with them. If we buy into them, they gain power.
To break the cycle we have to refuse to engage, and starve the negativity of influence, by not giving those negative thoughts that we don't believe, any attention.

The Key Questions

We can reframe unhelpful thoughts rather than suffer as victims.
When negative thoughts arise, write them down, then ask,
- *Is that true?*
- *Is this fact or feeling – e.g. fear?*
- *Is the thought helpful or harmful?*
- *What will be the impact of these negative thoughts?*

For example,
"I'll mess up this presentation."
turn into
"I've succeeded before, and one mistake won't define me."

We can challenge ourselves as we reframe our thoughts,
- *"Is this realistic?"*
- *"What evidence supports, or disproves this?"*

Practice nightly check-ins each evening. Nightly reflections can help to reframe patterns and activate positive reinforcement at the end of our day.
- List the negative thoughts we had.
- Ask. *"Without this thought, how would I feel?*
- Then, list 3 things that went well for us today.

Turning negative thoughts into accurate ones isn't about being overly positive, it's about staying grounded, in honest real truth. It frees us from **limiting beliefs** (127) and helps us think, feel and act from a place of clarity and authenticity.

Positive or negative thinking is a habit, our minds follow different highways. Some lead to optimistic realism, while others get stuck, or detour into self-doubt and rumination.
Let's shift from roadblocks to open highways in our mind.
So, which road are we travelling?

Time to load up the tyres to pick up a slipstream, overtake!
- Consider changing to a different compound. Soft Tyre.

I hope I can feel more energised and focussed...

The Wake-Up Call

Awakening our Senses

Dashboard The Green Light indicates: All Clear!

I know it's a big ask to start our day with a cold shower.
Begin by aiming for 20 seconds of full immersion in cold water, then gradually increase the duration each week until we can shower for up to two minutes. Just 120 seconds, a small habit with a big impact, can set us up mentally and physically for the day.

Cold exposure shocks our system, triggering a release of endorphins that leave us feeling energised. With a natural boost of dopamine, serotonin, and other 'feel good' hormones, it's one of the most effective ways to invigorate our soul and recharge our spirit. The power of cold exposure strengthens our immune system and supports our mental health by reducing stress, boosting our mood and combating fatigue.

Awakening our senses with a burst of cold is the ultimate wake-up call to kickstart our day!

Time to load up the tyres to pick up a slipstream, overtake!
- Consider changing to a different compound. Soft Tyre.

I hope I can maximize my resources ...

H_2O

Mental Quencher

Dashboard The Green Light indicates: All Clear!

The quality of water is important and makes a difference, especially if it contains electrolytes.

We can survive without food for up to three weeks, yet we cannot survive without water for more than three days.

Our **brains** (72) (approximately 80%) are composed of water, and fat.
Water helps improve the brain's efficiency and enhances short-term memory function. It is essential for our bodies, particularly during periods of intense studying. We must maintain hydration to sustain focus and concentration, which in turn increases our performance by improving endurance. Water also helps prevent headaches, let's stay ahead of any obstacles.
On average, one and a half to two litres of water per day will serve us well, especially given the demands that this level of mental intensity places on our bodies. However, be aware that too much water can dilute the sodium levels in our blood; everything in moderation.

We can find natural electrolytes in drinks like coconut water and watermelon water.
The more we stay hydrated, the more our body learns to crave it.

I hope I don't feel anxious ...

Nutrition

Kick starts the Day

Dashboard The Blue Light indicates: Leisurely Slow the Pace Down! 🔵

Yep! Breakfast is the most important meal of the day.

It is vital that we eat breakfast within the first 90 minutes of waking up. If we skip breakfast and deprive our body of fuel, this puts the body under stress. The body starts to panic, and if we are prone to experiencing anxiety or anxiety attacks, this is the perfect invitation to encourage anxiety and stress levels to rise and interfere with our day. Ninety percent of our serotonin is produced in the gut, so eating the right foods is essential for supporting mental health.

For example, we can't go wrong with most of the ingredients of the full English breakfast, the vegetarian or vegan version, depending on our preference. A nutritious fish dish with high protein, fibre and vegetables can also provide essential vitamins and minerals. Porridge is a good alternative, as it slowly releases energy throughout the day. What we eat for breakfast usually sets the tone for the rest of the day.

If we eat unhealthily, we are likely to experience sugar spikes, crave unhealthy foods, and subsequently consume more high-calorific food that fails to satisfy our appetite, creating an unhelpful cycle. High-protein **foods** (254) help keep us alert and energised, making them a much better alternative than high-sugar/caffeine-laden energy drinks. If we struggle to eat a large portion in the morning, try a boiled egg, or an omelette.

A little is better than nothing.

Fuel our engine to start the day. Ensure we eat three balanced meals a day and graze on protein -rich and plant-based snacks throughout the day.

Give our body the right nutrition, and it will go the distance!
Keep the engine purring and be kind.

    ⚫ Consider switching to a different compound. Soft Tyre.

Student

I hope I can lift my mood and maintain routine ...

Sunshine Vitamin

Cast some light on the Subject

Dashboard The Green Light indicates: All Clear!

Whether we're owls or larks, it's healthy and helpful for students to get outside and soak up some natural daylight the day, whether it's before breakfast, or lunchtime.

Walking in nature can soothe and de-stress us from exam pressure and help break up the monotony of revision.
A daily twenty-minute walk, run, or even just sitting outside, is a winner. If we get some fresh air, and are exposed to direct daylight, it provides us with our daily vitamin D requirement. Depending on skin tone and location, Caucasian people typically need twenty minutes, whereas people of colour may need up to forty minutes.

The sunshine vitamin boosts brain function and our mental health by regulating our mood and reducing risk of depression and anxiety. It increases our cognitive performance by improving memory and focus during studying. Vitamin D helps calcium absorption, strengthens our bones, supports muscle strength and endurance. As a bonus, it helps regulate our body clock to encourage sound sleep at the end of the day.

Foods such as, fatty fish, eggs, and mushrooms help to maintain healthy vitamin D levels which supports our body, brain and immune system.

Vitamin D is vital to staying sharp, strong, and resilient!

🟢 Consider changing to a different compound. Medium Tyre. Driving on the limit!

The Beloved The Sun Rising 🎵

I hope I can unwind after intense studying ...

Unwind

Rest our Brain

Dashboard The Blue Light indicates: Leisurely Slow the Pace Down!

Give ourselves time to unwind, de-stress, and switch off after revision, or the daily stress. Anxiety and intensive **brain** (72) activity may not allow us to fall asleep straight away.
Allow ourselves time to train our body to know when
it's time to switch off.

No more reading, memorising, planning, arranging, solving, or overthinking. Let's give our brains the rest they deserve.
Allowing our mind to disconnect from tasks is essential. It reduces stress and recalibrates our brain. Boosts creativity and problem-solving by allowing our mind to disconnect from tasks which sparks 'incubation' time. This lets new ideas surface and solutions to emerge – hence, why the best ideas come from walks. Loosening up improves our mood and boosts feel-good hormones, serotonin and dopamine, reduces our negative thoughts, helping us to manage our anxiety and frustrations better. Mindful relaxation, such as meditation, improves our sleep quality by quietening a busy mind before bed. Unwinding helps us to show up in our relationships. By calming our mind, we create mental space to be fully present, and patient which encourages deeper connections.

It's in our best interests to plan productively for tomorrow. Whatever activity that helps us unwind, maybe a bath, gaming, playing music, meditating, or shifting our focus to something effortless can be beneficial.
Unwinding isn't a pause or a break, it's a powerhouse that fuels creatively, emotional resilience, and healthier relationships.

Switch off, unwind and rest the brain!
Be kind to keep our engine purring.

◉   Consider changing to a different compound. Wet Tyre.

Zero 7 Give it Away ♫

I hope I can learn how to spend my spare time effectively ...

Down Time

Time to Refuel

Dashboard The Blue Light indicates: Leisurely Slow the Pace Down!

When life is tough, it's time to engage in a bit of fun and escapism, be it watching films, reading books, listening to podcasts, paintballing, walking in nature, dancing, or simply just leaving those four walls, out of the house to meet some new souls. It's important to know that when we have a deadline to meet, we're fully focused, not being distracted, looking left or right, keeping our heads straight ahead, staying in our lane. Yet our spirits still need time for rest and relaxation, to re-energise from being on the go at full throttle.

A good sign is 'cabin fever', when things are becoming too beige, when we've seen the same four walls for too long and haven't been outside, been stuck doing the same rounds of work at home, or simply going from work to home with nothing in between. That's the time a break is overdue.

Take a day or half a day out of our schedules to do something entirely different from our plans. Somewhere we can fully switch off, step away from our current environment and surroundings, and reintroduce a different landscape to stimulate, energise, and revitalise our souls. Consider catching up with friends, getting lost in a different landscape or scenery. To see, hear and experience new and different things without considering the coursework we're undertaking. Leave those behind at home, switch off, and enjoy stepping out of our bubble and having some quality time with people that matter. If we choose to be with ourselves, go find a view that inspires us, breathe in the fresh air, and get ready for starting again.

> Sometimes we have to slam on the anchors; to take the time to revitalise, lift, and reboot our spirits.

Recognise that love, **care** (191) and attention to ourselves are what get us over the finishing line. When we pull over into the pits and take time to refuel ourselves to go back on track. It won't feel like we've been driving on standard 95 octane, we'll be fuelled and boosted back on super-unleaded.

Time to apply the brakes. We can set the fastest lap.
  🌑 Consider changing to a different compound. Intermediate Tyre.

Xavier Rudd Follow The Sun ♫

I hope I don't fall back on work ...

Master Momentum

Prevention is better than Cure

Dashboard The Green Light indicates: All Clear!
Be uncompromising in protecting our mental health and wellbeing.

The only time we may lose our balance is when we fall behind. It's crucially important that we stay on top of things and keep one step ahead to look after our mental health, to keep **anxiety** (220) and **stress** (164) under control. With preparation and consistency, we won't need to burn ourselves out, experience, stress, anxiety, panic attacks or crashes, or withdraw, fall into **isolation** (169), lose friends, lose social contact, and develop depression.

Stay focussed and master our momentum.

Don't waste our three years. It's an expensive three years of both our time and money. There will be times when it feels like a slog, but we're absolutely worth it.

Get a healthy balance between our 'down time' and our 'time to flex'. It's a win win!!

Keep up the pace. Time for more downforce.
Put our foot on the accelerator and go!!
  🏁 Consider switching to a different compound. Soft Tyre.

Graduation's coming our way!

Baz Luhrmann Everybody's Free (To Wear Sunscreen) ♬

iHope

Chapter 13

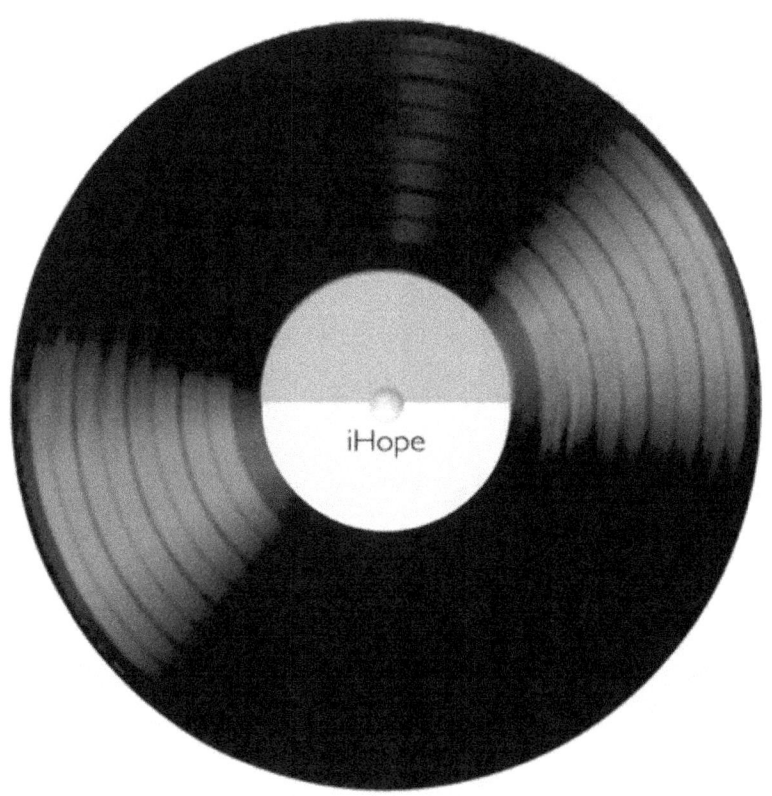

Wheel Ups

The Wheel-Ups Chapter motivates ...

Wheel Ups!

Create our own playlist.

Music has the power to heal, motivate, and inspire us. It can be the soundtrack to our lives, providing us with the energy to overcome challenges, reflect on our journeys, and celebrate victories along the way.

The *iHope* playlist is a curated selection of songs that speak to the highs and lows of life. Songs that lift us up when we're feeling down, push us forward when we feel stuck, and help us find clarity when the road ahead seems uncertain.

This chapter focuses on the positive impact of music on our wellbeing and how we can use it to stay on track towards our *iHope*. Just as a car needs fuel to keep moving, music can fuel our emotional, mental and physical progress.

358 **Wheel Ups!**
361 **Playlists**
370 **iHope 101 Playlist**

I hope I can catch a vibe to keep me on point

Wheel Ups!

Rinse and Repeat

Dashboard The Green Light indicates: All Clear!

"If music be the food of love, play on!"
(Duke Orsino) Twelfth Night – William Shakespeare

Music is medicine.
Motivation is not just about mental strength; it's about the state of our entire being, our mind, body, and soul. Music has the incredible ability to cleanse our minds, heal our hearts, and elevate our spirits.

When life comes at us fast and we find ourselves facing tough times with no one there to support or encourage us, we often need an extra boost. This is where music steps in providing motivation, inspiration, and validation through its powerful melodies and lyrics. Listening to a track that resonates with our current experience can make all the difference, re-energising our souls, helping us stay on track, or even encouraging us to exit a situation gracefully.
Music is not just a backdrop; it's a driving force that can keep us focused, accelerate our progress, to push us toward our goals. It's time to 'Wheel it up,' to let the music speak for us, shout for us, lift us, and elevate us to navigate us to the finishing line.

The 'Wheel Ups' playlist reflects my insights and wisdom about life's challenges, intertwined with references to cars and different aspects of car culture. Inspired by Formula 1, this playlist uses the metaphor of cars to give us the energy and the push we need to keep moving forward.
Each song in the playlist is carefully selected to support the themes and advice offered in the chapters. Fuelling us to clear our misty windscreens of sadness, regret, disappointment, hurt, fear, and frustration, and keeping our eyes on the prize with clear focus. Whether we need to boost our motivation, find solace in our struggles, or simply keep moving forward, the *iHope* playlist offers the soundtrack to guide us through our journey, providing the right notes to keep us on track and the power to reach our desired destination.

The power of music can change our state of mind.

It's an art form that transcends boundaries, crossing all cultures and acting as a universal poetry that unites us. At the same time, music is deeply personal. It weaves into the fabric of our lives, connecting and translating our individual stories. A song can reflect a pivotal episode in our journey or transport us back to a memory, much like a Kodak picture etched in our minds. Whether through the lyrics, melody, harmony, riff, or bassline, music has a remarkable ability to evoke emotions and guide us down 'memory lane'.

Music is art, and like all art, it is subjective.

It's beauty lies in how we, as listeners, choose to interpret it, drawing from our own frame of reference to find meaning and connection. Through its power, music becomes more than just a sound; it's a bridge to our emotions, a mirror to our experiences, and a source of healing and inspiration.

Music can penetrate our souls. If our hearts are under arrest, music can turn us inside out or make our hearts purr and take us on a journey. A happy place, help us get into our feels, release pent up emotions, validate our thoughts, encourage us to connect with our inner child and have fun, sing and dance. Music keeps us moving and pushing; it lifts our vibrations and reduces stress.

Music from all different genres has its place. Before House music was born there was Hip Hop, Soul, Ska, Punk, Rare Groove, Disco, Reggae, Glam Rock, Motown, Folk, Country, Rock n Roll, Rhythm and Blues, Blues, Jazz, Gospel and so on.

What is our preferred choice of music?

Being a 'House Head' some of us may wonder what this means or where House music comes from. House Heads are known for loving House music. It's one of my favourite genres of music.

As an example of how music evolves, House music goes back to the 80's. After the revolution and demise of disco music, a new underground movement was born in a small warehouse in Chicago, called House music. The term 'House' music came from the name 'Warehouse'. The style and genre became synonymous with Chicago producers that Knuckles influenced. DJ Frankie Knuckles is the godfather of House music, he worked at Warehouse, a small club in Chicago.

Warehouse was originally a club that primarily catered for the LGBTQAi+ community, along with African American members and other ethnicities that frequented the club to dance and feel safe in the 80's. The dancefloor was a joyful and liberating space to express themselves, dance their blues away, to celebrate and have fun. The dance floor brought people together from all walks of life to create a community, a space I like to call the adult playground.

House music began as a mix of rock beats, disco break loops, drum machines, keyboards, and R n B songs, that advanced to strings, vocals, piano and a baseline arrangement. A simple formula that became the dominant sound of House music. When House hit the UK, this underground scene went under the radar, it wasn't on the radio here. We had to sniff out the small clubs or early raves, even abandoned warehouses or fields. It changed the pulse of underground music that had an energy all its own.

House has influenced genres such as, EDM (Electronic Dance Music) to Acid House, Afro House, Tech House, Latin House, Balearic Beat, Rave music and many more. They all emerged to stand on the shoulders of House music. Many other genres of music were created and came into existence in a similar way, from one division of music emerging into another sound of music.

Playlist 101 is an eclectic mix of music from mainstream to House, Indie, Dance, Alternative, Hip-Hop, Soul, Rock, Classical, Pop, Jazz, Afro Beats, Garage, Reggae, Folk, Drum and Bass. Each track is connected to the various themes explored in this book. Care has been taken to minimise profanity or offensive language; some tracks featuring motor-themed references are in keeping with the spirit of Formula 1. Along the way, we may discover songs that shift our perspective, spark a sense of purpose, or ignite our motivation.

The *iHope* playlist is a collection of powerful songs from inspiring artists, celebrating life, love and positivity. Music is a deeply personal art form, how we experience it is shaped by our own journey, allowing each of us to connect in a unique way.

The tracks have been thoughtfully selected to reflect the book's core themes. Some have been intentionally left blank, inviting us to connect them to our own story.
As we listen, we may recognise parts of ourselves in the lyrics or melodies. If a song strikes a chord, let it fuel our momentum and encourage us to fly.

Louie Vega I Hear Music in the Streets ♫

I hope I can find a song that supports my space...

Playlists

The playlist is designed to inspire and motivate, tailored to support different projects or stages of our journey.
In our lives, music is a powerful tool for enhancing focus, boosting creativity, or providing emotional support during a task. Whether the project is short-term or long-term, having a playlist with songs that reflect the subject matter or evoke the right feelings can help maintain momentum and spark new ideas.
Here's how we might approach creating this kind of playlist.

1. **Define the project's mood** – What is the subject matter or the motivational landscape of our project? Is it introspective, energetic, nostalgic, or goal-orientated?
   The playlist can mirror these qualities.

2. **Select tracks to match the stages of the project** – For long-term projects, we could have different phases of music.

   Beginning – Tracks that energise and inspire, setting the tone for a new start.
   Middle – Songs that maintain focus and keep us on track – more emphasis on being steady, and introspective.
   End/Completion – Music that celebrates achievement and encourages reflection.

3. **Personal connection** - Pick songs that resonate with our experiences. If they trigger breakthrough memories or align with our current project, they can be powerful motivators.

4. **Variety to suit the environment** - If we are working in a fast-paced, high-energy environment, we might want upbeat songs to keep us moving. If we need calm, softer, instrumental tracks might work better.

5. **Flexibility for the journey** - The playlist is dynamic, so we can adapt it as we go. Sometimes, we stumble on a particular song on a low

day that gives us exactly what we need to keep going. On other days, a different song might spark new ideas.
If we are on the move and need encouragement, the playlist can be tailored for both short-term and long-term goals.

Here are some clear examples of how we can simplify and organise them.

1. Playlist: Short-Term Project

Beginning – Set the Tone

- **Mike Cruz** Most Precious Love
- **Sounds Of Blackness** Optimistic
- **Marshall Jefferson & Solardo** Move Your Body
- **Steppenwolf** Born to be Wild
- **Anastacia** Welcome to My Truth
- **James Brown** The Boss
- **Kendrick Lamar** I
- **Basia** New Day for you
- **Bon Jovi** It's My life

Middle – Push through

- **Eminem** Lose Yourself
- **Kate Bush and Peter Gabriel** Don't Give Up
- **Wookie (feat Lain)** Battle
- **Sterling Void** It's Alright (House Mix)
- **Folly and The Hunter** Lose that Light

End – Celebrate

- **Celine Dion** I'm Alive
- **Theresa Phondo** Blessings
- **Milk & Sugar Feat Lizzy Pattinson** Let the Sun Shine
- **Thee Sacred Souls** Live for You
- **Primal Scream** Moving on Up

- **Nina Simone** Feeling Good

2. Playlist: Long-Term Project

Beginning – Inspirational
- **NF** Hope
- **Jasmine Sullivan** Dream Big
- **Sounds Of Blackness** Optimistic
- **Des'ree** You Gotta Be
- **Green Day** Good Riddance (Time of your Life)
- **Donae'o** I

Middle – Focus
- **Pharrell Williams** Piece by Piece
- **Whitney Houston** Step by Step
- **Sade** Keep Looking
- **Ariana Grande** Breathin'
- **Beautiful Chorus** Inner Peace

End – Reflect
- **Deadmau5 & Kaskade** I Remember (Extended Version)
- **Thundercat & Tame Impala** No More Lies
- **Coldplay** Warning Signs
- **Christina Aguilera** Hurt
- **Pearl Jam** Rearviewmirror
- **Nina Simone** Feeling Good

3. Couples Playlist

The playlist can be a powerful tool for couples to communicate with each other without confrontation.

Amber, 34 and Hendrix, 34 are facing their first major relationship challenge as a couple. Amber avoids confrontation and struggles with **decision-making** (202). They're finding it difficult to initiate a conversation about it. A great icebreaker might be playing a song that's related to the topic that reflects their situation.

Hack

That hack that captures this issue might be **Couples** (292), the soundtrack for this subject is:
- **Louie Vega** Can We Keep This Going

Another hack that captures this issue would be **Decisions Decisions** (202) the soundtrack for this situation is:
- **Heatwave** Mind Blowing Decisions

This is a playful approach for couples to ease into conversation, creating a more comfortable space that encourages open, and honest dialogue.

Here are a few common scenarios that couples often encounter in therapy, where music can act as a transformative and therapeutic tool. This may help them to uncover suppressed emotions, find the words they struggle to speak, and encourage a stronger sense empathy and connection.

Music can provide a safe and navigate the intrinsic layers of relationship dynamics that are sometimes too overwhelming to address through conversation alone.

A. Unheard or Overwhelmed with Responsibilities

Javier, 44, and Chaya, 39, – Javier feels overwhelmed by the mental load, handling everything on his own, carrying all the responsibilities, and managing the household alone. Anger and resentment towards Chaya have been building, and despite having the same conversation repeatedly, the last ding-dong felt like the final straw.

- **Jamiroquai** White Knuckle Ride (Monachy Remix)
- **Heatwave** Mind Blowing Decisions
- **Amerie** 1 Thing (instrumental)
- **Coldplay** Warning Signs
- **The Jimi Hendrix Experience** Crosstown Traffic

B. Emotional Distance

Sergio, 42, and Darcy, 33, – Sergio has been finding it difficult to open up to Darcy. He's been bottling up his feelings for too long, and doesn't know how to express what he's feeling He can't quite pinpoint the cause of his low mood, only that he's been feeling increasingly down, as though he's sinking towards rock bottom. Now, he realises that he needs both her support and professional help, and is beginning to consider therapy.

- **Mr Probz** Waves (Robin Schulz Remix radio edit)
- **Lewis Capaldi** Survive
- **Germaine** Rose Rouge
- **Tracy Chapman** Change

C. Past Issues – Trust

Marvin, 34, and Lillybet, 36, – Lillybet's been carrying emotional from past experiences. Old wounds that were never fully healed are resurfacing, creating barriers and preventing her current relationship from moving forward. Trust issues are triggering waves of anxiety and fear making her feel emotionally guarded. She recognises in order to move forward she needs to heal from the past events, for herself and for a healthier and more secure connection.

- **Christina Aguliera** Hurt
- **Pearl Jam** Rearviewmirror
- **Freddie McGreggor** I was Born a Winner
- **Sade** Keep Looking
- **Doves** There Goes the Fear
- **Ram Dass (feat Krishna Das)** I Am Loving Awareness

D. Sexual Frustration

Harmonie, 38, and Orson, 40, – Orson has stopped trying, becoming too comfortable and stuck in his old ways. As a result, things have changed in the bedroom, causing friction, and affecting confidence. This led to disagreements and feeling disconnected as a couple.

- **Lil Wayne & Babyface** Comfortable
- **Scissor Sisters** Comfortably Numb
- **Tony Bennet & Lady Gaga** Let's Face the Music and Dance
- **Louie Vega** Can We Keep This Going

E. Parenting Challenges

Brogan, 35, and Xander, 33, are under pressure from mounting debt, which has intensified stress within the relationship. Xander's emotional distance and rigid parenting style often leaves Brogan feeling unsupported and inadequate, causing frequent arguments. Brogan finds herself constantly trying to keep the peace, juggling responsibilities and emotional strain, and in doing so she feels she's slowly losing herself in the process.

- **Radiohead** Reckoner
- **Joan Armatrading** Show Some Emotion
- **James Vincent McMorrow** Higher Love
- **Lola Young** Messy
- **Florian Christl** Natural

By using music as a medium to reflect and express our concerns, couples can create an emotional connection and facilitate conversations that might otherwise feel too difficult to initiate.

Tyre Playlist

Life is like a race. The tyres we choose represent how we navigate different situations. Just as in racing, we must switch compounds to adapt.

The red tyre represents bursts of energy and focus. The white tyre represents balance and maintenance. The green offers support, and the blue tyres bring calm and relaxation. Choosing the right playlist of strategies ensures we stay in control and keep moving forward.

Blue Compound

- **Mike Cruz** Most Precious Love
- **Cymande** Dove
- **Ariana Grande** Breathin'
- **Cleo Sol** Life will Be
- **Travis** Writing To Reach You
- **Asake** Peace Be unto You
- **Hans Zimmer** Now we are Free
- **October London** Mulholland Drive
- **Beautiful Chorus** Inner Peace

Green Compound

- **Mike Cruz** Most Precious Love
- **Madonna** Nothing Really Matters
- **Marshall Jefferson & Solardo** Move your Body
- **Tracy Chapman** Change
- **Wookie (feat Lain)** Battle
- **Cymande** Dove
- **Germaine** Rose Rouge
- **Freddie McGreggor** I was Born a Winner
- **Thee Sacred Souls** Live For You

⚙ White Compound

- **Mike Cruz** Most Precious Love
- **Marshall Jefferson & Solardo** Move your Body
- **Alysa Marie** The Woodland Realm
- **Cymande** Dove
- **Yung Wylin** Good Energy
- **October London** Mulholland Drive
- **Flawed Mangoes** Somniferous
- **Thee Sacred Souls** Live For You
- **Theresa Phondo** Blessings
- **Travis** Writing To Reach You
- **Larry Heard** Can You Feel it (Instrumental)

⚙ Yellow Compound

- **Mike Cruz** Most Precious Love
- **Marshall Jefferson & Solardo** Move your Body
- **UB40** Food for Thought
- **Milk & Sugar** Let the Sun Shine (Terrace Club Mix)
- **Flawed Mangoes** Somniferous
- **Franky Wah** Boundaries

⚙ Red Compound

- **Mike Cruz** Most Precious Love
- **Marshall Jefferson & Solardo** Move your Body
- **Eminem** Lose Yourself
- **Des'ree** You Gotta Be
- **Asake** Peace Be unto You
- **Alysa Marie** The Woodland Realm
- **Franky Wah** Boundaries

- **UB40** Food for Thought
- **Sounds Of Blackness** Optimistic
- **James Brown** The Boss
- **Pharrell Williams** Piece by Piece
- **Jasmine Sullivan** Dream Big
- **Franky Wah** Boundaries

Use the tunes to keep us on track and remind us, to stay focused.

Alternatively, we can refine our own playlist according to our goals. Here's *iHopes* top 101 jams to pick, mix or add to our rotation.

Take this as an inspiration to create our own playlist to support our *iHope*.

It's time to Turn it up, and drop our waistline!

I hope there is a listing of music ...

iHope 101 Playlist

Rinse and Repeat

Jend Backseat
NF Hope
Basia A New Day for You
Cultural Warriors & Errol Dunkley A Little Way Different
Frank Sinatra That's Life
The Verve Bitter Sweet Symphony
Justin Timberlake Let's Take a Ride
Steppenwolf Born to be Wild
Limp Biztic Rollin'
Sash Adelante
Ed Sheeran Drive
Pulp Common People
Mr Probz Waves (Robin Schulz Remix radio edit)
Primal Scream Moving on Up
Annie Lennox Little Bird
HNNY Kindness
Children of Zeus Vibrations
Massive Attack Unfinished Sympathy
Serial Killlaz Traffic Blocking
Kate Bush and Peter Gabriel Don't Give Up
Snow Patrol Chasing Cars
Alanis Morissette Thank U
Solange Cranes in the Sky
Donae'o I
Madonna Notting Really Matters
Little Simz Woman (feat. Cleo Sol)
John Lennon and Yoko Instant Karma (We all Shine On)

Wheel Ups

Ram Dass (feat Krishna Das) I Am Loving Awareness
Harry Styles Lights Up
Eagles Desperado
Farafina Mousso Lubiana (Acoustic Version)
Freddie McGreggor I was Born a Winner
Jungle Keep Moving
Bon Jovi It's My Life
Keala Settle & The Greatest Showman Ensemble This Is Me
Lil Wayne & Babyface Comfortable
Rozni Wykonawcy John Williams: Schindler's List
Villagers Courage
Micheal Kiwanuka Love & Hate
Yung Wylin Good Energy
Alex Serra Human
Tony Bennet & Lady Gaga Let's Face the Music and Dance.
Dua Lipa Scared to be Lonely (Acoustic Version)
Celeste Hear my Voice
Thundercat & Tame Impala No More Lies
Manic Street Preachers If You Tolerate This Then Your Children Will Be Next
Scissor Sisters Comfortably Numb
Nitefreak, Imad & Clubhouse (Black Coffee feat Shoba) Not the Same
49th & Main Self Sabotage
Joan Armatrading Show Some Emotion
Radiohead Reckoner
Utah Saints My Mind Must be Free
Gwen Stefani What You Waiting For? (Jacques Lu Cont's TWD Mix)
Jamiroquai White Knuckle Ride (Monachy Remix)
Fleetwood Mac The Chain
Bob Marley Who the Cap Fit
Raye & Hans Zimmer Mother Nature
Cat Burns Live More and Love More
Khalid & Disclosure Know Your Worth
Ezra Collective Ego Killah

iHope

Alexis Jordan Happiness
Christina Aguliera Hurt
Jill Scott Comes to light (Everything)
George Michael Let Her Down Easy
Seal Get it Together
A Tribe Called Quest Stressed Out
Coldplay Warning Signs
The Police So Lonely
Faithless Salva Mea
Folly and The Hunter Lose that Light
Marvin Gaye Got to Give it Up, Pt1
Brandon Flowers I Can Change
Pearl Jam Rearviewmirror
Lola Young Messy
James Vincent McMorrow Higher Love
Mike Cruz Most Precious Love
Maze Changing Times
Des'ree You Gotta Be
Foo Fighters Wheels
Eminem Lose Yourself
Brandy Best Friend
Heatwave Mind Blowing Decisions
I Virtuosi Italiani & Daniel Hope Experience
Pharrell Williams Piece by Piece
Radiohead Airbag
Terri Walker Fearless
Flawed Mangoes Somniferous
Mahalia Terms and Conditions
Franky Wah Boundaries
Beautiful Chorus Inner Peace
Sade Keep Looking
Doves There Goes the Fear
Amerie 1 Thing (instrumental)

McAlmont & Butler Yes

Mr Fingers Can You Feel it (Instrumental)

Take That & Sigma Cry

Whitney Houston Step by Step

Alexia Chellun The Power is Here Now

Marshall Jefferson & Solardo Move your Body

Sounds Of Blackness Optimistic

AMC Time

Lewis Capaldi Survive

Ariana Grande Breathin'

Koelle The Void

The Allman Brothers Band Jessica

UB40 Food for Thought

Jorja Smith Little Things x Gypsy Woman - (L Beats Mashup)

Adele Rolling in the Deep

Oasis Stop Crying your Heart Out

Cymande Dove

Air All I Need

Tom Rosenenthal It's Ok

Florian Christl Natural

Wookie (feat Lain) Battle

D'Angelo Cruisin'

Thee Sacred Souls Live For You

Milk & Sugar Feat Lizzy Pattinson Let the Sun Shine (Terrace Club Mix)

Olivia Dean It isn't Perfect, but it Might Be

Justin Timberlake Suit and Tie (radio edit)

Germaine Rose Rouge

Tracy Chapman Change

Louie Vega Can We Keep This Going

Oliver $ & Jimi Jules Pushing On

Travis Writing To Reach You

Played-A-Live The Bongo Song

James Bay Let it Go

Asake Peace Be unto You (PBUY)

Kendrick Lamar I

Sterling Void It's Alright (House Mix)

October London Mulholland Drive

James Brown The Boss

Elmiene Light Work

Alanis Morissette You Oughta Know

Olivia Rodrigo Driver's License

The Blessed Madonna Shades of Love (feat. Joy)

Alysa Marie The Woodland Realm

Anastasia Welcome to My Truth

The Chemical Brothers Galvanize

The Jimi Hendrix Experience Crosstown Traffic

Cleo Sol Life will Be

Butcher Brown Ibiza

Celine Dion I'm Alive

Theresa Phondo Blessings

Riccardo Muti & Vienna Philharmonic Freiheits-Marsch, O. 226 (Live)

Deadmau5 & Kaskade I Remember (Extended Version)

Jasmine Sullivan Dream Big

Hans Zimmer Now we are Free

Stormzy Blinded by Your Grace Pt23. (Feat. MNEK)

Jill Scott Golden

Green Day Good Riddance (Time of your Life)

Self Esteem Focus is Power

Olivia Dean Time

The Beloved The Sun Rising

Zero 7 Give it Away

Xavier Rudd Follow The Sun

Baz Luhrmann Everybody's Free (To Wear Sunscreen)

Louie Vega I Hear Music in the Streets

Nina Simone Feeling Good

Soul Central (Danny Krivit Re Edit) Strings of Life

iHope

Chapter 14

Summary

I hope you crossed the finish line and achieved your iHope!

Summary

It's not about our position in the race,

but the race itself

As we reflect on our journey, we begin to see the pitfalls we've encountered along the way, moments where our choices led us down the wrong track. The lessons we either dismissed or learned too late, and the obstacles that slowed our progress. These moments add up, forming the number of times we "lap the track", or experience a setback, or fall short of our goals.

- How many times did we face a 10-second penalty because of poor decisions?
- Did we pause our race because of burnout, heartbreak or fear?
- We may have been held back, overtaken, or delayed by self-sabotage or life's many challenges.
- Did the relentless hustle puncture our momentum, forcing us to DNF?
- Were we navigating slippery situations, or were we simply cooling down our tyres' temperature?

These scenarios reflect how we can become our own obstacles, holding ourselves back from realising our *iHope*.

Perhaps we've felt the sting of a broken heart after a relationship ended, or found ourselves caught in cycles of self-neglect or toxic habits.
Maybe we've ignored our emotions, made choices that strayed from our true desires, or allowed the safety of our comfort zone to hold us back. The pain of breakups, self-sabotage, lack of boundaries, or poor choices. Whether it's ignoring our instincts, struggling with low confidence, discounting our voice, or overstaying our welcome rather than quitting. There are so many ways that life, and sometimes we, can stand in the way of us reaching our full potential and crossing our finishing line. Despite how difficult life can be, this does not mean the race is over. It's a chance to stop, recalibrate, and reflect on how we can make the necessary adjustments to get back on track.

As we look ahead, it's important to acknowledge these challenges not as failures, as opportunities to learn, grow, and realign with our *iHope*. It is essential to learn the art of acceptance, forgiveness, and setting boundaries.

These are the pillars that sustain our mental, emotional and physical health, allowing us to drive forward with purpose and resilience. Rather than disagreements and disputes forcing us into the role of a backseat driver, it's crucial that we are behind the wheel of our lives, tooting our horns, making the decisions that guide us toward our true destination.

How was your Grand Prix?

Life's twists and turns often take us on unexpected journeys. Even with the best plans in place, we can't predict what's around the corner. What we can control is how prepared we are, how mentally, physically, and spiritually strong we are to handle whatever challenges arise.

I hope your journey hasn't been marked by too many collisions, setbacks, or storms that have deterred you from reaching your finishing line, just enough to support our growth and self-development. Most importantly, I hope it's been a road less travelled that has equipped you with the tools and courage to cross the finishing line with hope, while learning to love yourself along the way.

The life hacks shared in this book are designed to keep you going until the chequered flag. They offer a toolbox of strategies to help you stay in control, buckle up securely, and navigate life with clarity and intention. By clearing our windscreens of fear and letting go of regrets in the rear-view mirror, you can focus fully on the road ahead. Discovering who you are, and how you tick, and knowing that's good enough.
You've won!

"Remember Red.
Hope is a good thing, maybe the best of things, and no good ever dies. I will be hoping that this letter finds you well. Your friend. Andy."
Shawshank Redemption

We each travel our own unique paths, facing a mix of challenges, triumphs, setbacks, and milestones. These experiences shape who we are, creating unique frequencies and energies that guide us. Yet, despite the diversity of our journeys, we all share a universal goal: to cross the chequered flag, representing our personal triumph and success.

Mission accomplished, take pleasure in the victory lap!
Enjoy the champagne feeling.
Cheers!

Nina Simone Feeling Good ♪

The Road Not Taken

Two roads diverged in a yellow wood,
And sorry I could not travel both
And be one traveller, long I stood
And looked down one as far as I could
To where it bent in the undergrowth.

Then took the other, as just as fair,
And having perhaps the better claim,
Because it was grassy and wanted wear.
Though as for that the passing there
Had worn them really about the same,

And both that morning equally lay
In leaves no step had trodden black.
Oh, I kept the first for another day!
Yet knowing how way leads on to way,
I doubted if I should ever come back.

I shall be telling this with a sigh
Somewhere ages and ages hence:
Two roads diverged in a wood, and
I took the one less travelled by,
And that has made all the difference.

Robert Frost

Summary

To acknowledge, I thank you for your wise words...

Attributions

Dr Martin Luther King Jr "I have a dream...", 6.

Tina Turner "The future belongs to those who believe in the beauty of their own dreams.", 6.

Steven Bartlett *"The first step to getting somewhere, is to decide you're not going to stay where you are."*, 11

Maya Angelou "If you are always trying to be normal, you will never know how amazing you can be.", 21.

Tony Bennett "Life teaches us how to live, if you live long enough', 23.

Steven Bartlett "Quitting is a skill. Knowing when to quit, change direction, leave a toxic situation, demand more from life, give up on something that wasn't working and move on, is a very important skill that people who win at life all seem to have.", (LinkedIn, 2024). 65.

Dr. Gloria Wilcox Feelings Wheel, – (1982?), 42-43 and 306-307.

Sigmund Freud "Before you diagnose yourself with depression or low self-esteem, first make sure you are not, in fact, surrounded by assholes", 101.

Warren Buffett "You will lose a lot of friends when you get serious about your life goals. That's why the Lamborghini has two seats, and a bus has 50", 102.

Queen Elizabeth II "Grief is the price we pay for love", (Public statement – September 11th, 2001), 123.

J.R.R. Tolkien "All that is gold does not glitter, not all those who wander are lost, the old that is strong does not wither, deep roots are not reached by the frost." – (The Lord of the Rings - The Fellowship of the Ring) - (1954), 135.

Shunryu Suzuki "Leave your door and your back door open. Let thoughts come and go. Just don't serve them tea.", 164.

Prince "Don't be fooled by the internet. It's cool to get on the computer, but don't let the computer get on you. It's cool to use the computer, but don't let the computer use you. You saw the matrix. There's a war going on with the battlefields in the mind and the prize is the soul, so just be careful." (1999 Interview with Tavis Smiley on BET Tonight), 172.

Denzel Washington "At your highest moment, be careful. That's when the devil comes for you." at the 2022 Oscars., 198.

Muhammad Ali *"It isn't the mountains ahead that wear you out, it's the pebble in your shoe."* 154.

Hermann Hesse "If you hate a person, you hate something in him that is part of yourself. What isn't part of ourselves doesn't disturb us" (Demian – 1919), 209.

Mel Robbins' The Five Second Rule', 257.

Alan Yentob "If you're going to succeed you need to know about failure", 259.

Micheal Waltrip "Typically, you learn more when you lose than when you win" (2010), 260.

Mark Twain "Anger is an acid that can do more harm to the vessel in which it is stored than to anything on which it is poured.", 298.

RuPaul "If you've got one foot in the future and one foot in the past, you're pissing on the present. Be in the moment!", 300.

Christine Caine "Sometimes when you're in a dark place you think you've been buried, but you've actually been planted.", 326.

Iyanla Vanzant "Until you heal the wounds of your past, you will continue to bleed into the future.", (Yesterday I cried: Celebrating the lessons of Living. And loving - 1998), 382.

Thich Nhat Hanh "Silence is essential. We need silence just as much as we need air, just as much as plants need light. If our minds are crowded with words and thoughts, there is no space for us.", (Facebook post – 27.01.15 Thich Nhat Hanh official page OR The Power of Quiet in a world full of Noise – 2015), 396.

Davina McCall "Menopause was an age thing, and now I realise it's a woman thing.", (Davina McCall: Sex, Myths and the Menopause – C4 – 2021), 400.

Marriella Frostrup and Alice Smellie "Watch out for the menopausal woman, for she is driven and passionate, and she seeks pastures new."
(Cracking the menopause: While keeping Yourself Together - Marriella Frostrup and Alice - 2021), 404.

Ram Pass "I can do nothing for you but work on myself. You can do nothing for me but work on yourself!", (Be Here Now – 1971), 416.

John Burroughs "I go to nature to be soothed and healed, and to have my senses put back in order.", 423.

Gary Chapman Love Languages, 1992 – Northfield Publishing, 432.

'Nudge Words' Professor Cass Sunstein and Richard Thaler, 2008 - Nudge, 445.

The Serenity Prayer Reinhold Niebuhr (1932), 457.

St Bernard of Clairvaux "The road to hell is paved with good intentions." (1090-1153), 463.

William Shakespeare "If music be the food of love, play on!" - (Duke Orsino) – Twelfth Night, 481.

iHope

With my sincere gratitude, I would like to thank...

Acknowledgements

I never planned to write a book, just as starting my own practice wasn't intended at first. But both were driven by passion and creativity. With so much to share, the words flowed effortlessly, and I finished the book in a few months, shaped by my experiences, a true blessing. I owe my thanks to the angels who scattered their dust around me as I wrote this book, mostly in the still of the night. Watching the dawn break as I wrote is a vision I'll always cherish.

Thanks to the music. You stirred the very molecules within me. Grateful to the amazing musicians, songwriters, and artists whose creativity has been a constant source of inspiration. Thank You!

Growing up, I was captivated by iconic music shows like Top of the Pops, The Old Grey Whistle Test, Soul Train, No Limits, TFI Friday, Never Mind the Buzzcocks, Solid Soul, The Tube, Entertainment USA, MTVBase. Looking back, those shows were pivotal for me, they opened my world to new sounds and helped shape my identity through music. Tuning into stations like, KissFM, Choice FM, Radio 1and 2. Thanks to the amazing broadcasters like Robbie Vincent, The Dream Team, The 'Madhatter' aka Trevor Nelson, Pete Tong, and Giles Peterson, who shone a light on the underground music scene. Your shows opened my ears to new sounds and cultures, and reminded me how music can connect, heal, and uplift the soul. Thank You!

Thank you to Formula1, for fuelling my passion and creativity.
To Sir Lewis Hamilton - The G.O.A.T! Thank you for demonstrating excellence, resilience and drive on and off the track.

To my wonderful friends and family, thank you for your patience and unwavering belief in me, and for supporting me through this process. Thank you!

Here's to all the varied strings to my bow, each one who has played a part in this journey's story. Thank you for helping bring this book to life.
Thank you to Lynne Hollingsworth, Gary Ward, and Touqeer, for all your expertise and technical support. To Craig and Jane, my first supporters on this journey. A heartfelt thank you for turning the key in the ignition.

A heartfelt thank you to all the souls who have entrusted me with their hearts and minds, sharing heartfelt stories in search of meaning, purpose, freedom, or peace. It has been a privilege and honour to witness your souls brighten and your lives transform. Though our paths may not cross again, I trust you will live a full and healthy life. I celebrate my difference with all the amazing unique souls that have crossed my path. A special thanks to Helen, who's inspirational story gave rise to the title iHope, first for you, and now for so many others.

To Eric Berne, M.D., thank you for your groundbreaking work that has deepened my understanding of myself and others. To my teachers, I am grateful for your positive impact on my life, for shaping my character and nurturing my hope. A piece of each of you is reflected in this book, and your teachings continue to guide me as I serve others. I am deeply thankful for your lasting influence. Lastly, to all my readers, and go-getters! Young, old and those in the middle, thanks for choosing to spend your time with my words, letting me step into your world for a little while, humbles me deeply. I hope this book gave you what you needed and made the journey worthwhile.
I wonder which songs became the soundtracks of your journey.
With that, I wholeheartedly say a loud and resounding,
Thank You.

If there's one thing, I know to be true, passion can take you anywhere!

Soul Central (Danny Krivit Re Edit) Strings of Life ♪

This book is dedicated to Marcus and Coco

marcocoadvice.com

www.ingramcontent.com/pod-product-compliance
Lightning Source LLC
Chambersburg PA
CBHW050327010526
44119CB00050B/699